The Emergence of MODERN IRELAND 1600–1900

L. M. Cullen

HM
HOLMES & MEIER PUBLISHERS, INC.
New York

For Eva and Christine

First published in the United States of America 1981 by
HOLMES & MEIER PUBLISHERS, INC.
30 Irving Place, New York, N.Y. 10003

Copyright © 1981 by L. M. Cullen
ALL RIGHTS RESERVED

Library of Congress Cataloging in Publication Data
Cullen, L. M. (Louis M.)
  The Emergence of Modern Ireland, 1600–1900

  Includes bibliographical references.
  1. Ireland—Social conditions. 2. Ireland—Economic
conditions. 3. Ireland—Politics and government.
I. Title.
HN400.3A8C84   941.5   81-6548
ISBN 0-8419-0727-7   AACR2

Printed in Great Britain

Contents

Preface		8
1	**Introduction**	11
2	**Castle, countryside and social change**	25
3	**The landlord's world**	39
4	**Village and countryside: landlord and settler**	61
5	**Social structure and evolution**	83
6	**Social and cultural frontiers**	109
7	**Diet in a changing society**	140
8	**Hospitality and menu**	172
9	**Settlers and natives: conflict**	193
10	**The '98 rebellion in Wexford and Wicklow**	210
11	**Education and cultural change**	234
12	**The character and identity of modern Ireland**	250
Notes		257
Index		285

Preface

This book is less an effort to summarise the results of recent or ongoing investigation — though it is in part that — than an attempt to integrate the varied themes of Irish history into a general framework which will make its complexity and evolution more intelligible. In consequence, the book ranges widely and some of its incursions were originally unintended and the conclusions unexpected. Ireland, an ordinary country in many respects, is none the less fascinating. Old traditions, long dead elsewhere, have lingered on, while at the same time Irishmen have seemed to abandon habits and institutions with a lack of attachment which is quite chilling in comparative terms. At the same time as old traditions and a lack of a sense of tradition lie warily side by side, a more fundamental racial awareness than in other European countries exists, embodied in the very landscape and in physical institutions as well as in thought and sentiment; religious differences have also stubbornly refused to soften with the same startling rapidity as in northern Europe. When the slanting sunlight of evening falls on the countryside, it frequently reveals a haunting profusion of overlapping layers of indigenous and external settlement imposed within a handful of generations: the country's complex microgeology is thus compounded by a striking lack of cultural homogeneity. Differences in the landscape parallel differences in thought and behaviour. If the novelist Aidan Higgins recalled in a broadcast some time ago his awareness as a boy of 'Protestant' gates, a Russian cultural attaché recently observed that Catholic social occasions ended later than Protestant ones.

None of these features is intrinsically unique to Ireland. In the cauldron of the middle ages changes no less profound took place in Europe at large, but Ireland's cultural changes have been so recent that they can be documented in abundance in written sources or even in direct observation, just as many of their effects are still living. They thus have a interest not only as the last but as the best documented stage in the profound intermingling of cultural and social developments that shaped European societies into the rich and vibrant force they became.

Of the many debts contracted in the course of writing this book, a special one has to be acknowledged to the students taking my special subject in Irish history with whom many of the issues were broached, and to whom some individual acknowledgments are made in the notes. I am grateful to my colleague Dr David Dickson, Dr A.P.W. Malcomson of the Public Record Office of Northern Ireland, and Mr W.H. Crawford of the Ulster Folk Museum, for much information; to Rev. R.B. McCarthy and Mr Salters Sterling for helpful observations; to Monsieur Alain Braastad of Jarnac for information about the Delamain family and the potato in south-west France; to Professor Isac Chiva of the Laboratoire d'anthropologie sociale, Collège de France, for bringing several sources to my attention; to Mr John Brooks of Messrs Jarrold, Norwich, for the benefit of a photographer's trained eye; and also to Dr M.J. Craig for observations on some sections. A posthumous debt exists to one of my former teachers, Professor Síle Ní Chinnéide of University College, Galway, for access to invaluable information from her transcripts of the de Montbret diaries. I am indebted to my wife for guidance from her knowledge of Irish cooking and its development in what has been a long-drawn-out attempt to make the evolution of Irish diet intelligible. The obligations to my daughters have been acknowledged in the dedication: they have been the companions of many forays into the countryside in search of lost villages and landscapes. Many people in the countryside have helped in many ways, both large and small, from bystanders on the roadside, to lecture audiences and the chatelaines of houses both modest and great, and many of the chapters of the book have taken shape with their help over the last two decades. A special indebtedness exists to Mr A.W.R. Seward of Messrs Batsford for many suggestions for improvements in the text, and to Miss Muriel Sadlier of the Modern History Department and Mrs Alice Tunney and members of the Central Secretariat for dealing with drafts of the book over the last four years.

Trinity College, Dublin
March, 1981

L.M. Cullen

1
Introduction

Ireland's history is clear-cut in the sense that it is dominated by certain well-defined themes. However, beyond these themes it dissolves into complexity and unpredictability. In 1914, when a home-rule parliament seemed guaranteed for a future date after the return of peace to Europe, few could have foreseen the momentous events which were to herald not only the emergence of modern Ireland but the first stage in the break-up of the British Empire. Even fewer could have anticipated, in the mid-sixties in the calm atmosphere of the Lemass-O'Neill meeting, that Ulster was about to enter a period of strife and tragedy whose outcome is still not clear. The dominant theme of Irish history is Anglo-Irish relations. The effective English conquest of Ireland, however, took place only in the 1580s and 1590s in response to the fear of Spanish invasion, and hegemony was put beyond challenge only in two further campaigns — the prolonged war of the 1640s and early 1650s and the military campaigns of 1689-91 in which for a while Ireland was the main theatre of a European struggle. The cost of conquering Ireland was enormous: more than any other single factor, the cost of Elizabeth's Irish campaigns set parliament and crown on the course which culminated in civil war in the 1640s. The personal participation of English rulers in Ireland was itself a measure of the importance Irish events had assumed in the seventeenth century: Cromwell campaigned in Ireland in 1649, and William and James faced each other across the Boyne on a fateful day in July 1690.

Anglo-Irish relations were meshed into a pattern of racial conflict in Ireland, in which the old division between Norman and Gael was perpetuated in a new and sharper guise. English settlers had taken the place of the Anglo-Normans, and the fusion of Anglo-Normans and Gaels was accelerated by religious and military resistance to English rule in the 1640s. The three great wars were each followed by plantation in which, over something more than a century, the bulk of land in Ireland was transferred into new hands: the Munster and Ulster plantations of the 1580s and 1610s, the

Cromwellian plantation of the 1650s, and the Williamite in the 1690s. Settlers came in with new landowners, but much settlement was quite independent of the plantations. Indeed in many respects, particularly in Ulster, immigration rather than plantation was more decisive in achieving durable change, although changes in ownership did of course provide an environment which reduced the risks for Scottish and English settlers who ventured across the Irish Sea. As will be shown in chapter 2, English plantation policy which had laid a heavy emphasis on immigration in the Munster and Ulster plantations, was less and less concerned with that aspect in the more secure conditions that held after Cromwell's crushing defeat of resistance in Ireland. The sole direct preoccupation of Cromwellian policy was the provision of Irish lands for the adventurers who had underwritten the costs of the Irish campaigns and for the unpaid soldiers. Thus the greatest of Irish plantations, the one which involved the most wholesale transfer of land, was also the first one in which immigration ceased to be a prime consideration of policy. If immigration proved to be large in the 1650s, it was a consequence of irresistibly cheap Irish land and of domestic difficulties in Scotland and England. A disproportionate number of immigrants from England were dissenters with no great love for conditions at home; the Scottish Presbyterians were also significant in the overall inflow. The Williamite confiscation was an even more nakedly financial operation, divorced from social policy. The only large influx in the 1690s was from Scotland, and even it would have been less sustained but for the four hungry seasons in Scotland from 1695 to 1698. The shift in the 1650s from sponsored immigration to independent immigration laid the basis for a growing gulf between on the one hand the Dublin government, the country landowners, and established church and on the other hand the growing number of nonconformists. In particular, a rift emerged between the north of Ireland and the Anglican establishment in Dublin, remote from its religious and social interests. The attitudes of Archbishop King mirrored the change more graphically than any other leading figure of the time. At this time he was the Bishop of Derry, which had been metamorphosized by the 1690s from a bastion of English and Anglican culture into a Presbyterian stronghold.

The eighteenth century, at least until Hoche's great invasion fleet was seen through the mists of Bantry Bay at Christmas 1796, represented the apogee of Anglican dominance in

Ireland. The decisive defeat of the French and Jacobite forces in 1689-91 made the prospect of invasion remote, and the Protestant establishment, which penalized Catholics, also felt strong enough to adhere to many of the restrictions on Presbyterians imposed when it had taken fright at the scale of the Scottish influx in the 1690s. Confidence radiated out from the landed class, both in the countryside and in the capital. In the countryside, the houses and demesnes appeared which only now, in the twentieth century, have begun to crumble into dust; the landowners also engaged, as chapters 2 and 3 show, in a wide variety of experiments in social engineering and economic improvement. Dublin, the focal point of the social life and political ambitions of the greater gentry, expressed their self-confidence even more forcibly. Its planning began earlier, was more sustained and on a greater scale than that of Edinburgh, and was perhaps unequalled by that of any other city in eighteenth-century Europe. Its new parliament house, opened in 1729, was more impressive even in the eyes of disinterested English visitors, than the mother of parliaments. The successive erection across the century of the modern buildings of Trinity College, the largest single mass of collegiate buildings in the British Isles, the Four Courts, centre of the administration of justice, and finally the King's Inns, intended to provide a legal education in Ireland for the sons of the gentry who heretofore had had to resort to London, were other monumental expressions of this self-confidence. Most majestic of all was the Custom House built in the 1780s — the building no less than its promoter drew the fire of the opposition in parliament, pointing as they did to the confidence and arrogance, as well as the taste and ambitions, of Dublin's ruling oligarchy. The elegant, serene and mellowed atmosphere of Dublin in the prints designed by the English artist Malton in the early 1790s represented the qualities which their purchasers in the upper class thought they found in their political and social environment.

The one nagging fear, even if for most of the century it was relegated to the background, was that of invasion which, if it ever took place, would be likely to kindle every resentment and could well be backed by the Presbyterians, the radical qualities of whose philosophy were more than ever suspect after the American Revolution of which they were the backbone. The year 1745 was in fact much tenser beneath the surface than the external calm suggested. The abortive landing by Thurot with a small force at Carrickfergus in

Introduction

1760 played a role in promoting the strange fears and happenings in Munster over the following six years. While these were to discredit Protestant ultraism until the French Revolution, it is significant that disavowal of them, though effective, operated in embarrassed silence and even in uncertainty rather than publicly. The background to the Volunteer forces recruited in the late 1770s to protect the country denuded of troops for the American campaigns, was compounded of fears of domestic disorder as well as of resistance to foreign invasion. The Volunteer companies created a heady involvement for many below the level of the gentry, and after the momentous displays of 1780-82, a rift developed in the movement, drawn largely between north and south. After 1783 the Volunteers were disbanded or disowned, depending on local circumstances, by the landed establishment which had established or officered them, though companies lingered on as a focal point of emerging radical protestant opinion where such was sufficiently strong. Catholics were more in evidence in the movement too, a reflection both of the triumph of radical thought and of their self-confidence. Radical opinion, already better-defined in the 1780s, grew at an alarming rate in the 1790s, especially in the north where it represented the culmination of Presbyterian disillusionment with the Dublin establishment. The union of the two islands was imposed in the aftermath of the 1798 rebellion which had illustrated the failure of the Anglican establishment to control the country. The Union was opposed by the politically most influential elements of the landed establishment, and though Protestants came to accept it as a guarantee of their survival, at the time it seemed a clear surrender of their power to the British government. It was in these circumstances that Catholics at large welcomed the Union, and that the Presbyterians in the north, recently in rebellion against the government, remained mute during the great transition which dramatically altered Dublin's place in Irish political life. Retrospectively, the Union in fact marked the first stage in the crumbling of the influence of the landed classes in Ireland. Effectively in the interests of order in Ireland, British influence had prevailed over the Orange establishment who in the first aftermath of the rebellion had thought they had savoured a great triumph. In every future crisis in Ireland imperial considerations prevailed against the protests of the Irish landed class who in the course of the next 120 years were to see Catholic emancipation introduced (1829), the Church of Ireland disestablished in 1869, a flood of radical land legislation from 1881, and the long-drawn out movement by the British government between 1886 and 1920 towards self-government in Ireland.

The flood tide of Anglican dominance after the Restoration in 1660 coincided with a remarkable expansion of the Irish economy. The Elizabethans had difficulties, cultural as well as military, in coming to grips with Irish society, so primitive did it appear to them. But over the next two centuries Irish society evolved decisively. Population grew in a sustained fashion, and between 1600 and 1800 foreign trade likewise increased very rapidly. Several factors accounted for the rapidity of the transition. The increased contact of a primitive society in trade and culture with the more advanced outside world was one. Another was the role of the landed classes who in a paternalistic age financed and superintended many of the changes in the countryside. A village structure grew up, largely built on the fringes of the new or expanding estates of the country's landed magnates. The character of the villages was influenced by the role of the landlords in financing activity away from the land itself, and their functional lay-out, no less than their general character, reflected the role which landlords played in contemporary society. In the more developed societies of western Europe, no parallel existed in this period for village creation on this scale, or for a comparable dominance by the landed class of the establishment, and the progress or failure of villages and small towns. Even as late as 1746, the account of two English gentlemen travelling in Ireland testifies to the intrusion onto the visitor's attention of this aspect of landlord activity.[1] It is a major feature of seventeenth and eighteenth-century change, and is described at length in chapter 4. Another feature in the change was the impact of sustained immigration on a scale unparalleled in Europe. By 1700 no less than 27 per cent of the population was of Scottish or English origin or descent compared with a mere two per cent in 1600, as chapter 5 shows. But the support for change came from indigenous classes as well. Poor by western European standards, the ordinary people were compelled to make sustained changes in their diet, and in acute need of cash, they also responded readily to the intense pressures of commercialization which seemed to put some cash in their path. The indigenous landed classes were equally open to change, in fact, in one respect more so than immigrant land owners. Compelled by the problem of disposing of agricultural surpluses to become engaged in trade or intermarried into town merchant families through the problems of chronic indebtedness, they had a much closer association with trade than the new English landed families; a fact reflected also in the career outlets of their sons.

Changing so rapidly in conditions of relative shortage of cash, the orientation of this society was, from the outset of this changing period highly commercialized. A very high proportion of output was marketed; internal trade was intense, and one of the contrasts between Ireland and France from the pages of Young's tours in both countries, is the heavy traffic on Irish roads, and the almost deserted ones of France.[2] At the most basic level, that of diet, many commodities were retained for domestic or local consumption in France, whereas in Ireland, the poorer society, everything which could be sold was disposed of. In the last analysis, the spread of domestic textile industry which provided cash for the poorer inhabitants, supported the creation of local cash food markets, at least seasonally. Even the landed class, as already mentioned, were influenced by these forces. As a result, especially in the hinterlands of the ports of Galway, Cork and Waterford, there was a close interaction between trade and land: sons were as likely to enter trade as the army, church or law, and the descendants of the older landed families in these regions often had a more cosmopolitan window on the world than the Anglican landed families which began to emerge in Ireland in the seventeenth century. Before they lost much of their land in the upheavals of the seventeenth century, this pattern was already well-established and the growth of foreign trade and of colonization in the Americas was responsible for the family network becoming even more extended with sons in the West Indies and in Europe as well as in trade in Irish ports and in London. In time, a highly elaborate network of families emerged overseas reaching from the Mediterranean to the ports of France and Spain and to the West Indies. It was the most far-flung mercantile network of the period, more extensive than either the Huguenot or the Scottish one. In fact, the intensely commercial orientation of this group was in conflict with the values of the Dublin landed establishment which dominated parliament. The 1756 banking act was anti-mercantile.[3] It was only as late as 1800, ironically when its own political defeat was in sight, that the social values of the Anglican landed class which sought to distance themselves from trade, began to become universal among the Irish landed classes. In the process of adopting the dominant social values of the Anglican landowners they also adopted their political stance. The Catholic converts to the Established Church had dominated social and political life in Galway which was liberal in political outlook and closely allied to trade through a farflung network of kin. But from around 1800 all changed: the Dalys, for instance, liberal in the eighteenth century, were political leaders of the Protestant establishment in the county by the 1830s. Lukewarm in their adopted religion in the eighteenth century, they also gave the Church of Ireland one of its greatest bishops in the following century.

It will be obvious from all this that the Irish social structure, faced with profound transition, must have been a highly fluid one. The social pressures and tensions in such a society are described in chapter 6. Society was dominated at the outset by large landowners and minute tenants except in the south-east and in the Pale (a region embracing some or all of four counties surrounding Dublin), where some tradition of yeomen or comfortable farmers existed. The only social group interposed between the minute tenants and the landowners were the middlemen whose emergence was very much part of the process of intense commercialization in the period. They were either immigrants who were keen to promote agriculture in a colonial setting or younger sons of gentry already within the country, for whom large tracts of land at low rents offered the avenue to a gentry style of life. Indeed, as Catholic landowners lost possession of their land, they were able to maintain a gentry social standing by becoming such tenants. Such individuals, especially in the south-west, where in contrast to Connaught few Catholics held onto land, or in contrast to Kilkenny where they were challenged by yeoman farmers, were an essential component of Irish social life. Their social standing, further confirmed by the gentry-type careers of sons at home or abroad, was frequently clear-cut and accepted by all. Below these great tenants, were the ordinary people who at the end of the seventeenth century were mainly tenants of rather menial condition who provided labour services to their immediate landlord, and who were often housed in village clusters. All this changed during the eighteenth century. As farming advanced, comfortable farmers emerged in greater numbers capable of taking over the acres of the middlemen. Middlemen were highly vulnerable from this competition which they had dreaded from an early date. This competition was much better-defined in the 1790s: it was the threat to their

Introduction

social standing which made the small middlemen of north Wexford and south Wicklow so aggressive, and which set them on a course which in parishes fairly evenly divided between two religions, inevitably led to religious strife. Landlords were frequently eager to replace them too; especially as middlemen with their precarious vested interest in the existing state of affairs were opposed to social changes. This determination was, however, mitigated by the fact that middlemen and landowners were frequently related or that landowners were reluctant to replace Protestant tenants.

As social changes took place, the old communal structures broke down. Communities organized on a 'village' basis disappeared, the community being replaced increasingly by a combination, on the one hand, of large farmers and graziers and on the other of landless men. Thus, at one level the farmer encroached on the interest of the middlemen; at another the farmer entered into conflict with the landless men who resented the loss of their small stake and of some communal rights such as commonage. A class war emerged in the countryside, most pronounced in the more advanced regions of the country, and much less evident in other regions where the survival of middlemen ensured easier access to land for small men. The prevailing causes of social conflict changed. In the middle decades of the eighteenth century, when re-organization was afoot, rural unrest frequently represented resistance to the process of social change; at a later date, with the new social order triumphant, rents of plots and wage rates were more commonly the issue. The economic development of a region was reflected in the nature of the issues, clear-cut in the developed regions, confused and complex in regions still in the process of social re-organization.

Such a society experienced change even in the most intimate details of existence. Diet and hospitality are two features of life which have received little attention from historians and contemporaries alike. Yet both changed, and because of the gulf between Irish and foreign standards, they were more commented on by visitors than was normally the case. The impact of the most sustained demographic expansion in Europe was accelerated by commercial pressures: these entailed the sale of food surpluses, which in turn created the necessity to replace readily saleable foods by new foods on a substantial scale. The consequence was that Irish diet over the last three centuries has been much less stable than that of other countries. Butter which could command a ready sale was replaced by grain and, as grain too could be commercialized, by the potato, a bulky and perishable item which had only a local market. In all of Europe grain was already, and remained, the basis of diet. But in Ireland, although it was of course important, it neither established nor retained this position in the general diet. Moreover, many food traditions which had been quite strong wilted in time: fish and cheese, once prominent in the diet, declined; and among beverages, ale and cider which had been well known in the countryside failed to hold their own. For these reasons diet merits close attention: the transition was unique with no close parallel elsewhere in modern Europe, and its dynamics were complex (chapter 7). Hospitality, a more significant function in a primitive society than in a more modern one, could hardly avoid change both because of the cultural influences brought in by immigrants and because of the general economic changes (chapter 8). A sharp cultural gap in hospitality was evident to contemporaries, and by 1800 a sense was general that age-old patterns had slipped into the past. Thus hospitality itself embraces simultaneously both dietary changes and wider mores within the society. The most arresting change of all relates to whiskey, now regarded as a traditional drink. In fact, whiskey before the eighteenth century was a ritual drink of great occasions — the poor could not afford to commission its manufacture — and of the tables of the great: even at their tables it was never the sole drink. Its prestige was conferred by upper-class connotations, and through the seventeenth century grandees crossing between Ireland and England often paid customs duties on several gallons on landing at Chester. Only in the middle of the eighteenth century did whiskey become a significant commercial product, bought rather than distilled within a comfortable household. The cash resources which became more plentiful at that time meant that the poor could purchase such a socially prestigious product, and the emergence of the market made it worthwhile for manufacturers, legal or clandestine, to come into being to cater for it. Even then, its diffusion was at first very uneven; the addiction was most marked in the north (the most cash-oriented part of rural Ireland), and spread out from the north-east.

This society was divided into two contrasting segments: a receding native one, and a modern one, the latter itself a confused amalgam of intrusive forces and of changes in indigenous society. It was also characterized by tensions, racial or religious, in which rivalry not only led to individual tragedy but to actual conflict. This aspect of Irish life is analyzed in chapters 6 and 9, and its ultimate denouement, the rebellion in Wexford and Wicklow, in chapter 10. The 1641 massacres were long commemorated by Protestant society — with renewed fervour in the 1760s, as again a century later — and the bloody ferocity of the 1798 rebellion hung ambiguously over subsequent history. Both events loomed large in nineteenth-century controversy, though in a divided society they meant quite different things to the two sides of Irish society. The sectarian divide ran deepest in co. Armagh and in co. Wexford and in both counties things came to a head in the same decade — the 1790s. Armagh represented the most complex mix of cultural influences in Ireland — Gaelic, English and Scottish. It was the centre of the most intense Anglican settlement in Ireland in the seventeenth century, and this in turn was reflected in its reproduction of the hierarchical character of English society. Its pattern of numerous and relatively small estates in the eighteenth century was the outcome of the activity, a century previously, of numerous small entrepreneurs, each with his dependants creating a small society of demesne and village. It was more immune to radical Presbyterianism than any other county in the north; the Orange Order took shape in 1795, and despite its popular origins it quickly assumed the hierarchical order of Anglican society in the area. It is surprising at first sight that county Wexford, remote from Armagh and socially very different in its economy and society, should respond so speedily to the tensions in Armagh and that the Orange Order should take shape there too so quickly. In fact, Wexford and the adjoining region of south Wicklow had been the region of the most successful and sustained Protestant settlement outside the north of Ireland. Moreover, this settlement was almost exclusively Anglican, consisting not of a dependent population but of largely self-sufficient farmers, many pretending to gentleman-farmer status. This Protestant community was thus receptive to the idea of defence of the Protestant establishment in the 1790s. It was doubly so because a family network of well-connected large Catholic farmers and minor gentlemen survived along the borders of Wicklow and Wexford. Through sons who pursued successful careers on the continent or in Dublin, these families imbibed revolutionary ideals in the 1790s. Their drift towards radical ideals and membership of the United Irishmen accelerated the support by Protestant families for the Orange Order. Thus, conflict in Wexford and Wicklow, when it occurred in 1798, had nothing to do with agrarian disorder, as has often been asserted, and much to do with the destructive competitiveness of minor Protestant and Catholic *notables*.

The 1798 rebellion in Wexford was a reflection of tensions created by successful Protestant settlement. Elsewhere, outside the north, the fortunes of such settlement were both uneven and precarious. Protestant colonization was much more evident around demesnes and landlord villages than in the countryside at large, as chapters 4, 6 and 10 explain. Dublin itself, more particularly at the outset of the eighteenth century, was largely a Protestant city. In the countryside, except where substantial farmers had been attracted in the original settlement, as in counties Wexford and Wicklow, Protestant society consisted largely of smallholders, artisans and servants: hence it was vulnerable to collapse as the fortunes of patronage or industry fluctuated, in the same way as Dublin's large Protestant artisan class faded away in the nineteenth century. In counties like Meath and Kilkenny, with their entrenched prosperous rural Catholics, it was already long fading before the end of the eighteenth century. Indeed, in county Kilkenny, the most monolithically Catholic county of all, dominated also by the large and partly Catholic caste of the Butlers, it never really took deep root. In Kilkenny the Catholic Church had reasserted itself even in the heady days of Anglican hegemony after the Restoration and in 1704 about half the registered Catholic clergy in Ireland had been ordained by the Catholic bishop of Ossory.

Protestant settlement was very precarious in most parts of Ireland except in the immediate post-Restoration decades when both landlords and immigrants were sanguine about its prospects often even in unpromising locations. Paradoxically settlement was most vulnerable where it was strongly supported by landowners, because the people they brought in were frequently smallholders or artisans with little resources, likely to melt away at the first difficulty. The success of such settlement depended heavily on the larger tenants, frequently the so-called 'middlemen' of Irish society about whom so much has been written.[4] With some economic resources, a knowledge of farming and a strong commitment to the survival of local Protestant institutions, they were the real backbone of such communities. But such men were already vulnerable to changing circumstances even in what were for them the relatively favourable situation of Wexford and Wicklow in the 1790s. The pressure they experienced in the 1790s was translated into collapse in many of the weaker centres in the early decades of the nineteenth century. The crisis of this class represented a significant stage in the collapse of a viable rural protestant society, and more particularly of leadership in it, as is argued in chapter 5.

Thus, on account of the many transitional elements of its character, Ireland was an unstable society. Central though immigration was to Irish history and cultural development, the balance between the two religions was unstable at local level. This was evident even in strongholds of Protestant settlement in Armagh, Wexford and Wicklow. The only exceptions in the 1790s were Antrim, Down and Derry, Presbyterian regions which, ironically, were highly suspect to the establishment in the 1790s, as sources of radical sentiment. Secondly, the religious profile of the rural community was closely allied to a changing social structure in which thanks to commercialization wealth was spread somewhat more evenly in the countryside. This entailed the transfer of land, income and status to farmers, who were often working their way up the social scale, from individuals in the groups who had been the heirs of immigration or of Protestant hegemony in the countryside. The vulnerability of the favoured group of middlemen in the countryside, Catholic and Protestant, accounts for their aggressive behaviour in Wexford and south Wicklow in the 1790s. This shift was also very significant on a wider social plane. The middlemen had been brokers, as chapter 5 explains, in all aspects of local life: connected to the landed class by kinship or marriage ties on the one hand, they were acceptable on the other hand to the ordinary man because in a land-hungry society they subdivided part of their lands to small men who sought leases or contracts for a number of years. Their departure widened — in a sense created — the gulf between landlord and tenant, just as the success of the tenant in taking over the acres of the middlemen ensured that small men increasingly could no longer aspire to land on a secure basis, having instead to accept small plots for a year only. Farmers were more central to economic life than in the past.

The changes in social structure were in turn allied to other changes. The middlemen, with uncertain pretensions to gentility, were the class among whom lavish hospitality died slowest. The change to more modern attitudes coincided broadly with their departure. Changes in hospitality, a transition from a simple lavishness, archaic by comparison with the western European economy, were overshadowed by changes in diet. A backward economy with an archaic diet, experiencing demographic growth, had to innovate. Hence diet in Ireland lacked the conservatism and relative stability characteristic of it elsewhere. Moreover, a sharp contrast emerged between social classes; between on the one hand the comfortable farming class, whose position was becoming more assured and who both retained butter and meat in their diet and adopted the potato, and on the other hand the poorer inhabitants of rural Ireland who in many cases proceeded from butter and porridge to the potato without ever having a strong association with the European tradition of cereal bread. Irish diet was in many respects unique, but this character could only have existed in the general circumstances of social change in Ireland. Social values were also changing. The archaic values of this society of patriarchal landlords and profligate middlemen were waning rapidly as the century wore on. Gentry figures had led their tenants in faction fights at the outset of the century, and abductions were commonplace. But fighting and abductions were successively abandoned by the upper classes, the change incidentally widening the gulf between classes, as the lower classes abandoned these age-old habits more slowly. The literature in which the virtues of the upper classes were extolled by poets, whose compositions survive in manuscripts alone because they were never printed, was beginning to lose its vigour after mid-century, largely because landowners lost interest in patronage of poets and transcribers. The first popular schoolteachers emerged from this archaic milieu of literate men, who resorted to teaching as patronage died. They could do this because a demand for literacy was spreading rapidly at the end of the century. The phenomenon arose of the teacher practising the language of the manuscripts for a narrow circle, and the language of the printed book and of commerce for the school room. Literate in two languages, the teachers usually produced pupils literate only in one. They bestrode two worlds, the old, almost medieval world enshrined in the great mass of manuscripts compiled in the eighteenth century, and the modern one which cherished the ideals of the French Revolution. However, while their modest background and literacy combined made them apostles of the ideals of the Revolution, their

Introduction

cultural background made them heirs of the resentments of leaders of the old Gaelic landed class. It was through them that the democratic ideas of the nineteenth century were dressed in the backward looking ideals of the old Gaelic world which had existed before the land upheavals. Few countries had experienced as complex a cultural change as did Ireland in the eighteenth century, and none one so compounded of elements of the archaic and the modern. In that regard it reflected the whole character of Irish society, whose late but powerful modernization is characterized by sustained contrasts for which no parallel can be found north of the Alps and Pyrenees.

2
Castle, countryside and social change

Ireland grew with remarkable rapidity between the seventeenth and early nineteenth centuries. The crudest measure of growth, but still one of the most significant, is of population with a probable six-to-eight-fold rise in numbers between 1600 and 1841. In comparison with other countries, Ireland's advance was very striking. France, perhaps twenty times more populous than Ireland in 1600, was only four times more populous in 1841. Scotland probably had as many inhabitants as Ireland in 1600, but only one third Ireland's population in 1841. Ireland's growth was more than a relative population explosion, and makes sense only in a wider social and cultural context. It was, in essence, the transition from medieval to modern. Because it was belated in comparison with western Europe at large, economic and social expansion when it got under way necessarily appeared in the transitional period more rapid than in its neighbours. In effect, a social and cultural transformation took place of what was the last western European country to abandon the medieval world.

Its exports in 1600 were still among the most unsophisticated of any European country. At that date one of the country's three key exports — hides — was the produce of an uncommercialized livestock production in which the hides alone had a monetary value; a second — fish — was the harvest of its water resources, and the third — wool — which alone represented an intensively export-oriented agriculture, still came principally, as it had for centuries, from the Norman lands of the south-east. Skins still figured prominently in the country's exports in the sixteenth century, coming from the large woodlands which covered much of the country. In this circumstance lies much of the explanation of the rapidity of the transition of agriculture and of foreign trade in the seventeenth century as dry cattle, dairy cows and wool encroached on the rapidly receding forests.

Towns were small, there was little rank order in size — Dublin was not much larger than other major towns and most towns were isolated with few, if any, urban settlements in their immediate hinterland. Drogheda and Waterford with five and seven towns, respectively, in their backlands, were unique. The relative proximity of two major towns — Dublin and Drogheda — was paralleled in the entire island only by the relationship between Waterford and Kilkenny. The fewness, smallness and isolation of Irish towns is eloquent testimony to the backwardness of Irish society. Beyond Waterford and Drogheda, the only towns regularly compared by contemporaries with Dublin in size, trade, or opulence, the sole really significant town was Galway in almost total isolation on the west coast. Scotland itself was a relatively backward country but there was a fundamental contrast between the largely unurbanized Irish society and the small-scale but closely-knit urban life, the 'many royal boroughs yoken on end to end'[1] of lowland Scotland.

The transition from medieval to modern entailed profound changes. One of its motor forces was the growth of trade and of the mechanisms of trade — markets, fairs and towns. Beyond the realm of trade, change was evident in the long-drawn-out process of enclosing the countryside into fields shaped by ditch and hedge. At a more personal level, it was to be seen, simultaneously, in the profound transformation, one or two centuries behind most of western Europe, in domestic architecture and home comforts, most immediately and impressively among the upper classes but percolating downwards unevenly but definitely to the rest of the population. The landed classes, where they did not live in long one-storey thatched houses, lived in cramped tower-houses at the end of the sixteenth century; at a lower social level people occupied a one-room cabin without even the luxury of a chimney. In the next two centuries the landed class moved from tower house or thatched dwelling to the modern country house. In popular housing, the chimney became commonplace, and the addition of a second or third room — a modest imitation, with a time lag, of the improved living styles of the rural upper classes — implied a revolutionary change in popular attitudes to privacy. The upper-class demand for privacy — a key measure of the progress of civilization in Europe before 1500 or in Ireland between 1600 and 1700 — had by 1800 percolated down to more than half the population.

In 1600 the transition had scarcely begun in Ireland. Tower houses were still being built as late as the first half of the seventeenth century. In 1672 Petty could count four out of every five houses as chimney-less. But transition was powerfully evident from mid-century. At various dates over the next century and a half, the occupiers of tower houses abandoned them for more modern dwellings, and given the lateness of the transition, the tower-house has often survived, either as part of a more modern building or in proximity to it. Ironically, it has often outlived the building of Georgian or Regency times. At Moyode, near Athenry, the ruined Persse house is a few hundred yards from a well-preserved tower-house within the demesne; at Castlegrove, six miles from Tuam, the ruins of a demolished Georgian mansion are concealed in the exuberant planting within yards of a perfect tower-house. The new and old stand, or until recently stood, side by side, evidence of the protracted survival of archaic life styles and of an abrupt, although regionally and individually uneven, transition to the modern.

The link between old and new was frequently close or intimate. Dinely's sketches of Ireland, c. 1680, are full of tower-houses with modern two-storey quarters with large windows added to them. The process of adding more spacious living quarters to tower houses continued into the eighteenth century, the cost of the addition amounting to about £1,000 in the early decades, and the physical dependence of the new on the old has been one of the factors which has helped to ensure the survival of the old. Such composite dwellings were frequently the habitations of the lesser gentry, unable to afford or unwilling to make, a complete break with the past. But even richer, reforming gentry were sometimes content to compromise. Robert French of Monivea — in the mid-eighteenth century the foremost moderniser west of the Shannon — and his descendants, were content to live in a great tower-house extended in two directions at right angles in the late seventeenth and early eighteenth centuries. Even when the mighty moved decisively to a new dwelling it was sometimes in sight of the old. One of the most dramatic vistas in Ireland is the view from Newberry Hall built by the fashionable amateur architect Nathaniel Clements some time after the marriage in 1747 of Mary Colley, heiress of Castle Carbury, to Arthur Pomeroy. Castle Carbury itself, a large fortified house of c. 1600 standing on an eminence less than a mile away, was abandoned within a few years, its chimneys and roofless walls still reaching to the sky to-day. Only Dunluce Castle on the Antrim coast is a more haunting spectre of the past. Castle Carbury, a nucleus of early colonization in the midlands, had been occupied by the Colleys from the 1560s. The decision to build the new house was accompanied by an urge to modernize the estate. Mrs Pomeroy and her co-heiress sister, Mrs Glover, as well as two aunts, in 1747 endowed and built a Charter School, clear proof of a personal commitment to change.[2] The abortive village of Castle Carbury, already a visible failure when the ordnance survey mapped the location at the end of the 1830s, and the survival of a substantial nucleus of Protestant settlement, are both evidence of the high intent and wide ambitions inextricably intertwined with something, at first sight, as purely personal and intimate as domestic architecture.

The tower houses, like their only alternative, the long rambling one-storey houses, had thatched roofs. Thatch lingered unfashionably into the eighteenth century in upper class dwellings. Even as late as 1709 the building of a two-storeyed, mudwalled house by a large gentleman tenant was regarded by the surveyor of the Courtenay estate in Limerick as evidence of improvement.[3] When Mrs Pendarves (the future Mrs Delany) visited the west of Ireland in 1732, she remarked on 'the thatched cabin' of a man worth £1,500 a year near Castlegar who kept a man cook, and less than a fortnight later while in the Killala region, took shelter in the course of an outing in the thatched cabin of a man worth £2,000 who, nevertheless, was refined enough to be able to refresh his unexpected guests with tea.[4] Mrs Delany expressed disappointment with houses in Ireland. However, on her first visit the cumulative effect of house building was still limited, and refinement itself frequently did not reach beyond the erection of a slated dwelling amid surroundings as rustic as their predecessors. Had she made her observations twenty years later, the sustained improvements of the second quarter of the century would have justified a more favourable judgement. By the 1750s the old was fast disappearing. Smith's histories of Cork, Kerry and Waterford illustrate vividly the mass of recent and current building and demesne improvement in three counties. The thatched gentry residence had disappeared, and the thatched house built by Isaac Corry at Derrymore in 1766 was a mere pleasant conceit. In the remoteness of Iveragh, the O'Connells erected the first slated house in 1745. Not only the gentry but many of the large farmers and middlemen were housed in slated dwellings. A step down in the social scale, Arthur O'Leary, (a relative by marriage of the O'Connells, but one whose marriage with their daughter was sharply disapproved of) at the outset of the 1770s lived a few miles outside Macroom, in one of the compact small Georgian houses whose erection illustrates the diffusion of modernity. Lower still in the social scale, the poet Eoghan Rua O'Súilleabháin, born on the neighbouring Cork/Kerry border, whose poetry was well-known to the Gaelic upper class of the region, offered the inducement of a slated house to the lady courted in the imagery of one of his poems: the aspiration was now a general one of the rural upper class. The obligation to erect a slated dwelling was frequently imposed in leases on the large tenant; as early as the 1740s newspaper advertisements of farms out of lease in advanced regions suggest that such slated houses, set amid orchards and outhouses and surrounded by enclosed fields, were already not uncommon among the larger occupying tenants.

For the demographer the period is dominated by its rapid population growth; for the economic historian by the sustained rise in trade and output which laid the financial basis to support sustained change, and for the social historian by the refinement in houses, furniture and decoration, which engulfed the upper classes. The period is refreshing because while the changes reflect or anticipate the relentless effort to be fashionable characteristic of the better-off in all modern societies, the changes in the eighteenth century correspond not merely to changes in fashion but to a revolution in life styles involving an emphasis on sophistication and comfort whose significance went far beyond the superficial aspect of fashion. It is no accident that the period was characterized by an intellectual ferment less compelling perhaps by its innate originality than by its wide social diffusion: ideas and people both circulated. Parliament, which had rarely and fleetingly met in the seventeenth century — and did not meet at all between 1667 and 1692 — met regularly for an extended session from October to May every second year: the press of business made necessary an annual session from 1771. Dublin, whose growth had almost stagnated in the 1680s and 1690s, was already expanding rapidly against a background of dire economic depression in the nation at large in the first decade of the eighteenth century: its new-found social and administrative importance gave it immunity against the crisis which paralyzed the economy. A coach route to Drogheda existed from the seventeenth century, one to Kilkenny came into existence later and the inception of a coach service twice a week to Kinnegad in 1717[5] signified the lure of Dublin for the upper class of the wide reaches of the midlands, west and north-west. Political ferment led to an explosion of ephemeral literature in the 1720s. While only two Irish writers of the period — Berkeley and Swift — were to find a lasting place in literature, the contrast between the lively controversial pamphlets of the 1720s and the virtual absence of public debate previously illustrates the range of interests of the writers of the 1720s. A real if narrow public opinion had emerged to which appeal was made. During the reign of George I no less than 33 newspapers were launched, and in contrast to the ephemeral journals of Anne's reign, almost half can be regarded as successful ventures.[6]

Some of the ideas concerned economic matters, the economic crisis of the late 1720s calling forth several pamphlets in 1728 ranging widely over economic issues with a novel sophistication. In the following year, in the aftermath of the famine of 1728-29 and simultaneously with Swift's *Modest proposal*, the two most original pamphlets appeared — those by Prior and by Dobbs (with a second part in 1731) — which were to underlie, along with Berkeley's *Querist* and Madden's *Resolutions and reflections proper for the gentlemen of Ireland* in the 1730s, the economic thinking of the entire century. An informed public opinion was emerging, the Dublin Society in 1731 being the inevitable outcome. Its membership was small — only 267 at the end of its third year.[7] By contrast, in Brittany, almost as populous as Ireland, a similar society, the first in France, emerged only in 1757 and collapsed in 1770. Moreover, the members of the Dublin Society were the influential gentry, who spent their lives between their seats and Dublin and who were the leaders of public opinion in their counties. Their example in practical support for the linen industry and for improved husbandry on their own estates supplemented the spoken and printed word. Prior, an improving landlord on his estate near Rathdowney, author of *List of the absentees of Ireland*, the most reprinted pamphlet of the eighteenth century, typifies the society's vigour. But many of its other members not only supported its didactic work on agriculture or industry, but sponsored the linen industry on their own estates, or the foundation of the Charter Schools which were intended to stress with equal emphasis knowledge of spinning and weaving and the religious tenets of the established church. At the very least, such men were immensely influential among their colleagues on the Grand Juries in the counties.

The intellectual upheaval, much of it practical in its emphasis on social issues and economic improvement, was itself part and parcel of the emerging revolution in housing. Berkeley, though highly censorious (in his *Querist* in 1735) of extravagance in all its forms, unreservedly supported expenditure on building and decoration, because it gave employment, and the severely practical Madden, quoting the example of Colonel Newburgh, approved of stucco in place of wainscotting and plaster arches in place of timber because they reduced the fire risk.[8] The new modes in housing and decoration were in harmony with intellectual developments, and both changed at the same time. A decisive change in upper class housing was beginning in the second decade of the century — too recent for its cumulative effect to influence Mrs Pendarves' judgment; and the houses of the 1710s and 1720s are themselves mute testimony in stone to the changing world and outlook mirrored in the flood of ephemeral literature of the 1720s and 1730s.

Cultural changes depend on education, and in turn on economic wealth to finance their physical embodiment. It was inevitable that the changes of the century should be first evident among the gentry, and that even among them acceptance of change should be uneven. The gentry who visited Dublin — and only wealth guaranteed regular travel — were to the fore: the new aspirations began to seriously influence the lesser gentry with some delay, so that changes, while bringing about in the long run a general revolution of outlook in the upper classes, in the short term actually multiplied contrasts. The dominant cultural role of the upper classes has been frequently attributed to their recent English origins, but it was in fact more a consequence of the wealth — and the advantages that wealth conferred — of the landed classes, whether of recent immigrant stock or long-established. Inter-marriage also spread new influences and Irish and Anglo-Norman gentry were already remarkably flexible in outlook and economic management in the seventeenth century. Even a wholly Gaelic chieftain like O'Flaherty in Connemara was not immune to change. While Dunton visited him in a smoke-filled 'habitation', the O'Flahertys excused it by observing that 'they had newly put up this for a booley or summer habitation, the proper dwelling or mansion house being some miles further near the sea'.[9] The primitive life style and housing, redolent of Elizabethan times, of a chieftain visited by Cuffe of Ballinrobe and friends, when they crossed the Corrib in the 1750s, was already an anachronism:[10] a survival of a life-style already rare before the end of the seventeenth century among the upper classes even of the most remote regions. The O'Sullivans of the Eyeries on the Bere peninsula were lawless petty gentry in the 1730s; a recapture by them of contraband was the occasion in 1733 of the largest mass proclamation of 'tories' in the eighteenth century, and as late as 1754 a member of the family, Morty Oge O'Sullivan, son of the leader of the 1733 gang was hunted down after the sordid dispute in which he killed his former smuggling confederate, John Puxley, a minor Protestant gentleman turned thief-catcher. But by 1790 the O'Sullivans had so changed in their life style that the visitor Coquebert de Montbret found their social vanities ridiculous.[11] The fact that social changes were inevitable whatever the composition of the ruling gentry has frequently been overshadowed by the revolution in landownership in the seventeenth century which in two generations transferred the bulk of Irish lands into the hands of new owners from England. This abrupt change overshadowed the deeper pervasive forces which were quite independently leading to economic and social change.

The new owners are said to have imposed outside standards, and, eager to make a profit, to have quickened commercialization. This, while not wholly untrue, overlooks the intimate involvement of the older gentry in foreign trade from at least the sixteenth century — both Galway and Waterford families were meshed into an intricate family network in which merchant and landed origins were indistinguishable, and younger sons moved abroad to the plantations or to foreign ports. In Galway, in particular, where no revolution in landownership took place, landed continuity was responsible for a striking survival of the pattern well into the eighteenth century.[12] In a family such as the Blakes, speculative involvement in trade was looked at askance only from the early nineteenth century[13] as the region experienced to the full the exaltation of landed respectability already established in eastern Ireland and in England.

There is of course everywhere evidence of the impact of landed upheaval — resentment by the dispossessed, insecurity among the new proprietors. The former landowners resented change, a fact illustrated in the Munster poetry which mirrors their aspirations for a restoration of their lands and the dispossession of the upstarts, as they regarded the new owners who had replaced them. The land system which came into existence as a result of landed settlement in the seventeenth century has been represented as a degradation of the rural population, but this view cannot correctly be drawn from the Munster poetry which laments not oppression, but dispossession. Leases were deplored, but simply because, set, in their view by the wrongful owners, they were the legal expression of the new system. In poetry which is not aristocratic, far from the lease being regarded as oppressive, leasehold was viewed as a token of security. Tenants on the whole benefited from the spread of leasehold in place of the arbitrary and more uncertain tenures hitherto common. Where they did not, it was generally a consequence of the collapse of prices, as in the dire first decade of the new century, when after prices fell abruptly, rents, reasonable at the time of leasing, overnight become oppressive in their incidence.

The dispossessed landowners, while suffering degradation in their status, usually retained sufficient working capital to stock large farms and to gain them preference over less solvent bidders for land. Both the landlord preference for large tenants who were believed to be less likely to default in rent payment and the entrenched social position of the old gentry in their region ensured their survival in dairying and cattle raising districts (although less certainly in mixed or tillage regions) as gentleman tenants. Paradoxically, it was precisely their ability to survive in gentle status, which accounts for the strongly expressed aspirations in the poetry of the region. In the tillage — and socially less archaic — regions of the east, or regions of mixed farming like Kilkenny, large working farmers were too numerous to leave an outlet for middlemen of large acres and aristocratic pretensions. In Waterford, Cork and Kerry, however, the large middlemen tenants, with the finely-tuned social awareness of an archaic society and frequently occupying as tenants the lands of which they regarded themselves rightful owners, found their circumstances galling. But having an assured, though reduced, social and economic position to lose, they were cautious of disloyalty. As always it was those who emigrated who were most likely to talk treason, and the prospect of war always led to loose talk among the Irish in France, Spain and even in London. Among those who remained at home, there was only a handful who openly adopted provocative attitudes, most notably James Cotter (executed in 1720), Morty Oge O'Sullivan (killed in 1754) and Arthur O'Leary, killed in 1773. Sir James Cotter, executed in 1720, was the only one of one of these three propertied in fee. Born in 1691, the son of a Jacobite leader in Cork, his behaviour and death seem part of the legacy of the 1690s, and his execution in 1720 took place in the aftermath of a projected Jacobite invasion. The O'Sullivans, on the other hand, in relatively modest circumstances, and Arthur O'Leary, probably a profligate younger son, represented a reckless element, whose behaviour was unrestrained by economic calculation and even by coherent political purpose: they both died in years of peace when invasion was not on the horizon, and in O'Leary's case when Jacobitism no longer had a meaning for Catholics. O'Sullivan and O'Leary were not representative of rich or rising Catholics: the O'Connell disavowal of Eibhlín Dubh Ní Chonaill marriage to Arthur O'Leary seems clear evidence of the active dissociation by rising Catholics from such disedifying co-religionists. The upper class was, except in 1744, very conventional in the expression of the aspiration of restoration: only the greatest of Jacobite projects of invasion led some to abandon their detachment.

If the native Irish have been represented as oppressed, the counterpart has been the representation of the eighteenth century as 'an age of insecurity' on the part of the Anglo-Irish landed class. The insecurity, while it existed, can be exaggerated. It was most clearly defined by Fitzgibbon in the 1780s for a political purpose: in an attempt to frighten the Munster landed class from lending countenance to the popular uprising against tithes. Just as for the dispossessed the greatest fervour for restoration was evident abroad, insecurity seemed greater viewed from London than from home. The Charter Schools drew heavily on English financial support — much of it from Anglo-Irish families in London — and while the agrarian unrest in the 1780s and early 1790s received a calm reaction from the landed classes in Ireland, it seemed much more frightening viewed from Bath, where 'we think you all in a state of anarchy'[14]. As late as 1795 a complacent brother among the Clements, alarmed for their safety in lawless Cavan, maintained that the guns being seized from Protestant households were for hare shooting in the mountains.[15]

The variation in attitudes of the landed classes between and within counties is striking. It was a selective rather than a general fear, paradoxically most evident where Protestants were numerous rather than where they were few. The attitude to Catholics by landlord or agent was most illiberal in the north where Catholics were usually in a minority, and in varying degrees was less marked elsewhere. Even in the south, where sectarian tensions were intermittently very evident in several counties, they were closely related to the traditional support of Jacobitism; they were gentry-manipulated, spreading to Waterford and Tipperary from Cork through family ramifications, and reached their peak in the 1760s. A landed sense of insecurity was not responsible for the accelerated sectarian tensions of the late 1780s and 1790s. Quite apart from the fact that they began in the north, they followed a period of pronounced landlord complacency in the 1780s, and bore in upon the landed classes by a novel and alarming momentum of their own acquired in the 1790s. The heightened insecurity of the 1790s was a response to a novel combination of factors — a more self-sufficient, literate peasantry, a decline in deference, and the disturbing implications of contemporary revolution in France, itself a subtle catalyst of class relationships in a delicately balanced and complex situation. It exacerbated differences of opinion among the gentry themselves — liberals favoured reform even more fervently, conservatives regarded reform as surrender to the forces of demagogy.

The relationship between Ireland and England was of course colonial — profoundly colonial in fact not only because Ireland was subservient politically and economically, but because Ireland received civil and ecclesiastical administrators, more humble immigrants, and ideas from England, and in turn many Irish migrated to London in search of fame or fortune. Sheridan, Goldsmith, Barry and others pursued their careers in London; Irish absentee planters from the West Indies made their residence in England, and the Fitzgeralds, Nesbitts and many lesser, though still successful merchant houses, opened business houses or supported relatives in London. As ideas were imported to Ireland and were sometimes carried by Englishmen who moved to Ireland, the contrasts between old and new could be represented not as a consequence of unending change, but in strictly colonial terms. Social tensions or conflict could equally be expressed as part of a colonial relationship.

Understanding of the landed classes is however clouded by being cast in a colonial context. The role of the gentry, whatever its composition, was indispensable in the transition from medieval to modern, and had its counterpart in the modernizing role of the English gentry or of the continental nobility. The position of the Irish gentry was actually far less despotic than has often been represented; their powers as landlords more circumscribed than elsewhere.

In Scotland, for instance, the tenants enjoyed no such privileges as the tenants in Ulster, and Scottish landlords were dictators in comparison to Irish landlords.[16] The relatively favourable tenures in Ulster were, in part, a consequence of the conscious landlord attempt to attract immigrants in the seventeenth century to the most under-populated province in Ireland. But the landord's power, limited in the north because it had been an under-populated region, could not be exercised freely in the other provinces precisely because they were more densely settled. In such regions, though landowners were legally free to bring in outsiders, it was difficult to do so economically or successfully, and landlords failed in the most settled parts of the east and south both to establish a strong Protestant community and to bring about sweeping changes in economic or social structures.

One of the most arresting failures comes from the estate, on the rich northern bank of the Suir, of the Ponsonbys, whig magnates who dominated Irish political life in the middle decades of the eighteenth century. The estate village — Piltown — is poorly planned: Protestant tenants, though more numerous than in other south Kilkenny parishes, were relatively few by comparison with many estates elsewhere; and within a few miles of the great house, archaic fields and village patterns survived in the 1830s almost unchanged. Landlord ability to bring about change was therefore dramatically limited, and in particular, except where marginal land or under-populated upland was at hand, any strong colonies of Protestants which landlords had been able to establish, had been set up with few exceptions while the country was still comparatively under-populated in the first half of the seventeenth century. The co. Wexford plantation, one of the most successful of Irish plantations, was facilitated by the woodland conditions of North Wexford at the outset of the seventeenth century. In co. Louth, strong Protestant settlements had been effected before 1660 in the barony of Dundalk and more modestly across the border of Meath in Duleek, but the only significant new settlement in the eighteenth century was made by Baron Anthony Foster at Collon on land regained from upland waste. Later attempts at settlement themselves usually took place in districts where a significant pre-1641 nucleus already existed. There were few eighteenth or early nineteenth-century attempts to introduce settlers to areas which had been unaffected by significant pre-1641 immigration. Tensions, of course, existed in such areas — the 1641 rebellion with its attendant 'massacres' is a sensitive indicator of their presence. There emerged a sharp contrast between areas where a significant Protestant population, in the main introduced before 1641, existed, and other regions where Protestant tenant settlement was never large. Where strongly populated Protestant areas overlapped with Catholic areas, a cultural and settlement frontier emerged, where friction existed or remained dormant but could, as in 1798 in the Carlow, Wicklow and North Wexford region, flare up alarmingly. The continuity in Irish history is overwhelming, and because sectarian tensions are unattractive, depressing. The distribution of Protestant settlement did not change greatly from 1641, the tensions evident then having a painful persistence in much of the country, relieved in some areas only by the collapse of Protestant communities as a vigorous force even before the end of the eighteenth century.

1641 is, from a colonizing perspective, a high point in landlord influence. After 1641, the landlord role in sponsoring immigration was significantly reduced, and spontaneous as opposed to sponsored immigration gained ground for the remainder of the century. Significantly, the Cromwellian settlement, unlike previous plantations, imposed no obligations on recipients to settle specified numbers of settlers. By contrast, the highly formal plantations like the Desmond and Ulster plantations had defined elaborate obligations on beneficiaries to establish settlers on the land. The more informal plantations in Leitrim, Wexford and Offaly, though lacking in such specifications, were carried into effect by planters with a determination to establish a settler population on the ground. The official and the private will to bring in immigrants both appear to have weakened thereafter. The Williamite Settlement in 1691 legally took the form of an outright sale of land rather than a land settlement, and the purchasers were, in the main, Irish landlords or speculators. The Hollow Sword-Blades Company, based on London, came into the picture only when lands were selling slowly, and its huge holding, almost half the land distributed, was sold off in later years mainly to Irish purchasers. The main stream of immigrants in the second half of the century was of largely unsponsored Scots, coming in large numbers fitfully in the 1650s, at the end of the 1670s and massively in the 1690s, almost exclusively to the north of Ireland. A small stream of English non-conformity was evident in the south. The fact that Protestant communities in the south recovered after the 1641 rebellion, is in no small measure a consequence of a high rate of natural increase among existing settlers who had stuck it out or returned.

Landlords sponsored migration in the eighteenth century much more selectively than in the past — mainly of textile workers intended to occupy no more than a small plot of agricultural land and to be housed in villages. Sponsorship of purely agricultural settlement had become rare — largely on poorer land, often upland — and was quantitatively insignificant. While tenants introduced afresh by landlords could still exacerbate racial tensions between indigenous inhabitants and outsiders, there were no areas where landlords were able to introduce settlers in large numbers. Moreover, the diminished role of landlords was reflected too in unsponsored movement of Presbyterians from the northeast to neighbouring counties.

The religious and social ideas of Presbyterians had radical and egalitarian implications. The agrarian unrest of the 1760s and 1770s and the later background to the 1798 rebellion reflected as well as other causes an anti-landlord animus among Presbyterians. Agents disliked Presbyterians as much as Catholics and at times, in the troubled 1790s in the north, more. Everywhere that Presbyterians were numerous, landlord powers were subtly threatened after mid-century. The United Irishmen spread in areas where Presbyterian farmers and the independent weavers were relatively numerous; on the other hand the Orange Order, which supported the established order in Church and State unequivocally, first emerged in Armagh, where a higher proportion of the population belonged to the Established Church and the economic independence of the weavers had already been diminished by the spread of the putting-out system.

3
The landlord's world

The Georgian period in Ireland was essentially a period of economic growth. Exports in current values, a mere £400,000 in 1665, passed £1 million per annum in the 1710s, a compound rate of increase of 2 per cent. Slow growth between the 1710s and 1740s was followed by sustained growth. Exports rose dramatically by 150 per cent between 1743/4 and 1770/1 i.e. at a compound annual rate of 3.4 per cent. Thereafter the pace slackened. For the entire period 1743/4 to 1792/3 they rose only at a compound rate of 2.9 per cent per annum, and the rate of growth fell further to 2.6 per cent per annum for the period 1792/3-1835. Trade created wealth. While its immediate beneficiaries were the landed classes, the fruits of expansion were shared with others as time passed and, in the long run, landlords ceased to have a virtual monopoly of wealth. But that was not immediately evident, and in the short term the incomes of the landed class rose not only absolutely but relatively. The enhancement of the role of the gentry was dramatic in the second quarter of the eighteenth century — a rise in rents as a proportion of incomes, cultural or intellectual ascendancy and unchallenged political power in local and national politics. The shadow of the future Presbyterian challenge to the establishment was still beyond the horizon — the fear of Presbyterian immigration so evident in the 1690s had abated and landlords, apparently secure in their world, were from the 1720s actively enticing Presbyterian linen workers from the north to their own estates. Moreover, the rising influence of the gentry was spread across the entire class, not confined to the peers or magnates. The equality of peer and gentleman was much more marked than in the past: the political role of the latter, helped by the absenteeism of many of the peers, left local political management in the hands of the gentry. It was now rare for a great peer to be received ceremoniously on his return to his estate not simply by his tenantry, but by the surrounding gentry. The reception in 1742 of the Earl of Clanrickarde at Portumna, attended by the gentry of the region on his return, was already an anachronism.[1]

From mid-century, when the rate of economic growth quickened so sharply, some of its benefits were spilling over into the hands even of the poorest. In the short term this seemed to add to, rather than diminish the prestige of the gentry: while rising rents facilitated landlord investment, rising incomes at large created the comforting illusion that landlord initiative was successfully shaping the environment and was responsible for the general rise in living standards. Landlord initiative was dramatically widespread in the 1740s and 1750s: never again was landlord enterprise and investment to be channelled simultaneously in so many directions. The growth of trade was astonishing after mid-century — imports rose by 73 per cent between 1745/6 and 1753/4, and by a further 39 per cent by 1770/1. The contrast with the uncertain trends of the preceding decades and their culminating famine of 1740-41 and near-famine of 1744-5 was striking to contemporaries. The so-called 'gap in the famines' between mid-century and the famines of the nineteenth century, popularized as an interpretative concept by Professor Connell, has been attributed to diet, especially to the advent of the potato. But as dietary changes were immensely complex — with both early changes and retardation in their diffusion — it seems implausible to attribute a relatively sudden change in social trends to something proceeding as slowly as dietary change. A more significant factor was the unexpected economic improvement which in putting some savings or cash in the hands of the poorest raised them if only marginally above subsistence level in a bad year.[2] Even as early as 1746 — immediately after the bad harvest of 1744 and the uneven one of 1745 — a perceptive agent's comment in co. Cork dwelt on the economic situation not having been so good for many years[3]; the agent on the Abercorn estate in the north reported in 1748 that 'we have had a very good season in this country', the improvement by 1752 being astonishing.[4] The Sligo landlord, Charles O'Hara, noted a decade later how tenants were able to survive seasons which a few years previously would have threatened disaster.[5]

While landlords had hardly created the changing environment, they were acutely aware of all that was happening, a fact nowhere more evident than in the most fundamental activity of a landlord — leasing policy. When price trends had been indifferent and the great mass of rural inhabitants semi-pauperized, as in the seventeenth and early eighteenth centuries, landlords had favoured very large tenants at low rents in the belief that their resources were some guarantee of ability to pay the rent. Disappointment with such tenants led to a pronounced swing from mid-century to smaller tenants, among whom individuals able to stock a farm were now more numerous and whose ability to pay rent was facilitated by the remarkable general economic advance. Self-interest as well as considerations of economic improvement dictated this course. Tenants taking large tracts at low rents, on long leases and sub-letting on higher rents and shorter tenures had lived well, and landlords resented a situation in which much of the profits of economic advance went to an intermediary rather than to the head landlord. In time, with population growth and extensive sub-division, landlord policy changed again in emphasis, favouring moderate-sized tenancies for good farmers in place of small tenants and facing up with varying degrees of resolution in the pre-famine decades to problems of sub-division, pauper tenants and clearance. Thus, landlord policy moved sensitively in recognition of social changes — from a preference for large tenants when no other solvent tenants offered, to one for smaller tenants when general economic improvement, from 1745, created a significantly larger number of solvent individuals in the rural community; and finally, by the early nineteenth century, to a growing preference for proved farming ability as opposed to mere ability to pay the rent.

The landlord's unique monopoly of wealth could not of course last in a society where economic change distributed some of the benefits to many. It explains, however, the landlord's leadership at mid-century in mining, large-scale enterprise in textiles and the promotion of canal and road building. Landlord rent accounted, in the eighteenth century, for at least a third of the net income of the rural community. Some of the wealth of the landlord was syphoned off by townspeople and urban creditors. Urban incomes were disproportionately high, both because of an urban monopoly of trade — and high distributive costs in a relatively backward society — and because landlord expenditure and extravagance so often benefited urban creditors and suppliers. To assume that urban income was as large as rural income is not very wide of the mark. Landlord rentals accounted for about 16 per cent and more probably 20 per cent of total national income. If it is borne in mind how few non-agricultural capitalists existed outside the towns, and how poor relatively even the best-off of the tenants below the level of middleman were, the utter dominance of the landlord in mid-eighteenth century rural society is immediately evident. Rents as a proportion of agricultural output were high, and the equalization of gains and losses between seasons meant that tenant capacity to save was limited. Even in a county such as Meath, nationally recognized for its prosperous farmers, the 'clear profit' to a farmer of 100 acres was estimated at only £56 as late as 1802[6]. As an artisan — mason or carpenter — earned three shillings a day, he could earn almost as much in a year as the farmer. Of course the contrast is overstated, the artisan could not count on regularity of employment, at least in his declining years, while the farmer's security and cheap food gave him an advantage hard to quantify but reflected in the fact that farmers, but few artisans, could dower their daughters generously. But the farmer's actual cash income was not much larger than that of the artisan, and his high propensity to save, while it gave him a security and a status beyond the reach of the artisan, left him with a day-to-day living standard superficially not much different from the artisan's. Contemporaries were frequently misled by the same superficial similarities into concluding that farmers of even 50 acres were little, if anything, better off than the labourers they hired; as in the case of the larger farmers, a high propensity to save minimized the contrast in current living standards, the dramatic contrast in security and status often not being fully appreciated by the almost invariably socially remote observers of the period.

The dominant role of landlords not only over their tenants but over the economy is, therefore, hardly surprising. They dominated iron and coal mining — a landlord, a small one, Robert Hartpole, on the borders of Leix introduced the first steam engine in 1740 — not unexpectedly, perhaps, as the minerals lay below the land they held in fee. Equally, they were the main or almost sole entrepreneurs in the first factory enterprises, whether in flour mills in the 1760s or the early textile ventures, and as late as the 1780s they were well represented among the projectors of the new cotton enterprises.

Landlord income rose rather unevenly, reflecting the leasing history of the individual estate, and at national level, the bunching in leasing caused by the upheavals in the land market in the 1650s and 1690s. The falling in of the leases set at low rents in the 1650s and their renewal at higher rents 14 to 21 years later, explains the landlord ability to undertake the house-building commented on by Clarendon in 1686. In the difficult economic conditions of the late 1680s and early 1690s, many tenants abandoned their farms, Protestants frequently returning to England. There was massive resetting of land for several years after order was restored in 1691, usually at low rents because economic conditions remained uncertain till war ended in 1697. As the 21 year leases set before 1697 expired between 1712 and 1717 and the 31 year leases between 1722 and 1727, there was a sharp rise in rents in the late 1710s and 1720s. Stagnant farm income combined with rising rents was responsible for a redistribution of a static national income towards the landlords. It was this circumstance that accounts for the rapacity with which landlords were vehemently charged by their most hostile critic, Jonathan Swift. If rents rose, the amount of rent remitted to absentees rose automatically; the country seemed threatened with insolvency, if as was the case in the 1720s, exports were static. Comment on absentee remittances multiplied through the 1720s reaching its most fully developed form in the celebrated pamphlet by Thomas Prior in 1729, *List of the absentees of Ireland*. The improved economic circumstances of landlords — the source of criticism of the class in a decade of economic difficulty and, in its closing years, of dire poverty and even famine — account for the first general wave of house-building since the early 1680s. The 'genius towards building' of George Mathew at Thomastown in co. Tipperary was commented on in 1718, his house near completion 'full of joyners and carpenters, but he hopes to have finished all this summer, and then he will have the compleatest seat in this kingdom'[7]. His brother-in-law, Kean O'Hara, was building in co. Sligo at the same time. The Conollys who enjoyed the largest rental in Ireland laid in 1722 the first stones of Castletown which was to remain the largest house erected in eighteenth-century Ireland. Other great houses, Carton, Powerscourt and Westport, followed soon after. These houses set both the fashion and the style.

Leases for 21 or 31 years, or for 3 lives, set in the 1720s, fell in typically at various dates from 1740 to 1770. Rents were depressed — arrears mounted ominously — in the early 1740s but from the beginning of the 'economic miracle' in 1745 to 1770, rent rolls roughly doubled. The rise in the rental, occurring this time amid general economic advance, did not result as in the 1720s and 1730s in the absolute impoverishment of the rural population. The incomes of all rose, the incomes of landowners perhaps more than most. The building boom — still confined in the 1720s to the very rich or the very fashionable — had now become widespread; and though many of the landed classes rehoused themselves only in the 1770s or later, the modern house had made its appearance everywhere.

Significantly, the few architectural works published in eighteenth-century Ireland were concentrated in the 1750s[8]. John Aheron's book was in manuscript by 1751, in print by 1754; and the Reverend John Payne's more influential *Twelve designs for country houses* was in manuscript in 1753, in print in 1757[9]. Rents whose rise was halted during the difficult 1770s, perhaps doubled to £12 million between 1776 and 1813, lands set before the 1770s usually becoming due for renewal at some time during the sustained rise in prices between 1793 and 1814. The rise was slower than during the heady years of the 1750s and 1760s — the doubling was accomplished in almost twice the time — but the sustained rise made possible the continued housebuilding. In the 1770s housebuilding had very unevenly reached the upper classes, Young, for instance, commenting on the indifferent housing of many of the gentry. The box-like Georgian house of the late eighteenth and early nineteenth centuries made its appearance in the countryside during this period. It was, in a sense, a product for a mass market reaching far down the social scale of upper class affluence. Compared with the variations in earlier houses, it reflects the relative standardization of mass building: cheap, relatively unpretentious and functionally successful, drawing on the cumulative lessons of a hundred years of housebuilding for the upper classes. The general rise in rents halted after 1812. The condition of individual families varied enormously however, depending on the accidents of leasing history. Landlords with old leases which fell in after 1812 could still experience a rise in income; on the Downshire estate the rental, after a steep rise, net of newly purchased land, of 79 per cent between 1801 and 1815, rose by 40 per cent in the 29 years from 1815 to 1844.[10] It was a low rate of increase by eighteenth-century standards, but higher than on many less fortunate contemporary estates.

The rise in rentals before 1815 had triggered off the last wave of great house building: the Gothic mania of the early nineteenth century. Francis Johnston's talent was given free rein on new and old: Morrison covered the south; existing houses such as the Mathew house at Thomastown were

Gothicized, and vast Gothic mansions such as Gosford, Markree, Dromoland or Mitchelstown were erected. Even flour mills, frequently gentry-built, did not escape the fashion. While the Slane mill, the largest in Ireland in the 1760s, was built on the lines of a classical house, the mill complex of the Alexanders near Carlow, rebuilt and extended after 1814, the largest in Ireland at that time, was castellated as were a number of other mills. The Gothic mania reflects the fashionable urge at the top of the social scale, once new styles were general, to diversify. But it was of course an indulgence, and hence lacks the appeal of earlier Georgian houses which had heralded not only a fashion but more fundamentally a break-through in the standard of the home environment.

The landlords' role was all the more effective because they were in the main resident. A rapid turnover of property — in the 20 years after 1604 only one third of the 33 seignories in Munster remained in the hands of the original families [11] — was more a feature of early plantation, and some remained to accumulate impressive holdings. While absenteeism was not insignificant, it was far from progressive; typically it occurred in the second generation of a successful plantation family. Even in the early plantations, many members of the beneficiary families were resident, their presence in fact being indispensable for the erection and maintenance of the fortified dwellings characteristic of plantation in the first half of the seventeenth century. George Courtenay, for instance, resided in his castle at Newcastle, co. Limerick and members of the Digby family at Geashill, King's county. But the Courtenays ceased to reside; the large Digby estate was later managed by an agent, with some assistance from cadet Digbys; the vast Wentworth estate in south Wicklow shared the misfortune of its mighty landlord, the Earl of Strafford; the mansion at Tinehely was never completed, and the marriage of a Wentworth heiress in 1744 to a Fitzwilliam simply passed the property from one English absentee family to another.

The Courtenay, Digby and Wentworth estates illustrate, for different areas and in different contexts, not atypical developments. Immense properties such as the Orrery lands in Cork (the later Burlington estate) or the Petty-Fitzmaurice lands in Kerry, once built up by able, enterprising adventurers like the Great Earl of Cork and Sir William Petty respectively, were subsequently in the hands of absentee descendants, the vast Irish rentals supporting English pretensions based on equally vast possessions. Planters from the first plantations were after a generation joined by new absentees from the Cromwellian plantation, but the alarming rise in absenteeism towards the end of the century was of a once for all nature. If some were destined to leave, others including many of the new, mid-seventeenth century families, chose to stay. The change in the pattern of the typical village from the rudimentary settlement focused on a village green to a formally planned village, usually intimately related to a demesne, betokens a more permanent landlord presence. The rise in absenteeism was in effect contained. While the granting of land to corporate bodies such as the London Companies (or Dublin-based such as Trinity College) in the early seventeenth century, created an impersonal landed nexus from a very early date, the pattern was not repeated on the same scale in later times. The Hollow Sword-Blade Company, a body of projectors formed to purchase Irish lands at the outset and holding almost one half of the huge acreage involved in the Williamite Plantation, would have added to the weight of absenteeism, had the Company succeeded. But its failure meant that it had to sell most of its lands which passed into the hands of owners resident in Ireland. Thus, the upsurge in absenteeism was not reinforced by the Williamite settlement. The concern about absenteeism in the 1720s related to a static phenomenon, more the consequence of the rising burden of rent than of a rising number of absentees. In 1738, Madden, though not unconcerned about it reluctantly conceded that absentee remittances had been abnormally high in 1729.[12] The decline in absenteeism or in the absentee proportion of the total rental may have been a continuing phenomenon. The history of the land market in co. Cork in the eighteenth century, for example, concerns in the main the disposal of three great absentee estates to local purchasers.[13]

The crude contemporary estimates of rentals and absentee remittances seem also to betoken a decline in the proportion of rents remitted, from a third in the 1720s to a seventh in the 1770s. Residence within Ireland itself did not guarantee residence on the estate — many landowners possessed several estates, and had to make a decision on residence, in extreme cases residing on none but choosing to maintain themselves from their country rental in or near Dublin.[14] But residence was commonplace, and the splash of green denoting planting around a demesne and mansion is one of the most distinctive features of the county key maps in the ordnance survey of the 1830s and 1840s. Co. Cork had one to two hundred gentry families who dominated local social and political life.[15] Galway had a very large gentry, outstanding because they were almost all resident, and distinctive because not only did they hunt together (to single out one Galway trait already famous), but they transferred their social life to Dublin with their own dining club during the social season. Trinity College lands were often useful in helping to establish younger sons in a rural society. While they were legally tenants, they were for all practical purposes almost as secure as holders in fee — especially as the College, unlike private landowners, did not share the ambition to get rid of middlemen — and neither they nor their tenantry differentiated the holders of college land from owners in fee.

As a class, the gentry were therefore present to superintend change. The geographer's concept of a landlord-created landscape has a large element of truth.[16] It is evident most vividly in the demesnes, planted and walled typically at some time between 1740 and 1770, and scattered across the country with a degree of regularity, each presiding over its own region of property and influence. Visible change in rural areas by the landlord was not confined to the house and demesne. Most of the countryside was still open field in 1709. Even in Leinster, Molyneux could travel in 1709 from Dublin to Kilkenny largely through open fields.[17] But under landlord inspiration, expressed through lease-imposed obligations, the open fields were being enclosed in and before the 1750s. Much of this work was executed by the larger tenants, or middleman farmers. At Shrule on the Hartpole estate in Queen's county, John Bambrick, during the first three years of an advantageous lease taken in 1736, superintended the baking of bricks and the erection of a home costing £200 on a site (renamed Hollymount) with a walled garden. He cleared 'a great number of useless ditches which were not fences but covered with blackthorns and briars of various sorts' enclosing the land regularly, and manured the ground with 'lime, marl, dung and other manures'. He claimed that he spent £900 on these improvements and on farm buildings in 1736-8.[18]

It is the typical pattern of the period, in which landlord intent and tenant interest coincided to create a transformation of the landscape and of land use. The work was under way before mid-century, newspaper advertisements illustrating clearly the presence of newly erected slated houses and outbuildings and enclosed fields. It was carried to completion in the heady conditions of the late 1740s and early 1750s. Landlord hostility to middlemen as it emerged was most evident in the counties where middlemen were most entrenched, and where the middleman contribution was most uneven. In Leinster, on the other hand, middlemen were usually resident, their acreages relatively small — not above 500 acres — and they frequently represented a gentleman farmer, as opposed to large working farmers of lower social status. They were probably not as productive as large working farmers, and paying lower rents often on perpetuities (i.e. on leases renewable for ever), they were certainly less frugal. Their more ostentatious life style — approaching that of the gentry — was translated into the building of two-storey slated houses and the erection of modern farm buildings. Living in the countryside at no great remove from the people, their example inevitably influenced the social and business styles of the working farmers, and they thus contributed decisively to the gradual and almost imperceptible modernization of rural life.

Enclosure itself had troublesome preliminaries which could be solved not by the intervening tenant middlemen or the occupying farmer, but by the landlord alone. In much of Ireland the land was divided into strips either in vestigial remains of the open-field systems of Anglo-Norman areas or on the rundale pattern of more Gaelic regions where the occupiers had lived in village-type settlements, and the strips belonging to the individual tenant scattered across the parish, became ever more sub-divided as generation succeeded generation. Before land could be enclosed even by the tenant, the pattern of land use had to be reformed — the scattered strips of each tenant replaced by a more compact holding which could be enclosed into regular-sized fields. This was time-consuming work, and only personal attention by the landlord or by a trusted agent could bring about change. In 1762 Charles O'Hara referred as a matter of course, in one of his letters to Burke, to a day spent in the mountains personally dividing boundaries.[19] The extensive but uneven and retreating distribution of rundale suggested by Young's minutes of his Irish tour illustrates the effect of such work undertaken and executed silently with little surviving direct documentation of the operation. In much of the country it had obviously disappeared entirely, sometimes with a dramatic frontier between the large, regular landlord-created fields evident on the ordnance survey maps, and the small, irregular enclosures of adjoining upland. In an advanced county like Kilkenny, where some of the structures still survived intact as late as 1840, ruins of villages could be seen in 1802, where change had taken place 40 or 50 years previously.[20] In the more backward areas, early instances such as O'Hara's were simply precursors of later change, as landlord re-arrangement, often already completed in the more advanced counties, was still being vigorously conducted in the early decades of the nineteenth century. At the outset of the century, Vandeleur abolished rundale on his Kilrush estate in co. Clare. In counties Donegal and Leitrim landlords divided land into separate tenancies, Palmerston eliminated rundale on his Sligo estate and it was also disappearing on the western slopes of the Wicklow mountains.[21] Even in Mayo, partnership farming was said to be dissolving of late,[22] and the ordnance survey maps of c. 1840 reflect the contrasts created by the ongoing process of landlord-sponsored change in the most backward of all Irish counties.

The effort demanded of landlords was therefore sustained. They frequently gave their estates prolonged personal attention; the first Earl of Burlington spent ten years studying his father's deeds.[23] But for even the most work-prone, an agent (or agents) was indispensable. O'Hara had an agent on his Sligo property whose financial problems in 1765 and death in 1766 detained him in co. Sligo to a greater extent than he had wished.[24] As early as 1738, Madden referred to agents as 'entirely taken up in writing . . .'[25]. Mary Mathew, a socialite Dublin lady, found it difficult in 1772 to entertain her agent and his wife: 'he can only talk of farming, leases, accounts etc.'[26]

The emphasis on the lease and on mutual contract obligations entailed a fundamental change in landlord-tenant relationships, from the arbitrary dominion of landlord demands still characteristic of much of the rural scene in the seventeenth century to a highly regulated relationship, in which each tenant's place on the estate was first negotiated and thereafter determined by reference to a written contract. Agents varied immensely in quality or ability — ranging over the entire gamut from a salaried individual, sometimes a near relative valued for his gentry status, to the overpowerful tenant who not only held leases in his own name but managed the entire leasing policy of the estate, and to the mere rent-receiver, a solicitor or merchant from a neighbouring town whose regular appearances in person on the estate could be counted on only twice a year. But, however imperfect the execution of the agency, the responsibility was a specialized one conducted in large measure on the basis of written instruments, and devolved in a clear-cut fashion on an individual functionary. It was thus the basis for continuing scrutiny of the individual tenant and direct negotiation with him as opposed to the intermittent, unpredictable and arbitrary management of tenants, often collectively, in the past. The focus on the tenant was, of course, primarily on his ability to pay his rent, but it highlighted the contrasts in performance between individual tenants and implied consideration or preference for the more reliable tenant. It was only a step from this realization to the deliberate creation of an environment in which the tenant could more easily and effectively fulfil his obligations, to the mutual benefit of tenant and landlord. Thus in the middle of the century, the emphasis had already moved substantially from mere efficient but undiscriminating rent collecting to a positive involvement in actually shaping the physical structure of the estate and to an explicit preference for the more able tenant. But by the end of the eighteenth century, the relatively passive preference for the more able tenant had become a moral responsibility to raise the farming and living standards of the tenantry. The farming societies sponsored by landlords in many areas around 1800 are an eloquent but probably ineffective expression of this ambition. The demonstration effect intended by the building of farm houses and cottages, rebuilding villages, or efforts to impose more exacting estate regulations intended for the tenant's benefit (as defined by the landlord), illustrates the same aim, and some or all of the entire armoury of measures was implemented on estates in many parts of the country in the early decades of the nineteenth century. One of the most impressive attempts was on the Clancarty or Trench estate at Ballinasloe, with the rebuilt town and its strict regulation as to cleanliness, the neatly-built farmhouses whose erection was assisted by the landlord, and the personal 'moral' visits of Lord and Lady Clancarty to the tenantry.[27] The agent's role changed in sensitive reflection of the changing aims of estate management. The great 'moral' agents of the nineteenth century were emerging, unremitting in their attention to the entire range of estate duties and themselves committed to preaching the merits of their policy to the unconverted beyond their own estate. One of the first of the new agents in the second quarter was William Blacker, agent of both the Dungannon School estate and of the Gosford estate. His achievement was well known, not least through the vigorous literary apostolate represented by his own writing, but there are other equally dedicated, if less literary, agents. Steuart Trench, whose successive experiences on several Irish estates from the mid-1840s are outlined in his *Realities of Irish Life*, provided the most completely expressed record of this highly specialized compassion.

The most constant function of the landlord through all these changes was that of controlling settlement on the estate, whether on the individual farm or on the estate at large. Where a farm was vacant the landlord had, in theory at least, and in practice to a varying degree, the choice of the new tenant. This could extend to bringing in outsiders, either in isolated instances or systematically. As already indicated, the massive introduction of outsiders by the landlords had been feasible only before 1641 and even then only unevenly between regions. In the 1650s, with an underpopulated countryside, landowners were sometimes obliged to resume sponsored immigration, an uneven pattern of which can be traced into the 1670s or early 1680s. But massive sponsored immigration had been limited to the pre-1641 period, and in the next three decades was neither as large nor as general. The only significant sponsored immigration of the eighteenth century was of textile workers from the north for the linen industry, to be grouped in industrial villages, and intended to lay the basis of a strong protestant community in the south at the same time as they established the linen industry.

In the hey-day of sponsored settlement in the pre-1641 period, the Munster and Ulster plantations had envisaged the undertakers who received grants of land bringing in specified numbers of farmers and artisans. If the undertakers had observed their covenants, the original Munster Plantation could have involved an immigration of 15,000 persons. Although it is unlikely that the notional figure was attained, strong immigrant communities were established on individual estates in Limerick and also in Kerry and Cork. The number of English adult males in 1622 could have been 4,000, the total number of all sexes and ages, 12,000.[28] By contrast, the number of adult British on Scots plantation lands alone in the more recent Ulster plantation in 1619 was estimated at 4,420 in the six plantation counties.[29] Beyond the plantation counties unsponsored Scots were already established in Antrim: and in co. Down the Scottish landlord families of Montgomery and Hamilton, receiving grants of land shortly after the accession of James I, vigorously settled Scottish families. In the six plantation counties, the number of men in 1619 was 8,000;[30] in Ulster at large, i.e. including the three non-plantation counties the number of British males between 16 and 60 was estimated in the 1630s at 13,092 of whom 8,000 could bear arms.[31] Elsewhere plantation took place in Leitrim and Longford, in King's county, in parts of Westmeath and Queen's county and in north Wexford. These plantations were selectively implemented on the basis of challenged land titles, and in consequence were far less wholesale in execution than the Munster and Ulster plantations; but they were made more effective by the surviving vestiges of earlier plantation in adjoining areas of east King's and east Queen's and along the west flanks of the Wicklow mountains. Moreover, their thrust was supported by isolated grants of land elsewhere, and by private acquisitions, not solely the extensive ones by King's officers such as Richard Boyle in Munster or Wentworth in Wicklow, but isolated purchases by lesser individuals in smaller blocks, as far afield as Galway, Roscommon or Mayo, at various dates from the 1570s onwards. The failure of grantees to observe covenants of colonization was less universal than often admitted by historians. Even unconvenanted purchasers seem frequently to have sponsored the settlement of English immigrants on their lands, or as in Wexford to have introduced settlers from England although their covenants simply imposed an obligation to settle the land, without specifying immigration. The consequence of this pattern was the emergence of well-defined regions of sustained pre-1641 colonization, not only in Munster — and beyond the Desmond lands of the original plantation in the 1580s — but in three other fairly well-defined regions outside Ulster. The first was Wicklow and North Wexford, with pockets also in east Kildare and east Carlow. The second was King's and Queen's counties and, less uniformly, Westmeath. The third region was Leitrim and Longford, supported by less general colonization in Sligo, Roscommon, Galway and Mayo. The records of claimants after the 1641 massacres[32] define these regions dramatically as well as illustrating the presence of numerous small pockets elsewhere. Some of the most powerful foci of settlement in the east and west, moreover, were centres of informal rather than covenanted plantation: the Wingfield and Wentworth lands of northern and west Wicklow, the Bingham lands around Castlebar and the King estate around Boyle.

The aim of colonization was to settle an agricultural population on the land. The settlement was already quite significant, measured by the numbers who took refuge in the landowners' castles in 1641. In George Courtenay's castle at Newcastle, 1,000 persons took refuge, many obviously from beyond the village itself as the number of houses burned at Newcastle seems to have been only 40; 500 or 600 took refuge in Tralee castle; 900 in the castle of Birr[33], and reports of massacres, or refugees, or houses destroyed at other centres, provide a crude measure of numerous though less massive concentrations of Protestants in the 'colonial' counties. A single colonist, John Ridge, who bore losses at Boyle and elsewhere, employed before the rebellion 'three score and ten servants at least'.[34] While the Mountrath lordship (sold shortly after its formation to Charles Coote) was, in part, sustained by a non-farming population engaged in the iron industry, diligent farming by settlers 'newly come out of England' raised the rental in a few years three-fold.[35] Legacory, a non-iron working region of Queen's, was 'well planted with honest, religious Protestants'.[36] The promotion and success of pre-1641 settlement was, however, powerfully helped by the iron industry, and by other non-agricultural pursuits. Settlement along the river valleys of Cork and west Waterford had been determined by the iron industry, towns on the Great Earl of Cork's estates being built around the iron industry and at Bandon around textiles; along the Cork and Kerry coast, the fisheries — fish being still one of Ireland's main exports — sustained compact coastal settlements. Charles Coote employed 2,500 to 2,600 in the industry at three sites, the largest at Mountrath in Queen's, the others in Leitrim and Roscommon.[37] Wandesforde's settlement of immigrants in the barony of Fassadinin and across the border at Idrone in co. Carlow was based on the iron industry.[38] At Mountrath, Coote's fustian company was an added source of artisan employment; Mountmellick started as a centre of Adam Loftus' iron industry.

Wicklow/Wexford and King's county are of especial interest as they seem to stand out even with a predominantly rural character, as the centres of strongest settlement outside Ulster, although in the case of north Wexford and south Wicklow the original dense woodlands and ironworks suggest that many of the immigrants may also have been brought in by iron. The massive concentration of Protestants in Wicklow in later enumerations of population by religion seems retrospectively to indicate Wicklow's leadership.[39] The 1660 poll-tax gives King's county (14.8 per cent), Carlow (13.9 per cent) and Wexford (11.9 per cent) the highest proportions of English outside Ulster except probably for Wicklow for which the data do not survive. The incomplete returns for Cork county give a high proportion of Protestants (13.3 per cent), but elimination of the three strongly Protestant towns of Bandon, Kinsale and Youghal reduces the figure to 8.3 per cent. Moreover, the so-called 1660 poll-tax appears to have been based on status, and was not a simple poll-tax, and in consequence seems to have underestimated largely rural population in comparison to industrial or urban activities. The absolute number of Protestants in north Wexford and King's county seems surprisingly small compared with larger numbers in more urban or industrial townlands elsewhere, suggesting widespread non-imposition of the tax on the labouring and farming classes.[40] The rural emphasis of settlement in both King's county and Wexford is very evident. King's county had a single large settlement compared with three in neighbouring Queen's. King's had from retrospective settlement evidence an exceptional number of small rural villages, a circumstance reflected too in the fact that the settlers' fortifications in King's county were considered remarkably good.[41] The powerful North Wexford settlement had a single instance of urban incorporation — Newboro' or Gorey — and even village concentrations were few. The Ram family, responsible for the incorporation of Gorey, were the most powerful single family in the plantation of Wexford, but even in the vicinity of Gorey, their residence, they were not alone in sponsoring immigration. Walsingham Cooke had planted some 200 English families in the parish of Killenagh, five miles south of Newboro'.[42] The losses of Cooke's tenants, suggesting an average of £50 to £60 per tenant, give an impression of a flourishing and relatively highly-capitalized rural community. Wicklow presented an identical picture, no incorporated town being established on the Wingfield estate, or on the Wentworth estate, despite probably the most intensive colonization, on both estates, experienced outside Ulster. Moreover, Carysfort, the only incorporation in south Wicklow, failed to prosper despite the establishment of a royal school in the 1620s.

Pre-1641 settlement determined the future pattern of British settlement in Ireland. Despite the upheavals of 1641, settlers remained or returned: Petty's estimate was of 150,000 immigrants between 1652 and 1672 including the return of no less than '80,000 banished and expelled English'.[43] As the numbers of immigrants were relatively small, it seems likely that their society was marked by a high rate of natural increase of population: the age composition of immigrant populations, one would expect, was young, and early marriage was probably general. Both before and after 1660, the natural increase may have been sharper among the immigrants than among the native population.[44] The main post-1660 change was the dramatic shift in the pattern of the population of the north-east brought about decisively by the massive Scottish immigration of the second half of the century. In 1660, judging by the poll-tax, an immigrant population was in a majority in no county in the north-east, and outside Down and Antrim, on other evidence, English as opposed to Scottish cultural and racial influence was the dominant immigrant force. In the eighteenth century the pattern was reversed dramatically, with retrospective evidence from the religious census of 1831 and 1834, of massive Protestant majorities in the dioceses of Connor, Down and Dromore (approximately to the counties of Antrim and Down), Presbyterians being twice to three times as numerous as members of the Church of Ireland. In the other counties the Protestant population did not exceed a half, but the relative weight of post-1660 immigration in the composition of the Protestant community is reflected in the enhanced proportion of Presbyterians to members of the established Church: twice as numerous in Derry (a reversal of early dominance by the Church of Ireland), and only slightly less numerous in the dioceses of Raphoe and Armagh. By contrast, members of the Church of Ireland retained their dominance in the diocese of Clogher by three to one.[45]

Under the impact of Presbyterian immigration and diffusion,[46] a contrast emerged between areas which retained a Church of Ireland predominance among Protestants and areas where Presbyterians became predominant. Brought in originally by sponsors, or dependent on employment offered by sponsors, Church of Ireland members often held menial wage-paid employment, or occupied the inferior lands. As a body they lacked the mobility that capital-holding tenants enjoyed. By contrast, Scottish immigrants or their descendants had more resources and were consequently more mobile. Even in a South Tyrone parish like Clogher in a region where the Church of Ireland was the largest Protestant sect and where English settlement had preceded Scottish, Presbyterians occupied the best farm land from an early date.[47] The Church of Ireland remained immobile, retaining its predominance in relatively backward west Donegal, in Fermanagh, and the adjoining Clones region of Monaghan, but gaining no new areas to compensate for the loss of dominance to Presbyterians in many of the most accessible or fertile regions of Ulster. Presbyterians replaced Anglicans as the dominant force in Derry, in the rich lands of east Donegal and Tyrone drained by the Foyle, penetrating in force as far as the Clogher Valley, and in the emerging linen regions of east Tyrone dominated by Dungannon, the largest linen market outside the Armagh/ Lisburn axis. In east Ulster, the only area of Anglican dominance was north Armagh and south-east Antrim, long and most successful region of English settlement. Its village structure dating back to the early seventeenth century, a testimony to landlord sponsorship, was unparalleled in the rest of Ulster. Beyond that area, Presbyterians predominated over Anglicans not only in Down and Antrim but in mid-Armagh, with significant settlement testifying to their success further afield in the Fews and even beyond the Louth border in Ballymascanlan. Likewise, in Monaghan, although colonized extensively at a late stage — and more by migration than immigration — Anglicans surrendered leadership to Presbyterians.

Armagh itself was the cockpit of change. Long the strongest centre of Anglican or English settlement, it experienced much Presbyterian influx as well. The sharp contrast between Anglican dominance in north Armagh and Presbyterian in mid-Armagh, in what was to emerge as the most densely populated county in Ireland, may hold the key to its social tensions. The hostility to Catholics in the north may reflect the resentment of Catholic involvement in an industry, in the one region where the Church of Ireland was firmly identified with the industry. The dependence on wage employment as opposed to independent weaving, while it reflected the advanced nature of the region's industry, also reflected the region's relatively dependent nature right from the seventeenth century. Significantly, the Defender/Peep O'Day Boy confrontations in the 1780s were equally characteristic of mid-Armagh, and may reflect friction occasioned by the canalization of Presbyterian movement in Armagh southwards from the densely populated, high-rent, largely cottierized north towards the more open spaces and lower rented land of the less developed south of the county. The variety of surnames in Armagh as reflected in the tithe applotment books and the Griffin valuation is quite astonishing, being the cumulative effect of a mobility unequalled elsewhere in Ireland.

A frontier of settlement is evident. Such a frontier implies mobility and flux. The Scots continued a sustained pattern of advance from the seventeenth, well into the eighteenth century. Even before 1641, small numbers of Scots were to be found on the evidence of the 1641 depositions in Longford, Roscommon and Sligo. In the island at large, excepting later Scottish immigration, the first 40 years of the seventeenth century were the crucial years. Subsequent immigration, sponsored by landlords or unsponsored, did little to alter the southern pattern which after 1660 changed remarkably little. In the north the Scottish immigration was the dynamic behind settlement after 1660, and even there the advance of the settlement frontier slowed after 1700. In the parishes of Termoneeny, Maghera and Killelagh, immigrant-dominated townlands had emerged by 1740: the 1740 pattern of immigrant or native domination of individual townlands remained unchanged thereafter [48]. However, a shifting frontier of settlement remained even if after 1740 new migration failed to alter the character of the receiving townlands decisively. Armagh with its entrenched Anglican population in the north and its dynamic Scots in the mid-county is an instance. The settlement dimension of Armagh's unrest in the 1780s and 1790s is evident. Fermanagh Anglicans were no less intolerant of Catholics than Armagh ones, but intolerance in itself is not sufficient to spark off strife. The well-defined Peep O'Day Boy/Catholic strife seems to mark a sharp geographical frontier. Presbyterians fanned out beyond the north-east thinly into the adjacent counties of Leinster and Connaught. Their settlement in Sligo, interrupted in 1641, seems to have resumed in the 1740s — there were rather few Scots names in the county on the evidence of the 1749 census — and the linen industry spreading in the west and in North Leinster since the 1740s seems to have been the basis of their movement. The migration reached as far west as Mayo, and as far south as Loughrea in Galway. The growing dependence of the north-east on Connaught for both food and yarn from mid-century also helped to create an intimate circuit of exchanges of men and materials between the Connaught counties and Ulster. The movement of several thousand Catholics, expelled from Armagh in the sectarian troubles in that county in the 1790s, fitted into an existing pattern: [49] the only difference, apart from the relatively large numbers, was a change of religion in the bulk of the immigrants. Their participation on arrival in the linen industry in the west, said to have benefited from their arrival, seems to illustrate the not insignificant scale of the emerging Catholic role in the linen industry in Armagh on the eve of their expulsion. The link between the most crowded and the least crowded region in Ireland is itself a significant illustration of a complex pattern in which settlement is strongly implied. Before the Catholic exodus to Connaught in 1795, the use of the term 'Connaught' to denote both a district in Armagh and its trouble-makers represents an intriguing link with the west of Ireland [50]: perhaps journeymen weavers who had joined the movement to the western counties and had returned.

Early settlement, where sponsored, entailed the creation of villages: many early immigrants had little capital, and for the entrepreneur establishment of a village community was at once more economical as well as offering a better military protection of his investment in colonization. In addition, a high proportion of early settlers were artisans, sometimes being sponsored expressly for their skills, necessary to make even new rural settlement viable, quite apart from the more intensive demands of the iron industry itself, one of the major inducements to colonization. Comfortable farmers too were little disposed to move, and a high proportion of immigrants from England as of immigrants to America at the same time, were people whose lowly position and precarious prospects at home made settlement abroad attractive. Significantly, in districts colonized by the Scots, many of whom arrived as independent settlers, an early formal village pattern is harder to detect: a contrast seems to exist between the Scots coming into Ireland independently and moving to farmland, and the English settlers clinging more closely to their sponsor and protector. The Quakers likewise often settled directly on farms, although as a high proportion of Quakers were artisans, a tendency to village nucleation can sometimes be detected in their settlement. Some Quakers at the outset were able to rent farms of 500 acres [51], this class providing much of the Quaker entrepreneurial talent in the midlands. As early as 1709, Moate was reported to be 'of different ayre from the generality of Irish villages' with 10 to 12 Quaker families [52]. Its wide street and the adjacent demesne of its Quaker Clibborn landlord family give it the character of a typical landlord village. Ballitore, with a central square, seems not dissimilar.

The incorporation of boroughs is usually an indication of town creation, and while the privilege was granted because it denoted a royal purpose, the request usually reflected the aims of an ambitious entrepreneur landlord. Early colonization in Munster is marked by the creation of eight boroughs in the reign of James I, three on sites associated with the iron industry in the Blackwater Valley (Tallow, Lismore, Mallow), one on the Bandon river, at Bandonbridge, two coastal settlements (Baltimore and Clonakilty) and two towns in the Kerry/Limerick plantation region (Tralee and Askeaton). Later creations denote a uniformly rural character: Ardfert and Doneraile (1639), and — evidence of a short but intensive colonization based on landlord seats — four boroughs incorporated between 1670 and 1682 (Midleton, Charleville, Castlemartyr, Rathcormack). Colonization in the Longford/Leitrim/north Connaught region was marked by six incorporations in the reign of James I, and a new impetus to town creation, this time confined to Longford/Roscommon, became evident in the reign of Charles II in the incorporation of Tulsk, Lanesboro, Longford and Granard. In the Ulster plantation, a total of 17 towns were incorporated in the reign of James I and Charles I, no less than five of them in Donegal, plus three towns in the Scottish districts of north Down and three other Ulster towns. The incorporation of three south-west Antrim towns and one town in north-west Down in the reign of Charles II corresponds to particularly vigorous estate management evident in that part of Ulster in the Restoration. Outside the south Munster, north Connaught/Longford and Ulster regions, incorporations were surprisingly few — in the midlands only Banagher, Ballinakill and Kilbeggan — underlying the purely rural or industrial character and aims of much early settlement. The incorporation of Portarlington (1667) was the sole further development. In east Leinster several incorporation reflect real progress in colonization such as Gorey (1619) and Carysfort (1628) or after the Restoration on the Kildare/Wicklow borders, Baltinglass (1663), Blessington (1669) and Harristown (1681). Other east Leinster incorporations are confirmations of existing boroughs, but confirmation itself appears to point to a pattern of landlord entrepreneurial ability and colonization in Wicklow/north Wexford and across the borders in Kildare and Carlow, to pockets of settlement in Fethard, Bannow and Taghmon, and abortive but unsuccessful attempts at colonization in county Kilkenny. The marked decline in incorporation at the Restoration coincides with a decline in direct landlord investment in immigration, the post-1660 instances themselves corresponding to identifiable regions of active post-1660 sponsorship of colonization.

4
Village and countryside: landlord and settler

The village is one of the hallmarks of Irish society, its purely colonial aspects hard to dissociate from a more broadly modernizing character. In Scotland, some 150 planned villages were established between 1730 and 1830 [1]. In Ireland the number is even larger, and the period of establishment, beginning earlier and ending later, more protracted [2]. Scotland's economic development was uneven and uncertain in the seventeenth century, Ireland's sustained. An extremely primitive country in 1600, with few villages and certainly no regular pattern of village settlement, the protracted expansion of the seventeenth and eighteenth centuries has meant that most Irish villages can trace their origin to this period, and that a very high proportion of them were, to a greater or lesser degree, planned. Inland towns which had already existed such as Cavan, transformed their character under the impetus of their colonial and landlord tutelage to the point that they must be regarded for all practical purposes as seventeenth-century creations. Over two-and-a-half centuries, upwards of 500 artificial settlements were created or planned, the number being probably near 1,000 if very informal definitions are used. The exact number is difficult to enumerate both because documentary evidence is scant for their origins and because their early physical character — often eloquent of the origins of villages — has been obliterated or concealed by later development. Some early villages too have disappeared. Staplestown, co. Carlow was a compact settlement in 1680 with its landlord seat, inn, mill, its seven slated dwellings housing tradesmen bearing English names [3]. Even as early as 1840 it had disappeared from the map, a derelict demesne and two gentleman's residences remaining, its tradesmen's housing totally gone. At Court Matrix, the first site of the German Palatines at Rathkeale, the settlers were housed around a square, now virtually banished but still well-defined when the village was mapped by the Ordnance Survey at the end of the 1830s[4]. Carysfort or Macreddin, despite its location in the region of most intense colonization outside Ulster, its incorporation, and its royal school had also disappeared by 1840. A triangular green, the hallmark of early seventeenth-century settlement, survived, as well as a castle. To-day, neither survives, the fair green having been incorporated into a farmyard less than 40 years ago, with a prodigal use of stone walls on both sides of the road which traverses the site of the green.

In attempting to enumerate villages, quite apart from the formidable difficulties already mentioned, a conceptual difficulty remains: how to distinguish the formal from the informal settlement. The irregular huddle of houses depending on the patronage of a big house is itself a landlord village, and shades into villages planned with a varied degree of order. Belanagare, an Irish village supported by its modest Gaelic landlord, the O'Connor family, was falling into ruins in 1837 because the landlord has 'lately removed to a new lodge in the neighbourhood, since which the village has been neglected and is falling into decay'[5]. If such settlements were included, the proportion of villages classified as landlord-villages would be extremely high, as hardly any rural villages before the era of factory employment post-1780 were in fact able to survive without the sustained patronage, employment and succour offered by a resident landowner. Even confining study to the formal village, a satisfactory criterion embracing minimum conditions for identification is hard to come by.

Towns like Newmarket-on-Fergus, or Piltown, co. Kilkenny, are relatively poor in planned elements, but they are recognizably estate villages, Newmarket retaining elements of a planned and highly functional lay-out achieved in the main by 1768 [6]; Piltown, despite good late estate cottages, was functionally far inferior. Towns or villages like Ballyshannon or Carnew (except for the survival of its castle and bawn at the town centre) retain few early features, but are basically planned settlements. On the other hand, a village like Kiltullagh, a small huddle of houses at the demesne entrance of the Darcy house at Dunsandle, is not nor ever was, an estate village in a meaningful sense, let alone a planned village. Bray is hard to classify, because although built on the Earl of Meath's land and enjoying some continued functional dependence on him to the end of the nineteenth century, it seems to lack the pattern caused by artificial creation or sufficient functional elements of a recognizable estate village or town. On balance, Bray must be excluded from the category. Newtownmountkennedy presents a not uncommon situation because, despite having few visible planned features, it has a clear functional dependence on Mountkennedy house and a relatively high quality of housing [7]. The fundamental problem in determining the status of a village derives from the inherent ambiguity in distinguishing between, on the one hand, the planned creation of a village (with original characteristics which may not survive), and on the other hand, the existence or survival of ordered characteristics regarded as the hallmarks of good planning. Villages planned by landlords did not necessarily have (although they usually had) or retain good planning characteristics, but they were almost invariably planned in the sense of originally being laid out with deliberation.

There are essentially three types of planned village — the settlement village, the functionally planned village (which may be simple or complex in its layout) and the re-developed village (a village built at an earlier date but later re-developed). The rebuilding of villages was common whether as in the re-structuring in the late seventeenth or eighteenth centuries of earlier simpler settlements of tenants originally grouped around a village green, or at the end of the eighteenth century and in the early decades of the nineteenth century, in the cosmetic improvement of existing villages. Thus individual villages could pass through several stages. The green in Dunlavin which may have constituted the original settlement is underneath the planned village of the mid-eighteenth century dominated by a square with market-house. In a village with two greens, as in Laurencetown, two successive stages in its development were probably represented. Birr reflects all three stages — simple settlement, functionally planned village in the 1740s, further elaboration in the early nineteenth century.

The settlement village was established by early settler groups — or more accurately by their sponsors — in the first half of the seventeenth century. Given their insecurity they were housed in close proximity, convenience and protection both being achieved most effectively by grouping them around a triangular open space or an irregular square. The fact that a high proportion of early settlers were tradesmen made villages all the more inevitable. Some of the villages with fortifications in their immediate vicinity served to protect the more isolated farming population that fanned out into the surrounding countryside, their military and industrial role thus combining to sustain the emerging rural colony in their immediate hinterland. Many of the early settlements grew up in the shadow of fortifications (Birr, Geashill, Charlemont, Carysfort, or Shrule in co.Mayo, isolated examples drawn from the entire island). But the fact that many did not rely on fortifications for their survival illustrates that trading and industrial support for the surrounding rural community was no less and frequently more important than defence itself. The fact that some of these settlements such as Tuamgraney or Scariff, both in co. Clare, began as centres of the iron industry illustrates their complex function still further. The importance of the village and the fact that much of the early settler population congregated in villages has long been evident in the case of Ulster [8], but the pattern was equally true for other regions.

The early open spaces were not invariably triangular. Many of the early villages of the London companies in county Derry were laid out in a straight line, a pattern repeated in the midlands at Newtownforbes, Lanesboro', Killashee, Longford or Kenagh, or in Wicklow at Templestown (Roundwood) and in Wexford at Coolgreaney. The greens fluctuated between a triangular form and an irregular square, few having the clear-cut diamond pattern, evident as late as the 1830s in Pallas, co. Limerick or Durrow, Queen's county, but which survives in the name of some Ulster greens. The so-called 'diamonds' of Ulster are either squares or triangles, although a few have a complex pattern which may have begun life as a diamond. The triangular form was surprisingly common, its wide distribution suggesting that it was the basic form with the diamond and the irregular square as variants on it. It occurs across the entire country, suggesting a common cultural background as well as an almost identical approach by sponsored settlers in most regions to the challenge to their early establishment and to its economics. Approximately 120 villages with triangular or irregular open spaces can be identified either from contemporary comment, the ordnance survey or observations on the ground [9]. Because the village lay-out has often been modified in later history, the survival of the triangular village, not surprisingly, is more evident in regions where early colonization was very strong, but later development or change comparatively weak. County Limerick and King's county, strong centres of pre-1641 colonization but both weak foci of later immigration and economic change, contain the largest number and the best defined triangular villages in Munster and the midlands respectively. In Leinster, nuclei of such villages can be traced in three groupings — east

Leinster, north Leinster and the midlands. In north Leinster, a few are evident in Louth, north Dublin and especially in Meath where Oldcastle is the best instance; in east Leinster, the focal point was co. Wicklow with five of the ten villages in the county being on or close to the Wentworth/Fitzwilliam estate. Other villages were across the county border in adjoining parts of Kildare, Carlow and north Wexford. The midland group, corresponding to colonization in King's county/Queen's county, was impressive, and as late as 1802 the pattern was evident to Coote who commented on Geashill, King's co., being 'like other villages of this county of triangular form'[10].

In Ulster the triangular pattern was widespread in the Plantation counties. The English as opposed to Scottish character of the triangular pattern is confirmed by its relative absence from the non-Plantation county of Down. In fact, the early seventeenth-century villages in north Down on the Hamilton and Montgomery estates are quite out of character with Scottish colonization. The two estates are among the few where Scottish settlement was sponsored on a large scale and where villages played a key role in it. Villages such as Holywood, Comber, Bangor and Killeleagh were laid out in regular streets on a grid pattern usually with a market cross[11]; some of their artisans even appear to have been English. By contrast Newtownards[12], close to the Lagan corridor, or Lisburn, actually within Antrim, both originated in English colonization and triangular planning. In Lisburn, as sketched at a date between 1622 and 1678 but probably closer to the former, the green was dominated by the 'chief house', and there were in all 53 tenants, mainly English[13]. In Antrim, five villages with triangular greens can be traced in the region of predominantly English settlement in the Lagan Corridor and in the south-west of the county generally. Only two survived by the 1830s in Derry, although the more formal or urban character and higher ambitions of Derry colonization are reflected in the presence of regular squares in a grid pattern in Coleraine and Derry city, which prospered, and in Kilrea which did not. As rudimentary villages, many of the less successful villages may have simply disappeared in time. This may be the explanation for the rural location of a number of sites called Diamond in Ulster. Some of these, like the Diamond in the townland of Grange Lower in north Armagh — which gave its name to the famous riot of 1795 — were rural road junctions. No less than ten occur across the north of Ireland[14]. Some like Ardboe on the Derry shores of

Lough Neagh are at the centre of complex road junctions [15], and it is likely that they are lost villages which have retained their importance as road junctions. All these instances occur in regions of pre-1641 English settlement.

The settlement village was basically a simple community with an emphasis on the settler population rather than landlord residence. Some were modest ventures with no castle and at best a church. At Cloonacool in the west of Sligo, Lisnarrick in co. Fermanagh, and some of the King's county settlements, with few houses surviving around the green in the 1830s, for instance, not even a church seems ever to have existed. The decline of others seems to have followed the decay of the fort or church that once supported the life of the little community. Some like Carysfort (Macreddin) have disappeared despite an impressive original array of institutions. A number have survived as modest rural villages. In some cases such as Laurencetown, off main roads, the support of a powerful local landlord family whose role replaced the defensive purpose of the settlement, and was reflected in the fact of continued occupation of the castle, (still occupied in the 1830s) as well as the emergence of a big house and demesne, obviously accounts for its comparative success: it also acquired a second green. Others like Toomyvara on the main Dublin road to Limerick or Cloghan, in King's county, illustrate the commercial forces which could rescue the village from decline or from the total eclipse which has overtaken centres like Cloonacool or Macreddin (Carysfort). At Cloghan the coherence of the original green was obliterated by mid-eighteenth century roads, flanked by large late eighteenth-century houses and 'an excellent inn'. The more successful towns have usually benefited from both forces — an adjacent demesne and a good trading position. In some cases, the original village character has disappeared, as at Frankford (Kilcormac), now a relatively large village; in other cases, it survived in the form of a small compact village which continued to fully occupy its original site and to extend modestly beyond it.

The first category of village shaded into the second category — the functionally complex and consciously planned village. The settlement village was itself functionally planned; the grouping of a small community around a green reflects the economic and defensive dependence of its members on each other and was planned in its construction to meet these needs. The second category embraces a larger number of functions: landlord residence, the presence of a church, active or anticipated markets; and formal planning of the provision for these functions is reflected in the very definite hierarchy between house, church, markets, and village and its translation into a conscious, although not an inflexible, spatial relationship between these activities. The formal dependence of the village on the residence is usually expressed in the fact that it either flanks the demesne wall near to the entrance gate or stands on both sides of an approach road to the principal demesne gate. The church was usually sited close to the demesne entrance — the establishment in Church and State both confronting the village — and if sited elsewhere was sometimes intended to serve the role of an eyecatcher, closing the vista from the demesne gate. The houses were of good quality — usually slated at least at the centre, in contrast to the thatched houses that predominated in many of the settlement villages. Roads were straight in line, usually crossed at right angles, and squares, central in location, were regular or rectangular. The importance seventeenth and eighteenth-century landlords attached to markets seems to be reflected in the frequency of the provision of a market square and the conscious attempt to site it at the centre of the village. Settlement villages, of course, had some of these elements — the hierarchical progression from castle to church to green evident in Edenderry, Geashill or Newcastle West, to take three instances, embodies the basic characteristics of the estate village, but without residence the village could not have developed, very certainly, beyond its rudimentary basic character. While the Courtenays ceased to reside at Newcastle West, the town is unusual in its marked estate character. On the other hand, Geashill, King's county, visibly showed the adverse consequences of landlord absenteeism. Inhabited only by cadets of the absentee Digby family it illustrates the crucial importance of the landlord's ambition or wealth in sustaining a village. With its large formally conceived triangular green, Geashill, location of the Digby castle in a barony owned entirely by the family, was obviously a centre of importance at the outset which lost ground subsequently. Its houses were thatched, and its present striking landlord village character was acquired only much later in the second half of the nineteenth century under the direction of the great estate agent Steuart Trench. It should be contrasted with the adjoining village of Cloneygowan which retains much of its original simple character. In many cases where there has been vigorous landlord direction, early triangular greens have been incorporated into the later, more complex, town or village: in Newcastle West, co. Limerick, for instance, a presumptively triangular green had been softened by subsequent rebuilding, on later evidence, and its original character is still less evident to-day.

The pre-1641 villages were in the main simple rural settlements of artisans and farmers. Some distinction existed between such settlements, largely agricultural and defensive in intent, and others cast even at the outset for the role of market centres, and intended to attract merchants and professionals. Rathvilly, for instance, perhaps because its inhabitants were lowly, does not feature in the 1641 depositions at all, whereas both deponents from and references to neighbouring Hacketstown, a 'market town', appear. The more complex structure of Hacketstown, dominated by a small regular square, may reflect the more ambitious role either cast for it or quickly acquired by it. Likewise, some of the Ulster plantation villages were built on a grid with a market cross at the centre, quite apart from the obvious and highly ambitious cases of Londonderry and Coleraine. Moreover, though all these villages are to be found in regions of strong pre-1641 settlement, some can not be unequivocally put into the period, and it is just possible that a few villages on triangular greens may have been built as late as the outset of the 1650s for a small group of immigrants brought in by a sponsor who undertook to house them.

The planned village, as opposed to the simple settlement village, is primarily a post-1660 development. The building of landlord residences increased enormously after the Restoration. It frequently went hand in hand with the intention of creating a village and even where it did not, the more lavish expenditure occasioned by the greater pretensions of Restoration landowners helped to sustain village life. Significantly, too, there seems to have been a marked emphasis in post-1660 landlord expenditures on the erection of churches [16], whose presence was by no means universal in the economically conceived and frugally executed settlement villages. The more ambitious and grandiose plans of landlords were reflected in the first attempts to incorporate a regular square in the planning of villages. Virtually the only pre-1660 squares were in the three Londonderry plantation towns of Kilrea, Londonderry and Coleraine, two of which — the sole fortified towns of the plantation — were the object of special attention and were from the start the most successful urban creations of the Ulster plantation. It is significant that co. Down, which had few pre-1660 villages but a high level of landlord activity at the Restoration, has the largest number of towns with a regular square at their centre. Down is in sharp contrast to Armagh which, despite its many pre-1641 villages, has only two regular squares from the eighteenth century. In Down, free from the Armagh problem of incorporating existing lay-outs into remodelled villages, no less than ten regular or near-regular squares were created. Some of this activity in Down is not identifiably eighteenth-century and as several of the towns were certainly Restoration creations in one form or other, it is plausible to see a powerful Restoration impetus in village creation there. In Queen's county, Portarlington, laid out in 1667 for the Earl of Arlington, may have been the first regular square in the entire midlands [17]. Four other towns or villages in Queen's have later squares. Queen's has relatively few villages with triangular greens: only Mountrath, Maryboro, Durrow, Castletown and Ballickmoyler suggesting (among other things) that immigration was more evenly balanced between the pre-1650 and the post-1650 periods than in neighbouring King's county. Neither King's nor Wicklow, the focal points of pre-1660 colonization outside Ulster and South Munster, in fact, have regular squares from this period.

The square is by no means a universal feature of the estate village. In fact, the contrast should be made between the square conceived as centre of a grid, a characteristic of highly conscious or ambitious planning, and the square entered at right angles but not in a neat grid pattern. The full grid is indicative both of very formal planning and of a relative absence of an existing lay-out to cope with. In fact, in many instances, the square is to one side of a road, or straddling it somewhat unevenly, or sandwiched between two lines of road, clear evidence that the planner was coping with an earlier settlement and had to take existing features into account. Even where the square is the central feature of the village, it is necessary to distinguish between the full grid as in Portarlington, Killough (co. Down), or the 'new town' areas in Birr, Westport or Mitchelstown, and less formal lay-outs. While the square was a feature of many villages, their small size, incomplete execution (as in Dromana) or the physical constraints of existing structures and lay-outs inhibited either a full grid or the incorporation of the square at a central point. The basic feature identifying estate villages is the spatial relationship to the demesne. Except in the cases where the demesne gave on to a village built around a green, there are two basic structures. One was the erection of a village along a road flanking the demesne, or in a village on a very modest scale simply on the roadside opposite the demesne wall. Waringstown, Doneraile, Frenchpark, Borris, or Gormanston represent instances from different periods and on widely varying scales. The other form was the erection of the village in processional form on an approach road. Summerhill, co. Meath, is one of the most clear-cut illustrations of this effect — it was a minute village but laid out in highly formal fashion along a tree-lined avenue. Some villages like Celbridge achieved this effect casually and apparently with little formal direction; others like Monivea, one of the most dramatic estate villages in Ireland, in an elaborate fashion: the road flanked by two large greens each with its own service road, the vistas at the two ends closed by the demesne gates and by the Charter School respectively. Many villages depart of course from the ideal lay-out; not all are erected at the demesne entrance, but even in such instances the church usually stands between the house and the village. In some instances, the coherence of the original village has been lost by the move of the family at a later date to a new residence. At Boyle, the original village huddles at the gate of the great King house built in the 1720s, the family's link with the town becoming less direct when they moved to Rockingham, three miles away, sometime after 1787. In Newmarket-on-Fergus, the focal point of the town was not Dromoland Castle, two miles away, but a house and a park giving on to a square, the latter in turn overlooked by a church.

In some instances the estate character of a village can be seen only in its early history; the disappearance of the family later removing its sustaining force. Edenderry is a relatively fortunate instance. The relationship of the ruined Blundell castle and of the church to the village still speaks of its early history, but the estate was inherited by the Downshire family in 1799 who, though absentee landlords, gave it in the 1820s or 1830s the large square and market house which still retain for the town some of the character of its origins as a landlord creation. Given such circumstances, the sustaining forces behind the village could change over time, the village coming to depend on a more distant family than the founding family. In some instances the later prosperity of a village depended on the accidental presence in the immediate vicinity of more than one successful family. The small estate village of Clogheen in south Tipperary had four demesnes in close proximity. Some towns were owned by two landlords. Sixmilebridge, for instance, controlled by the Ievers on the east bank of the river, was linked by the bridge with an O'Brien township built around a roughly triangular open space [18]; the main street of Carrickmacross was the line of division between the Bath and Shirley estates, the market house standing on both properties.

The village can be simple or complex in its structure. The simple village was built on a flank road, an approach route, or around a green. The complex village involved a greater number of streets. It was first evident in the formal square, with feeder streets either in a grid or on a looser pattern which appeared at the Restoration, and became more common in the 1720s and 1730s when greater wealth and a conscious planning ethic gave the erection of such villages an impetus. In the simplest cases, two roads crossed at a neat right angle, creating in effect four streets; a grid of four streets from a central square produced the same effect on a somewhat grandiose scale. In some cases the street grid was very elaborate. Cookstown, with its wide street and five major rectangular intersections, laid out by Stewart who resided at the nearby demesne of Killymoon, is the most elaborate instance in Ireland. Gorey, developed by the Ram family through two centuries and flanked by two Ram demesnes, was the closest parallel elsewhere: a wide, straight street with four major intersections. Bagnelstown in county Carlow, probably also from the middle decades, is an instance of a remarkably compact grid of regular streets. Newtownbarry in the north-west of co. Wexford, with a square and mall and several regular streets, is another instance of midcentury planning, as is Birr where a square with a grid of streets stands beyond the infill of the original green in the shadow of the castle. The aim was to create an atmosphere of spaciousness, an effect which could be enhanced by putting a square at the centre of the grid.

Even in modest instances there was a quite common attempt to create a square, the bulk of the squares in Irish towns being laid out — if not before — in the third quarter of the century. Rosscarbery, for instance, already had its fine square well before 1788 since it stands at the centre of a fully-built-up street plan in the map of that year [19]. By 1812, even villages on the Bellew estates in Galway had been modernised, with a small square incorporated at Newtown Bellew and a half-octagonal square at Mountbellewbridge [20]. Octagonal squares had become a feature in ambitious planning, as in Johnstown and Slane in the 1760s,

Westport c.1780, Stratford-on-Slaney in the 1780s, or, at Bellmullet, co. Mayo in the 1820s in the remotest barony in Ireland. So important was the emphasis on spaciousness that landlords sometimes deliberately planned two squares, one decorative, the other intended to be the site of the market. The tiny village of Sixmilebridge, created by the Ievers in 1733 at a time when they were socially the second family of Clare and had begun the erection of Mount Ievers, though minute even in conception, had no less than two squares: Hanover Square, intersected by two named streets — George Street and Orange Street — and two roads, and at the end of George Street, Frederick Square, its triangular form dictated by the presence of the river. The two squares in Cox's Dunmanway, the modest Laurencetown, co. Galway, and the larger Monaghan, or the impressive interconnected squares of Portaferry and Castlewellan, both towns with highly ambitious or enterprising landlords in co. Down, illustrate the widespread urge to create open spaces. The half-octagon, or 'old square', was created at Castlewellan around 1760 — Thomas Russell commented on it in passing through the town in the early 1790s — and the new square intended to be a full octagon was created in and after 1810 [21]. In the late eighteenth century, several large towns were created, the most notable instances being Westport by the Brownes in the 1770s, Mitchelstown by the Kings in the 1780s and Tullamore by the Burys somewhat later. Tullamore has a large central square with a market house, a market square and a further very large rectangular space or mall. Mitchelstown and Westport are equally ambitious, but even more formal in their planning. Tullamore. Westport and Mitchelstown are characterized by regular streets, although in none of the three cases was the planning based on a rigid grid pattern. They represent a more fluid and imaginative planning than the linear grids of Cookstown and Gorey, the elaborate street grid of Bagnelstown or the simple grid dominated by a central square of the mid-century new district in Birr. Stratford-on-Slaney, created in the 1780s by the Earl of Aldborough, had two squares linked by a main street, one circular, one octagonal, a remarkably grandiose project for what was an ambitious but unsuccessful town. In many cases, where the village already existed, the fashionable effect of spaciousness could be achieved by the creation of a mall, essentially an esplanade whose amenity was uninterrupted by through traffic. In Eyrecourt, the mall, at right angles to the main street, was created probably at the time of the erection of the handsome court house. The Clanrickardes added a mall flanking the lake to Loughrea, seat of their agent and otherwise a somewhat informal town, and Kanturk, an inauspicious village because of the non-residence of its landlord, was enhanced by the addition around 1830 of Egmont Green on the far side of the river. In the early decades of the nineteenth century the addition of the Green and the Mall essentially completed the planning of Birr.

The effort to achieve spaciousness was the dominant feature of the estate village, at least from the late seventeenth century. The wide streets and open spaces have frequently been attributed to the need to accommodate cattle fairs in a pastoral economy. They are, however, almost invariably the consequence of landlord ostentation, and the distribution of villages with wide streets bears no correlation to the main centres of the cattle trade. Where towns are purely linear, wide streets are usually evidence of relatively late foundation or of rebuilding. The triangular greens were even less related to the cattle trade. They were a defensive grouping of houses in much the same spirit as the pioneer wagons in the American west were drawn into a circle to ward off Indians. The close dependence of the green on a castle illustrates the defensive purpose of the village. Instances such as Enniskerry, or Toomyvara, on the slope of only partly subdued hill country illustrate this very clearly, as does even more forcefully Macreddin (Carysfort) high up in the pass in the Wicklow hills from Aughrim to Rathdrum. The villages were built when the cattle trade was still in its infancy, and some of them were not on focal points of a successful cattle trade.

Of course, the green as the *Piazza del popolo* answered all the needs of the population. Just as it was part of the defensive structure of the village, it served also as centre of markets, fairs and entertainment and the term 'fair green' frequently came to be applied to greens serving, at least originally, a wider purpose. But fairs had certainly not been the purpose of the creation of the original open space. Both in the 'triangular villages' and in estate villages, a fair green was frequently added at a more peripheral location if cattle fairs prospered. Such fair greens were simple arrangements, usually in fact on the periphery of the town or village, a clear illustration of their later development, and some small villages with no planned structure acquired functional fair greens on their outskirts in the course of time. Fairs, although their locations actually increased in number in the eighteenth century and landlords frequently applied for patents, took place only a few times a year, and were too infrequent, and in many cases too small to warrant special steps to accommodate them. They were either held in whatever streets or open spaces were available, or, as in Cappagh White or Frankford, were accommodated on simple fair greens laid out at the periphery of the expanding village. Fermanagh, with few villages and poor urban traditions but a significant place in the cattle trade, had no less than five such greens in the 1830s, including a very large one at Enniskillen. Landlord concern, in a concrete sense, was more evident in the regulation of markets, which were held weekly and which brought money and people to the town regularly and for which they erected or projected market houses. The title 'fair green' was appropriated either by the peripheral purpose-designed greens of the prospering villages or by greens of less successful villages where the infrequent fairs somewhat overshadowed the regular markets of a poor or thinly populated village and its hinterland.

It is by no means surprising that the conscious planning of villages coincides with periods of rapid growth in trade. In the course of the rapid expansion of the linen industry in the 1720s and 1730s, textiles were the main attraction in village creation, and again in the late 1740s and 1750s when the economy boomed, both textiles and non-textile villages were the object of landlord investment. The 1720s and early 1730s were a key period. Pratt's textile village at Newportpratt, co. Mayo, peopled by Quakers from Leinster, was erected in 1720; Brown's village at Manulla with streets crossing at right angles and established in 1733 housed 80 Presbyterian linen families from the north [22]. Iever's village of Sixmilebridge was intended to be a textile centre also because of the projector's contemporaneous interest in textiles. John Daly had already in 1735 engaged 50 Protestant families from the north to carry on the linen manufacture in Mountshannon (Inishcealtra) [23]. The interest in establishing colonies of northern artisans was very widespread in these years. The first stage of the eighteenth-century development of Sir Richard Cox's Dunmanway dates from then. In newspaper advertisements landowners sometimes offered land cheaply to anyone prepared to plant northern linen workers. The Crosbies of Ballyheigue received a proposal in 1733 for the rent of their King's county estate from a Dublin man so that he could plant a colony of tradesmen from the north [24]. The creation of villages with textile workers living in them and exchanging commodities at the local markets with the surrounding countryside was advocated by the Dublin Society as the policy for landlords to follow [25]. Samuel Madden was almost certainly the author of this policy: 'if gentlemen could once be persuaded to build little towns on their lands . . . they would in the best manner possible, improve the circumstances of their own fortunes'[26]. He referred to the example of a number of towns in the north, and specifically to Cootehill, Lurgan and Monaghan, all of which show clear evidence of comparatively early landlord direction. Cootehill was obviously one of the model instances of the period: 'the town of Coote hill is like a pretty English village', wrote Mrs Delany in 1732, 'well situated, and with all the land about it cultivated and enclosed' [27]. Given the emphasis on industry, many Irish estate villages consisted of modest houses, the main innovation being that they were slated and had sufficient room to accommodate looms. A contrast must be made between towns conceived as industrial villages such as Innishannon and Monivea and better located towns where trade or assizes led to the residence of a small middle-class of merchants and lawyers. Durrow, for instance, which took its modern shape around the site of an earlier 'diamond' at the time Flower built Durrow House, has an impressive row of eighteenth-century houses flanking one side of the green; Eyrecourt, vigorously directed by the Eyres at this time, was losing the character of a modest Restoration settlement. Even from Mrs Delany, whose standards were very exacting indeed, the comment was drawn in 1732 that 'we passed a fine place called Aire's Court, a great many fine woods and improvements which looked very English' [28]. At this period, with Ballinasloe's development still in the future, it was certainly the showpiece of the west midlands. Although its later history was less impressive, with little trade and the estate in chancery from the end of the century, it benefited from the erection of several solid houses built by professional or monied people.

The rapid growth of trade from the 1740s, coinciding with a sustained rise in landlord fortunes, led to a more widespread and more ambitious development of towns. The first ambitious formal creations, such as Cookstown (projected however as far back as 1736 [29]) or the first planned extension of Birr, date from this period. The classic instances — classic in the sense that contemporary comment singled them out —

were all from these years: Cox's Dunmanway, Adderley's Innishannon, Grandison's Dromana, French's Monivea, Kenmare's Killarney, Shelbourne's Ballymote. In all six villages northern textile workers were employed. Many lesser settlements also took shape, and the interest in attracting workers from the north was widespread. In fact there was much greater mid-century contemporary interest in such villages than in formal planning unrelated to industrial development. In co. Cork, there were no less than ten landlord ventures in linen [30]. The interest in creating industrial villages was sustained with important instances such as Jefferys' Blarney and Foster's Collon emerging in the 1760s. The interest was still evident in the 1770s and in the 1780s with villages such as Cornelius Bolton's Cheekpoint, co. Waterford, Henry Brooke's Prosperous or Aldborough's Stratford. Mining had also been a source of towns. Wandesforde's Castlecomer was the most long-lived instance, but Boyd's Ballycastle was laid out in the 1740s when the hopes for Hugh Boyd's many industrial ventures were still high. Hunt's New Birmingham with a very fine square at its centre [31] on the Tipperary slopes of the Slieve Ardagh hills, and the elaborately conceived garden village built by the Grand Canal Company at Newtown in south Queen's co., both in the early nineteenth century, were the last two creations from the interest in coal mining.

In an age of improvement and rising landlord incomes, not all villages were conceived of as industrial villages by any means. Wesley noted in 1758 that on the road between Granard and James' town the proprietor of Drumersnave had 'formed the plan of a town, with a barrack at the end, and his own seat at the other' [32]. Cookstown, one of the major examples of planning, was undertaken in 1750, and the significant planning precedents of Bagnelstown, Newtownbarry, Gorey and Birr were probably simultaneous. Such towns were, however, unique, to be rivalled only in the great projects of the end of the century. Most towns were more modest ventures, with a single intersection at right angles, as in Banbridge 'a sweet little new built market town as I may say created by Ld. Hillsborough who has at his own expense built a very neat little market house', or a central square as at Hillsborough 'where the improvements are very fine and his town of Hillsborough will soon be a place of considerable trade' [33].

Industrial villages themselves, even if modest in the standard of housing, were frequently ambitious in planning.

While Adderley's Innishannon seems to have been a linear development along a single street, Grandison's Dromana had been intended to be a square around the church at which Lord Grandison appeared on Sundays 'at church with my weavers' [34]. Robert French's Monivea was grandiose. Aldborough's Stratford was a very elaborate village, and the family pride in village building is reflected in a letter from Aldborough to his nephew, apparently in connection with a second proposed village, to be called 'George Town after your name with Aldborough, Hartpole and other streets in it' [35]. While the purposes of industrial village and of market village were slightly different, there was no clear difference in planning. Monivea or Dromana, neither with a market house, are no less formal than the classic market or estate villages. Had they prospered — in neither village did industry outlive the original projector, and in Grandison's case the intended square seems never to have been completed — a market house would no doubt have been added in time.

A few villages reflected more specialised ventures. Killarney, in addition to its projected textile role in the late 1740s, was consciously developed by its landlord as a centre of tourism, the inn built by him, entertainments financed by him for the visitors, and boats on the lakes financed or regulated by him. The Trenches regulated the fairs of Ballinasloe, which under their guidance grew from a modest Anglo-Irish settlement of the early seventeenth century into one of the most prosperous inland towns in Ireland. The fishing boom off the Donegal coast in the 1780s accounted for the creation of Lord Conyngham's village of Rutland, whose prosperity was short-lived. Apart from Roundstone, co. Galway, built by the engineer Nimmo, for Scottish fishermen in the 1820s [36], it was the only village built around fishing, a contrast with the numerous short-lived fishing settlements off the south-west coast of Ireland in the early seventeenth century, or contemporary fishing villages in Scotland.

Seventeenth and eighteenth-century villages almost invariably involved the attraction and settlement of outsiders. As late as the 1780s the correspondence between the absentee Earl of Kerry and his agent at Listowel illustrates the mechanism of projecting an estate village. A 'new town' was proposed for the vicinity of Listowel Castle: houses were to be erected at a cost of £2,000 by an under-taker, the agent advising that advertising for settlers should be deferred till the houses were begun, because he remembered a case in which an advertisement had brought a throng of people, who finding nothing ready, had to disperse, only a few vagabonds remaining [37]. Seventeenth-century villages frequently relied on fresh immigrants from England. In the eighteenth century, the most typical example was the textile villages, attracting linen workers from the north, the last instance probably being Aldborough's village of Stratford in the 1780s. Religious refugees from abroad provided a stream of immigrants in the eighteenth century, the arrivals being channelled towards the new villages. As far as the Huguenots are concerned, Portarlington was the outstanding case of settlement, but Huguenots were settled in several other estate villages, notably Lisburn. As late as 1742, there was a lottery 'for the settling of the poor French protestants among us' [38]. French refugees were settled both in Innishannon and Dundalk and Baron Foster's first settlers at his new village of Collon in the 1760s were French protestants [39].

The German Palatines and the Moravians provide other instances of the attraction of religious refugees. There was only a single immigration of Palatines financed by the Commissioners for settling the Palatines in Ireland, which permanently settled some two hundred families. Despite the widespread interest in the venture, it would have failed except for Sir Thomas Southwell's readiness to take some 103 families on his own estates, 30 families being settled around a square near Rathkeale at Court Matrix, the remaining ones on farms at Ballingarrane and Killihen. The only other significant settlement was on the Wexford estates of Abel Ram, 15 families at Old Ross and 21 at the Ram village of Gorey. The most arresting feature of the Palatines is that once settled in Ireland, the original settlements provided the basis for migration to other centres. The name Palatinetown in co. Carlow bespeaks an early venture. In 1751 the Olivers settled Palatines from Rathkeale at Kilfinnane, the main village on their estates, and in 1769 the village of Glenasheen on the Oliver estate was built for a further colony of Palatines from Rathkeale. Sir Richard Quin established them at Adare, and the Blennerhassetts who had already settled some near Tralee in the 1740s, established them at Arabella, near Castle Island [40]. In 1773, a colony from Rathkeale was established by the Barker family who were related to the Quins by marriage, in their Kilcooly estate in a minute village, Palatine Street, at the top of the Slieve Ardagh hills. The last instance of a refugee settlement was the celebrated case of the Geneva refugees for whose settlement public monies were provided in the early 1780s, and for whom the building of the village of New Geneva was undertaken. As in the case of the Palatines seventy years previously, cumbersome administrative procedures, delays, and frustrated hopes on the part of immigrants in 1783-4, furnish a textbook illustration of the problem of refugee settlement on a large scale. In this case, in contrast to the Palatines, all combined to make the venture a failure: the migrants melted away, and the incomplete village, intended to contain forty double houses around a square, one of the two government-sponsored villages in Irish history, was converted into a barracks.[41]

The settlement aspect of the village was waning rapidly by the end of the century although 'Thomas Mullock, Esq.' was undertaking an ambitious industrial village of fifty houses at Bel Air, King's county in 1802 [42], and as late as that year the writer of one of the statistical surveys was still advocating weaver villages on almost the same lines as Madden seventy years previously.[43] The landlord industrial village was to have few new companions, but the foundation of purely rural villages received a new, though more localised, impetus from the invigorated landlord drive in backward areas against the residue of rundale. Land was redistributed to create compact farms around new houses, the old huddles of houses — or clachans — were sometimes cleared away, their inhabitants either moved to houses in the new compact fields or else rehoused, where the idea of a village was retained, in new houses in small villages arranged in neat linear form. Such villages were most numerous in backward areas, and it is not surprising that Mayo, the most backward of Irish counties, provides the most numerous instances of new town creation in the early decades of the nineteenth century. Villages such as Belmullet, Binghamstown, Balla, Clane, Carrowkeel, and latest of all, Charlestown, with very regular streets, some of them incorporating squares, are striking examples. Some of them are estate villages in the classic sense — on the edge of a landlord demesne; others represent rearrangement of land at points on an estate remote from landlord residence. The sharp contrast between these new towns and adjoining clachan-type villages illustrates the unfinished and recent character of this work. Clane was a minute estate village in the immediate vicinity of surviving clachans. The neat village of Louisburgh, a regular cross-roads, already in existence by 1812 [44] contrasts with the neighbouring clachan of Carrowmore. The same pattern emerged on crown land in Pobal O'Keefe on the borders of Cork and Kerry where rundale was abolished and where the village of King Williamstown emerged in the 1830s, the second of the two government-created villages. West Galway provided the examples of Roundstone built by the engineer Nimmo, and Clifden launched by the Darcys after 1815. In Donegal Glenties and Ardara on the Conyngham estate appear to be examples of such villages. Kerry provided two of the most curious instances of all — Ventry built by one of the evangelical societies to house converts from catholicism [45], and Cahirciveen, which fell back into the direct management of Trinity College and witnessed an anachronistic paternalistic attempt by the college in the 1860s to create a more edifying settlement. [46]

At the end of the eighteenth century, when the interest in creating new villages was in decline except on the fringe, interest in remodelling or rebuilding existing villages was emerging, these villages constituting the third category of village. The emphasis was no longer on attracting settlers or even industry. The interest in the village was simply a logical extension of the emerging interest among the more progressive landlords in raising farming standards and improving housing conditions. If some individual farm houses were built directly by the landlord with a demonstration purpose in mind, and tenants themselves were encouraged extensively to rebuild by various inducements, financial and other, it was inevitable that the village would attract the same attention. The nineteenth-century 'cottage' style for the individual landlord-built farm house became the village style as well. While there was an aesthetic urge — the remodelling of a village frequently coincided with the rebuilding of the mansion — tenant welfare was uppermost, many of the villages not being centres of landlord residence. The first instance was probably Abbeyleix, rebuilt on a slightly different and more healthy site in the 1770s by the de Vescis; the second Maynooth, remodelled by the Duke of Leinster in the 1780s. Kingscourt, co. Cavan, was rebuilt by the Pratt family at the end of the eighteenth century. Kilrush, built at a much earlier date, was dramatically developed by its resident landlord Vandeleur in the early years of the new century. Simultaneously with a new residence and vigorous abolition of rundale on the estate, a market square was laid out with a wide well-built street leading from it to the new harbour [47]. In Cootehill, a model village seventy years previously, the neglect of the intervening years was being made good: a market house was erected, and the town 'has already been improved with several very handsome houses and the old lease being extinct, the tenants are obliged to build after an adopted plan'.[48]. The pace of village reformation quickened with the passing years. The Mahon village of Strokestown in Co. Roscommon was rebuilt in a spacious manner reminiscent of Cookstown. Enniskerry was rebuilt around its two-hundred-year-old green in 1818, 'tastefully built in the cottage style', and Tyrrellspass, a nondescript settlement village with a long-established Protestant colony frequently visited by Wesley, was remodelled by Lady Belvedere in the 1820s on the plan of an elegant semi-circle. A distinctive style was emerging — the 'cottage style' of Enniskerry. But eccentricity could also enter into the picture. While most landlords were getting rid of thatch — the thatched village of Dunmore East, for instance, was about to be rebuilt by its landlord the Marquis of Waterford in 1837 — the Quins at Adare, replete with the monies brought in by a successful English match, were actually rebuilding the village with large thatched houses in what was conceived to be the English village style. Instances of landlord building or replanning of villages could be multiplied, the activity ranging from simple rebuilding of houses in villages such as Marlfield, near Clonmel, c.1820, to more ambitious undertakings such as Dundrum, rebuilt and extended by Lord Downshire, or the laying out of Malahide by the Talbots. Many of the villages on the estate of the London companies in county Londonderry were rebuilt as the estates reverted to direct management with the lapse of old leases. Some landlords proposed improvements which were never carried out; village remodelling was one of the hallmarks of the improving landlord. In Blarney, for instance, where Young in 1776 thought the landlord's endeavours 'would undoubtedly do honour to the greatest fortune'[49], and which declined in the next generation, the Jefferys in 1837 were reported to 'have it in contemplation to rebuild it on an enlarged and improved plan'[50]. Although the creation of new villages had virtually ceased except in the far west, the improvement of existing settlements was widespread. Landlord involvement in remodelling villages, in regulating building standards, or simply standards of cleanliness and hygiene, was more direct, and more intimate than at any period in the eighteenth century. As in the case of relations with rural tenants, the closer attention to the regulation of the village and its inhabitants was not in itself a novelty so much as an accentuation of a trend emerging well before 1815.

5
Social structure and evolution

Ireland's demographic change in the seventeenth and eighteenth centuries was very rapid. The rapidity of Ireland's demographic expansion is a function of its initial backwardness, and of the availability of underutilised spaces which could sustain new communities or continued growth in existing ones. The sustained rise of Irish population through two and a half centuries began in 1600, just a century after the decisive break with traditional demographic patterns in the more densely populated parts of Europe where, before the end of fifteenth century, marriage ages were rising and were progressively to reach the level of 27 for males and 25 for females.[1] This fundamental change in the outside world, which did not affect Ireland, helps to account for the surprise of visitors from England or elsewhere abroad: because Irish marriage ages were lower than those in their homelands — or to put it in simpler terms because the Irish seemed to take more pleasure in begetting children — they assumed that the Irish married at remarkably early ages[2]. In fact, marriage ages probably did not change at all, in itself a great contrast with contemporary England and western Europe: they appear to have hovered around 22 years for males and 20 for females. In its demographic patterns Ireland in 1600 was in fact more than a hundred years behind the rest of Europe, its marriage ages approximating to those which prevailed in western Europe in the fifteenth century. The fact that earlier marriages were prevalent in Ireland is reflected in the frequency of marriage among servants (whose practices would mirror those of the lower classes closely) in comparison with England where servants deferred marriages or even remained celibate, a point which struck Arthur Young in his travels in Ireland in 1776[3].

If population in Ireland increased more rapidly than in Europe it was not solely because the birth rate was a good deal higher. Its death rate fell sharply also, in some measure because its diet, very archaic by European standards, became more varied and stable. This change, however, was somewhat protracted, and the decline in epidemic diseases, especially the plague, more precocious in Ireland than elsewhere perhaps because of its isolated situation, was probably a factor in the sharp rise in population after 1600. A factor, even more exceptional than in western Europe at large, was immigration into the country on a scale which had no parallel in the rest of Europe. In fact, if its relatively low marriage ages were uncommon, immigration, the counterpart of its colonial or frontier-type demographic situation, was even more exceptional. By nineteenth-century standards this was of course small. It probably averaged no more than 2000 per annum in the first forty years of the century. Only at its peak in the 1650s may it have exceeded 8000 per annum. It fell thereafter to recover in the late 1670s and early 1680s although the 1650s peak was not again exceeded until the 1690s. Yet at these levels, its average rate probably made it the largest stream of migration in the entire north Atlantic world. Migration from the British Isles across the Atlantic — probably half of European emigration — only averaged 3000 per annum in the seventeenth century; [4] the Swedish and Teutonic migrations within continental Europe were both on a smaller scale. In fact, the gross figures for immigrants to Ireland were at times larger than the estimates for net immigration suggest because in the upheavals of 1641 and of the late 1680s there was a massive outflow of settlers. Immigration probably equalled the entire flow from Britain to America, even exceeding it in the decades before the 1640s when America was unknown and venturesome as it was to do again probably in the 1650s, late 1670s and the 1690s. In its peak periods it may even have greatly exceeded migration from or within the rest of Europe. It fluctuated wildly: people were attracted by favourable circumstances in Ireland, or by crisis, economic, religious or political, in their homes in England or Scotland, and also increasingly by the balance of advantage between Ireland and America as prospective homes for would-be emigrants. In the early seventeenth century, this gave Ireland an advantage, as it did decidedly even later in periods of war. But after 1660 the peace-time balance of advantage shifted positively in America's favour. Village building in Ireland corresponded in approximate fashion to the movements in immigration and to the readiness of landlords and entrepreneurs to finance the removal of immigrants even across the relatively short distances from Britain to Ireland.

Immigrants to Ireland tended to come from relatively well-developed parts of Britain because such regions experienced pressures which made it difficult for younger sons of lesser gentry and rich yeomen to maintain their social position at home, and at the same time had sufficient means to finance the installation of families and servants in a foreign land. Younger sons of lesser gentry and of rich yeomen, experiencing difficulty in maintaining their social position or anxious to enhance it, were prepared to try their luck in a new country. They and the financial backers they were able to obtain paid the passage money of the resourceless men who could be enticed to join them in their venture with the prospect of setting up as tenant farmers below them or as artisans. In fact, this dependent population was a large element in early immigration and was vital to the success of the colonising ventures of richer and more status-conscious immigrants. In the case of mining ventures the dependent population was still larger and more central to the success of the venture and represented a proportionately greater call on the resources of the entrepreneur. Whether it was Boyle in Munster, Chichester in the north or a host of lesser people, they established in Ireland the distinctive arable cultivation of their home regions, the heavy concentration of orchards in the areas of early colonisation by the English (but not the Scots) illustrating the predominant role of immigrants from the cider-rich south of England. As the economic development of the north of England caught up on the south from the middle of the seventeenth century, northern England began to experience some of the demographic and social pressures which had long been evident in the south: northern immigrants became predominant in the movement to Ireland. As the regional composition of immigration changed, so did the character of the immigrants themselves. The woodland and partly industrialised society of the northern counties of England was much less stratified than that of the south in which numerous small gentry and rich yeomen farmers were juxtaposed against small tenants and labourers. Independent artisans were more numerous in the north, and they became much more significant in the flow of immigrants. The character of immigration reflected this change: there were both fewer younger sons of gentry and passage-paid dependents, and more independent artisans and farmers. Immigration by families as opposed to individuals was probably also more common. Farmer immigrants were different too, less likely to be yeomen anxious to attain gentry status quickly, and more likely to be small farmers just sufficiently well-off to pay their own passage and installation costs. Having resources of their own, and coming from pastoral regions of England, they also placed a greater emphasis on pastoral farming than did the settlers from the south of England whose arable agriculture was more easily practised in a stratified society and whose stratified immigration had in fact been intended to help them to create an identical society and economy in Ireland. Sponsorship of immigration by gentry entrepreneurs, though it had not ceased (it always picked up in boom years like the 1650s, late 1670s or early 1680s), was now much less common, and the mid-seventeenth-century hold of nonconformity on much of mid and north England at one and the same time made Anglican entrepreneurs more cautious of sponsorship and would-be immigrants positively eager to avoid it. Thus, in and after the 1650s, a decided though by no means wholesale change in the character of immigration becomes evident: sponsored movement was giving way to independent immigration, and pastoral farming was more important than previously.

Less concentrated because less subject to the centripetal forces of sponsorship, the impact of the new colonists was at once both more evident and less evident. More widely scattered, their less concentrated presence is evidenced by the decrease in village formation; village creation was much slower in the 1650s and 1670s than it had been in the first forty years of the century, when the number of annual arrivals was perhaps only a fourth of the figure reached in the 1650s and probably smaller than the inflow around 1680. But if less concentrated it was frequently more durable because sponsored immigrants often melted away as adversity or whim reduced the resources of the sponsor. Independent settlers were much more durable. Settlement in the 1650s and 1680s was thus responsible for the success of much southern colonisation, and where settlers were at once both relatively numerous and prosperous as in north Wexford and Wicklow, they created dramatically resilient communities. If settlement in many of the centres of pre-1641 settlement succeeded, it was not because of the return of the pre-1641 settlers but of the addition to returning settlers of a newer and tougher breed of settler. The Anglican-dominated district in Longford or the Munster river valleys, partly because they had enjoyed the presence of an active, demesne-creating, Established-Church gentry, fared less well in attracting dynamic immigrants than did other areas where the landlord presence was less dominant. Possibly for this reason the midlands adjusted much more successfully to the virtual collapse of its iron-working industry than did the Waterford river valleys: south Leix, north Tipperary, north Wexford and Wicklow created what were to prove in the long term to be the most successful rural Protestant communities in Southern Ireland: these areas were all characterised by relatively few post-1600 villages, the populations were rural-oriented rather than village-based, and Protestant farmers were frequently the dominant group among the middling and large farmers in the countryside.

However, the more resilient type of immigrant evident from mid-century was attracted not only to Ireland, but to America where trade and settlement were now spreading rapidly. This breed of emigrant was also in a better position to contemplate the long passage across the Atlantic, and Ireland attracted a greatly reduced proportion, compared with the pre-1641 period, of the total number of emigrants from England. In fact, after the 1650s immigration from England weakened, and total immigration would have lost pace even more sharply but for the rising importance of the Scots. Perhaps half the inflow in the period from 1652 to 1672 was Scottish, and in the boom years of immigration in the remainder of the century the Scottish proportion was even higher. The Scots came from the lowlands; few, however, were from the highly stratified arable Lothians in the east, the bulk being from the more pastoral economy of south-west Scotland: Ayrshire, Dumfries and Galloway. They were in the main pastoral farmers, owning their own livestock, able to pay their own passage and choosing their own location. Few were sponsored. The sponsored element evident in some Scottish immigration in the early seventeenth century was now almost invariably absent: few of them settled in villages, old or new, around the house of a sponsor or his agent.

Immigration was thus a large element in the development of Irish society in the seventeenth century. In crude terms, the proportion of the population of Scottish or English blood in 1600 can only have been around 2 per cent; in 1660 the estimate, based by now on contemporary statistical evidence, was 18 per cent, and by 1733 it was of the order of 27 per cent. As there was little post-1700 immigration the latter proportion in all probability already existed by 1700. Thus not only did the population of the island grow rapidly in the seventeenth century, but in ethnic terms its composition became diversified to a quite dramatic degree. There was no comparable change in ethnic composition in the Scandinavian lands, where population grew rapidly; even in Finland under Swedish hegemony the implantation of a Swedish population had not proceeded far. Nor on the whole had the German intrusion into the Slavonic lands produced a comparable change within the time scale of a mere century.

The global impact of sustained population growth and of the presence of immigrants, not only numerous but motivated by an urge to improve their lot, could not but have a profound impact on Irish society. First of all, these factors accounted for the intense pace of commercialisation in a society which was imperfectly commercialised at the outset of the century but then had to absorb both rapid demographic growth and the intrusion of large numbers of immigrants from a developed region. The failure of English settlers to maintain forest land in the iron-founding regions was not due, as often suggested, to an eagerness to make quick gains in conditions of insecurity. Quite the reverse in fact: while iron-making was the concern of large landed entrepreneurs and of a numerous dependent wage-paid population, the non-sponsored settlers, present already before 1641 and much more numerous from the 1650s, were anxious to lay the basis of permanent arable and pastoral farming. Their interests, which implied confidence and determination rather than the reverse, prevailed. This was fortunate, as Ireland was necessarily a peripheral base for the iron industry; and also, from the point of view of successful colonisation, as the settlements firmly implanted in the countryside as farming communities proved by far the most dynamic and durable. Likewise the interest shown in pastoral farming especially by post-1652 immigrants, far from suggesting insecurity, made sense. It reflected the type of farming that as independent farmers from pastoral regions they had known at home. It also reflected an appreciation of the lessons learned by the first generations of colonists: the difficulty of intense arable cultivation in a wet climate, and the marketing problems posed by the absence of a large urban market at close hand in an era when foreign trade in grain was totally unpredictable, reflecting the wholly fortuitous combination of forces embracing the state of domestic supply and the level of foreign demand.

If rapid commercialisation was the first result of these changes, the second was the profound transformation of the cultural character of Irish society. No element reflects the sum total of cultural influences more succinctly than the linguistic situation, which was the vehicle not only of conducting business but of expressing outlook and attitudes. Despite its insular position, the most decisive of any Celtic community, and despite much cultural resistance by the indigenous population to the growing influences of British civilisation, the Irish language faded more rapidly as a spoken language than that of any other Celtic people in modern times, and the number of native speakers is today much smaller than it is in Wales or Brittany or even Scotland. Welsh and Breton have remained the spoken language of very large communities; even Scots Gaelic, despite an unpromising physical invironment and ultimately because of it, survived more successfully than Irish. Social continuity in these countries helped to guarantee the survival of the language. In Ireland itself the number of Irish speakers was relatively much larger in north county Dublin and in Meath, on the very doorstep of the largest city in the country, than in county Wicklow or in Westmeath and Leix where the language had virtually disappeared even within the seventeenth century. As early as the 1650s, the decade of maximum penetration of new settlers and of remarkably good economic prospects, the English language was making rapid inroads, as the satire of the rich Gaelic tenants, 'lost in admiration of a man who could speak broken English', in *Pairlimint Cloinne Tomáis* suggests [5]. In south Armagh the same process took place only in the first half of the eighteenth century, and the poets of the region, less familiar with the advance of English than the poets of the more advanced province of Munster, display a more startled awareness of its progress. In the form of sustained demographic growth and commercialisation, of widening cultural change, of large-scale immigration, and of a revolution in landownership, seventeenth-century Ireland had experienced a revolution in its whole being which is not only unparalleled in its extent in the Europe of its period, but can have few parallels in other centuries.

The apparently relatively straightforward fact of growing numbers of people conceals the complexities of changing social organisation. While some crude but increasingly reliable estimates of actual numbers across the sweep of the century are possible, the more subtle changes in the characteristics of the population are unmeasurable. But even without being able to gauge them accurately some insight into their significance is attainable. The most fundamental of these characteristics is that in growing the Irish population became a more sedentary one. Thus, the very mechanics of growth implied quite literally a simultaneous change in the horizons of the Irishman. Modern writers have usually believed that their Elizabethan predecesors, making their close acquaintance with Irish society for the first time, exaggerated the nomadic aspects of Irish life, and confused booleying, the highly regulated migration between summer and winter pastures, with nomadism. But in fact Irish society as late as the seventeenth or even early eighteenth century was noticeably less stable in terms of fixed residence than its English or continental counterparts. The movement of tenants on a large scale was quite common in the sixteenth century, tenants fleeing from a harsh landlord or being enticed to a new home by a lord anxious to people his estate.[6] This is the movement of good years, motivated by the attraction of better prospects and not by desperation. Even if the Elizabethans were guilty of confusing booleying and nomadism — which may not in fact be the case — the instability of residence became dramatic in years of economic crisis. In such years, Irish tenants simply abandoned their holdings, and disappeared in large numbers from estates. There is no parallel in the better-developed parts of Europe for mobility on this scale, which suggests at one and the same time open spaces nearby to receive them and a meagre investment in chattels or houses to retain them at home. De Cuellar, a Spanish castaway on the north-west coast of Ireland, noted that the inhabitants taking their effects to mountain refuges possessed, apart from their cattle 'no other property nor more moveables nor clothing'[7]. It was by European standards, if not a destitute society in normal years, one which left little surplus for saving or investment. Tenants under the old order appear to have held their land from year to year, but they normally counted on renewal, so that large-scale and concentrated mobility derived more from the tenants' lack of resources than from any other circumstance. The dramatic mobility of tenants even on lands in the richer parts of Kerry as late as the second half of the seventeenth century, throwing up their lands and disappearing from the estates without payment of rent arrears in years of cattle mortality, suggests a meagre amount of possessions, apart from livestock, to retain them in a year of disaster: their losses were smaller if they moved than if they remained and rent payment was enforced. This is really a subsistence society, not so much in the sense of an absence of commercialisation (quite the reverse in fact) but in the sense that over the cycle of good and bad years, the net saving was little more than equal to livestock replacement [8]. Even as late as the eighteenth century the hearth money returns afford some measure of the scale of mobility in the more backward parts of the country. The short-term fluctuations in the returns reflect mobility rather than mortality: in Kerry and Sligo, two counties far apart and representing the poorer but by no means the poorest economic conditions in Ireland, the returns fell by as much as a third in the crisis of the 1740s [9]. As late as the 1760s, even in the relatively advanced county of Monaghan, individual hearth-money collectors defended themselves against the charge of negligence in the collection of the tax on their walk by claiming that many of the individual householders had simply run away after the bad harvests of 1765 and 1766 [10].

The disordered nature of this mobility is reflected in the fact that migrants were often accompanied by their wives and children. The famine of 1728-9 was the last occasion on which mobility of this sort was evident on a large scale: it was the social consequences of this disaster which prompted Arthur Dobbs to write in 1731 the second part of his essay on the trade of Ireland, and the nomadism or post-famine movement which he describes was one of the factors which most clearly preoccupied him. His account can be seriously misunderstood if emphasis is placed on Dobbs' concern about the nomadic element, which was extensive only in the aftermath of largescale social crisis; equally it cannot be dismissed lightly without ignoring an underlying readiness to abandon home. However, the very fact that Arthur Dobbs for the first time in Irish literature directly tackled the problem, suggests that the scale of the phenomenon had frightened him and other contemporaries and that it was much less taken for granted than in the past. It is likely that it was already declining as a general feature of Irish rural society as a higher level of population and general economic development continued to alter the character of the Irish countryside. On the one hand, denser settlement limited the prospect of getting land readily farther afield. On the other, tenants with some resources were now more common: a more stratified society was emerging, with many farmers able to board male and female servants to assist with household tasks, and to recruit migrant labourers in the seasons of heavy outdoor work such as haymaking and harvesting. An interdependence was emerging between better-off and less well-off families. The wages living-in servants sent back home eased the pressure to abandon house, especially when combined with higher prices for young livestock and emerging new forms of income such as yarn spinning for the market. In Sligo, as Charles

O'Hara, a local landlord, observed, young girls especially were sent away as servants at an early age.[11] The social stratification was very evident even within comparatively poor regions such as Sligo itself. As the census of 1749 for the diocese of Elphin — which embraces much of Sligo and Roscommon — shows there was a clear division between servant-exporting and servant-importing parishes in addition to the distinction between individual families within a parish.[12] The seasonal movement of able bodied males for heavy farm work, as opposed to the half-yearly hiring of male and female servants, was geared more to the demands of large farms especially in the mixed-farming regions of Leinster and East Munster. Before mid-century such seasonal movement, not only from the west but from Monaghan and south Armagh to the rich farmlands of Meath, north Dublin and Kildare, was already well-established. Less dramatically a similar movement existed between marginal lands within Munster and the rich farming areas of Munster and Kilkenny.

The mobility evident in Irish society to a comparatively recent date underlines the fact that Ireland was by European standards a very poor society. In fact, this comparative poverty is of long duration in Irish history. It is due neither to English oppression, nor to the industrial revolution which favoured the mineral-rich regions of Britain and of Europe. It preceded them both. Irish per capita income relative to English incomes seems to have fluctuated in a range of 44 to 70 per cent in a series of reciprocating long swings over the period from the sixteenth century to the twentieth century, with high points in the 1650s, 1690s, 1770s, 1900s and 1970s and low points in the 1670s, 1840s, and 1930s.[13] It must have appeared a poor society to European visitors even at an earlier date. To the French visitor Creton arriving with Richard II at Waterford, one of the two most advanced urban centres of Norman Ireland, the impresssion was one of poor living conditions and a primitive organisation of work.[14] It was still a poor society in the sixteenth century: Hugh Brady, bishop of Meath in 1583, in bequeathing the use of his best pan to the poor inhabitants of Dunboyne and stipulating that the portrieve of the town should settle any controversy as to borrowing or keeping the pan too long, affords evidence of the lack of basic cooking utensils even in one of the richer regions.[15] Farther afield the poverty was much worse. De Cuellar affords an European perspective of this poverty on the north-west coast.[16] Much later, in 1733 the poverty of the inhabitants of Connemara was very evident to Edward Smith, captain of a man-of-war stationed off the coast of Connemara: landsmen recruited for the British navy were virtually naked, having a single shirt and requiring shoes and hose before boarding the vessel to take them to England.[17] Arthur Young provides something of the measure of the relative state of the two rural societies of Ireland and France: only once in his tour of France, when passing through Peyrac in the Auvergne in 1787, was he prompted to say that he was reminded of the poverty of Ireland.[18] There was nothing in Ireland even remotely comparable to the French peasants painted by the Le Nain brothers in the first half of the seventeenth century. Though their housing was spartan and their clothes were torn, they were rich peasants with individual valuable objects including even glassware.

Population growth on a large scale within a relatively short period imposed changes in diet. There was less scope for the poor man's cow; diet had to change quite independently of the advent of the potato in the seventeenth century. Thus, the prodigal use of butter and milk in Irish diet was confined to a narrowing circle of people. Some change in diet was promoted by the fact of modernisation itself, but the basic reason was of course the pressure occasioned by population growth: grain and potatoes maintained a larger number of people than a corresponding acreage devoted to dairying. In this way the use of the potato, with its additional advantage that through being available as early as August it helped to spread the community's food supply more evenly across the year, and made it possible to retain the supply of grain for the spring, became in the long term much more heavy than it would otherwise have been.

The marked switch from dairying to grain and potato cultivation was not of course the only response by smallholders whose acreages were declining. Another response was increased employment in weaving and spinning, which gave a cash income independent of the acreage occupied, and which enhanced the ability of families to buy food when their own supply failed. Thus in the eighteenth century even poor families who were self-sufficient thanks to the potato in the autumn and winter entered increasingly into the market as cash buyers of grain from the spring onwards until the next year's potato crop ripened. Textile employment spread to a remarkable degree across the countryside in the eighteenth century, linen in the northern half of the island and in pockets farther afield, wool in the midlands and south. The better-off smallholders engaged in weaving; the poorer families in spinning. Most comfortable of all were the small hill farmers. Less engaged in arable cultivation than in the minding of animals, they had more leisure for the textile industry. They were often substantial producers of linen or woollen yarn or cloth. Having their own livestock including several cows, they also succeeded in maintaining a more varied diet and in retaining milk and butter in some quantity for their own use. The poorest families of all in the eighteenth century were frequently the labouring families in the richest farming counties of Ireland. Apart from the advantage of a cash wage, they had few supplements to their wage income and their diet was sparing, with little except potatoes and oatmeal in regular consumption. Even in a poor county like Mayo the presence of waste land made it easier to maintain a cow, just as the proximity of the ocean offered coastal dwellers the harvest of the seas. Extensive domestic textile industry underpinned this economy in Mayo: equally in neighbouring Galway both linen and wool were widespread across the county. Moreover, precisely because these counties were poor and families needed every penny they could lay hands on, they were much slower to abandon domestic activity than more prosperous counties as the returns in it diminished.

Even in the richer counties, widespread domestic activity had added considerably to the income and comfort of the poorer families and of many of the smaller farm families. For better-off families, it had a social stigma, and if engaged in at all was conducted only by servants under the supervision of the housewife. The woollen industry was entrenched in both Limerick and Clare in the eighteenth century. Protestant weaver-farmers were numerous in the Wicklow hills and Catholic ones in the hilly south of Kilkenny and adjoining parts of Tipperary and Waterford. Weaving and spinning, mainly in wool but also in linen, helped to maintain the incomes of the smaller landholders, as dairying swept across Tipperary and Kilkenny after 1750 and much of the land was concentrated progressively in the hands of large dairy farmers. Even as late as the 1820s, when it was well below its peak, domestic activity lingered on, and the fact that some 500,000 individuals returned their occupations as spinners in the 1841 census suggested that however underemployed they were, the aspiration to some income from spinning was still widespread. In 1828 the former condition of an evicted widow smallholder on the northern fringe of the Kilkenny textile region as recorded in her account in Humphrey O'Sullivan's diary [19], gives an idea of the living condition of such families: glass in the window of the house, pot, table, chairs, crops including potatoes, wheat and flax, livestock including cow and calf and yearling, mare, sheep, goat and fowl; the diet supplemented by pigeons and by eels and pike from the draining of the pool. Simple conditions no doubt but remote from the abysmal poverty described in remote areas like the Rosses, Iveragh or Connemara, the most disinherited regions in Ireland. In the case of the widow she had wheels for spinning both wool and linen.

The change of diet was significant in many directions, reflecting for instance the impact of outside standards as well as pressures which accelerated change. But it was particularly significant in its demographic import. Changes in diet, guaranteeing a larger food supply from existing land in the absence of sufficient marginal or waste lands, greatly reduced the pressures which would have otherwise dictated adjustment in Irish demographic patterns in the way which had already taken place in the more developed parts of Europe. The very fact that Irish diet to start with was archaic — one which in more evolved regions was associated with poverty — meant that the scope for increasing the food supply by greater reliance on cereals and potatoes was very large indeed, and the process of adjustment to a less archaic and more efficient food pattern would defer for a long time the advent of pressures which would directly impel a reduction in the age of marriage. The spread of domestic industry and of employment as servants for the younger members of poor families generally, and more particularly from the poorer regions, operated in the same direction at a slightly later date. [20] Thus the birth rate could have remained unaltered over a longer time, and a brutal adjustment in the form of a downward move in the marriage age was deferred. These circumstances would explain why Ireland had not only a more sustained growth of population over the seventeenth century than most of Europe, but was able to maintain it through the eighteenth century as well. Recent papers by Dr Cormac O Gráda and Professor Dupaquier have argued the likelihood of a sharp downward adjustment in marriage ages several decades ahead of the Great Famine [21]. A rise in marriage ages, however belated, could not be deferred indefinitely; social crisis among the poor, and faltering textile income in and after the 1790s provided the pressures to which it was within ten or twenty years a response. The very fact that the inhabitants of poor regions with waste land, sea or mountain on their doorstep often had a more varied diet than the poorer members of rural society within the richer counties, and that domestic industry declined more slowly in peripheral regions also helps to explain why adjustments in marriage ages came more slowly and less generally in the western seaboard counties than in the more easterly regions.

Of course, the fact that the birth rate did not fall could not of itself explain the rise in population because the already low marriage ages suggest the presence of archaic living conditions which should be reflected also in relatively high death rates. As in all primitive societies, the infant mortality would be likely to be high: even centuries previously, the care of young children among the Irish had been compared unfavourably with that of the Normans.[22] However, adjustment in the archaic diet helped to spread the enlarged food supply more evenly across the harvest year. This itself should have helped to ensure fewer years of deficit and fewer cases of food deficiency linked diseases. Thus the death rate is likely to have fallen also. If the birth rate remained stable in contrast to Europe but the death rate actually fell, perhaps more and from an earlier date than in Europe where there was not a comparable revolution in food supply, then the likelihood of more sustained population growth than elsewhere must appear certain. In fact, given its high mortality rates at the outset, it is possible to see the death rate as falling in two stages: the first in the seventeenth century, food-oriented and without close parallel in western Europe, the second in the middle decades of the eighteenth century, more closely related to the decline in mortality caused by infectious diseases. The fact that in some comfortable parishes the highest death rates were experienced in years of epidemic disease, not in or after years of harvest failure, seems to underline the potential significance of a decline in the toll of epidemic diseases.

While famine was in part war-induced in 1602 and 1652, it was not necessarily entirely so, and there was devasting famine in 1629. Between 1652 and 1725 Ireland was dramatically free of major food shortage or famine, the only possible year of famine seeming to be 1674. This was in striking contrast to most of Europe, especially in the decades of the 1690s or 1700s when Ireland experienced none of the crises which seemed to threaten many countries with dissolution. The switch from dairying for subsistence purposes to a more varied diet suggests that Ireland enjoyed a relative immunity from crises. The recurrence of crisis in 1728, 1729, 1741, 1744, 1757, 1783 and 1799-1801 suggests that the benefits of the changeover had been spent and that the more marginal members of rural society were increasingly vulnerable. In other words, a decline in mortality caused by infectious diseases would have been the operative factor in any continuing fall in the death rate. Ireland's vulnerability was now in contrast with the increasing ability of other societies to survive crisis, and suggests that while the dietary and agricultural changes in the seventeenth century had given the society a new resilience, they were not sufficient to enable it to absorb a continued rise in population numbers without living standards coming under threat. The quite dramatic growth in domestic textile industry, often in remote regions and generally among the poorer members of rural society, against a background of relatively poor industrial traditions and very recent commercialisation, suggests that the pressures were considerable. The fact that the upsurge in textile industry can frequently be dated to the 1720s and 1740s, the two decades of most severe crisis in the eighteenth century, seems to underscore the link between textiles and demographic or subsistence crises. The more northerly distribution of crises in the late 1720s, the more southerly in the 1740s is also persuasive in this context. Textile income did of course help to ward off crisis, and the fact that crises on the scale of those of 1729 and 1741 were not experienced again despite continued population growth in the eighteenth century is an illustration of its effect. The fact too that the finer branches of the linen industry spread in rural Ireland whereas in Scotland they were concentrated on the towns illustrates the lower rural incomes in Ireland and the reduced pressures in rural Scotland to add to income by industrial supplements. The fact that these decades are among the few intervals in which Irish population growth over the seventeenth and eighteenth centuries seems to have slowed significantly emphasises the underlying gravity of the demographic situation and points to the importance of the role of textiles as a means of deferring for another two generations any significant downward adjustment in marriage ages.

Social structures changed profoundly in Ireland over the period. The dynamics of development and population growth combined ensured that some elements in the farming class gained economically, the contrast sharpening between the stronger farmers who prospered and the smallholders and labourers who remained marginal. Stronger farmers in turn impinged even on the interests of the landlord class, because the downward mobility of many younger sons who rented lands ensured a clash of interest with the upward social mobility of farmers. Irish rural society can be understood only by analysis of the two groups which dominated it, one receiving rent for land it held, the other paying rent for a right to occupation. Study of rural society is bedevilled by problems of terminology because the terms landlord, middleman, and farmer are none of them clear-cut nor did the distribution of influence and the balance between these groups remain constant in the countryside over time. At the pinnacle of Irish society stood its landlord class, which is usually studied exclusively in terms of ownership of the soil and hence by implication, in a society where primogeniture was practised, of the eldest son. But if the younger sons and daughters are included, the study of the landlord class extends far beyond landowning, the younger sons entering the professions (including the church) or becoming large tenant farmers, the daughters marrying middleman landholders (in effect farmers of gentle status), or professionals, in a complex pattern embracing the upward or downward mobility of individuals or of entire families. But above all, whatever the fortunes of the individual person or family, the landowning families were the centrepiece politically and socially of a large interest group whose income and status by no means depended exclusively on the income from landownership.

Well-off, coming a generation or two back from more advanced regions in Britain, well-educated by the standards of the time, landlords were imbued with ideas from the outside and were the sponsors of much innovation in social and intellectual life. But because they were under no commercial pressure to modernize, they were often slow to alter their life styles. Thus more than any other group they stood quite literally in two worlds. Irish landlords, alien to much of Irish culture though they were, vied with older families in their liking for harp music, and welcomed Carolan royally as did the surviving old Gaelic families. The Brownes at Kenmare were patrons of the poet Aodhgán O'Rathaile and in much less perfunctory fashion the family of the Brownlows at Lurgan in co. Armagh both patronized poets and collected manuscripts. The traditions of hospitality of an older generation and culture died hard, and the Anglo-Irish families entertained with a profusion which was quite archaic by British standards and with an abandon associated also with an addiction to hunting more general and unsparing than in Britain. Right into the nineteenth century, visitors from Scotland and England, even from the top of society, were impressed with Irish hospitality. A concomitant of hospitality and hunting — servants and horses — was invariably on a lavish scale, and Arthur Young, an assiduous visitor of many of the great houses, commented after his Irish tour on the excessive number of horses and servants. Expenditure on houses and on industrial projects reflected some of this lavishness or lack of restraint. These characteristics were not of course exclusive to the Irish landlord class: the prodigal spending by the great English landowners on the high farming of the 1840s and 1850s, financed in part by mining royalties, as much as it was modern in expression, was archaic in the attitudes behind that expression.

Middlemen are almost invariably treated as a form of upper-class antithesis to the landed class. In fact, far from being part of a different segment of society, they were originally members of it. Many were the younger sons of the smaller gentry who sought to maintain a gentry style of life by renting a large tract of land and living off the profit rents created by the difference between their head rents and the subrents paid to them by their tenants. Many of the Catholics who became middlemen in the south of Ireland were descendants of the main branches of the dispossessed landed families, and their ethos and outlook was that of gentry, not of tenant families. Church lands offered another opportunity of acceding to land, as did the vast estates of Trinity College, Dublin, scattered across the country. The social identity of middlemen and landlords is reflected in the difficulty of making a clear-cut legal distinction between the two categories: many of the landlords who held land in fee, also held lands on lease. The extensive upheaval over the Tenantry Act of 1780, which made it easier to find defects in the title to land, was largely a conflict of interest within the landed class, between holders of land in fee and holders of leases for lives. It did not touch the occupying tenantry even remotely, and was an interesting illustration both of the importance of this form of tenure and of the conflict of interest it could occasion within the otherwise relatively cohesive upper-class. The middlemen played a vital role in landed society, and helped to maintain its viability. First, at a time in the early eighteenth century when humbler tenants were only gradually developing a commercial outlook and often had too few resources to stock land or even market their products effectively, the middlemen, often content to be paid in kind, helped to accelerate the spread of a stable market structure in the more remote areas. Their role in marketing produce was significant. It seems to have been the major point, even as late as the 1770s, stressed in defence of the system to Arthur Young, who was highly critical of their role. But the spread of a cash economy through the countryside and the enhanced ability of tenants to turn their products into cash without the direct liaison with merchants in a distant port which the middleman had maintained (strikingly illustrated in the 1770s in a reference in the imagery of *Caoineadh Airt Ui Laoghaire* where the merchants' wives are said to curtsy to the tragic hero of the poem), inevitably reduced their usefulness. In the dairying regions, the rising butter brokers, roving far afield and prepared to make cash advances to dairy farmers, were the effective harbingers of economic change. Viewed from the perspective of the more intensely commercialized late eighteenth century, the middlemen had an increasingly anachronistic air. But, given an undercapitalised tenantry, their contribution was vital to the spread of dairying at an earlier date; the fact that dairying spread rapidly in south Munster in the 1720s and 1730s, the region in which their role was most entrenched at a time when dairying contracted nationally and prices were very low and falling, illustrates their effectiveness at a crucial point in the growth of butter exports. Moreover, in this period not only did they often market the butter to the ports, but they provided the dairy cattle for the farmer dairymen as well as the land. Secondly, middlemen, accessible to their tenants and living among them, helped to popularise the living habits of the upper classes. Their houses, imitating those of the landowners but on a reduced scale, their kitchen gardens and domestic offices, provided the model which the larger tenant farmers were to imitate as they rose in the world.

This system was inherently unstable by its very nature. At one level, the emergence of better-capitalized tenants whose rise was facilitated by the much better developed economy of the late eighteenth century, threatened the survival of middlemen. Middlemen were a function of the degree of backwardness of a region, and were never entrenched in the more developed regions, such as Dublin, Kildare, Kilkenny and Meath, where large farmers cultivating extensive acreages existed, and there was little scope for the middlemen. In regions like north Wexford or Louth, they were small-scale operators who were in effect large farmers cultivating extensive acreages directly and adding to their income and status through some subletting. In the less-developed regions their role was threatened by the emergence for the first time of better-off tenants. At another level, their existence was threatened from the middle of the century by the growing urge of landowners to dispense with them, and to capture for themselves the rents formerly enjoyed by the middlemen. But this urge was itself subsidiary to the degree of development of the region and to the emergence of an alternative in the form of a solvent, improving tenantry to whom land could be let. Thus, the system was being challenged from above by the urge of landlords to eliminate middlemen and from below by the rise of a better-circumstanced tenantry ready to pay higher rents and no more likely than middlemen intermediaries to default on payment. Landlords were, however, very ambivalent towards the replacement of middlemen: they frequently envisaged their replacement, but when leases came up for renewal they as frequently relet the land to them. This ambivalence can be accounted for very simply by the fact that many of the middlemen were related by blood or marriage to members of the gentry families, or were Protestants whose replacement by occupying farmers in the more backward regions necessitated a departure from the long-established tradition of favouring the solvent Protestant tenant. But the break-up of the system was inevitable though it could be slowed down by the operation of family and social considerations. By the closing decades of the eighteenth century the system had become unstable: the bitter controversy over the Tenantry Act of 1780 is itself proof of that. In a highly developed area, where middlemen were marginal and their acreages small, competition between vulnerable Catholic and Protestant middlemen was responsible for the outburst of rebellion in north Wexford. The distinctions between various grades of gentlemen (true gentlemen, half-mounted gentlemen, etc.), which only emerged and were popularized at this stage, illustrate the social predicament in which the more marginal members of the gentry found themselves as both income and status were squeezed. The reluctance of landlords to get rid of middlemen was of course strong but after 1815 the collapse of farm prices accelerated the process. Middlemen who had often taken their farms on reduced acreages at inflated rates and in the boom of the Napoleonic wars relet at high rents to their tenants, now found their tenants unable to pay and in turn had difficulty in paying their own rents to their head landlords. Landowners, reluctant to replace middlemen as long as social considerations were uppermost, were less hesitant when overwhelming economic necessity forced them to act. And as always, once the inevitable was faced up to, it became much easier to continue the process. The title of tenants holding leases on lives was now scrutinized more closely, and technical faults helped landowners to rid their estates of them. What was a remote possibility at the time of the controversy over the Tenantry Act in 1780 had now become for the middle interest a fearsome reality. Only on the Trinity College estate did the middle interest survive successfully, the College like the non-institutional land-owners at an earlier date temporizing between its economic interests and the social interest imposed by its standing as, after the Established Church, the greatest Protestant institution in the island. The parallel went further. Prepared to temporize as long as social considerations were the dominant factor, in the crisis of the 1880s the College ruthlessly abandoned its tenants.

The increased hostility and difficulties in management which landowners experienced from the early nineteenth century onwards are explicable as a function of the breakdown of the middleman system. Middlemen had been in close day-to-day contact with their tenants. At one level, they had been for long, although they were now ceasing to be, economically useful members of local society, marketing agricultural produce and even in the south-west maintaining dairy herds and farms of their own. While the landowners were remote from the people because of their great incomes, lordly manors and demesnes, and their peripatetic social and political life, the middlemen mixed with the people both at a daily business level and in social contacts. Even the abductions of heiresses or daughters of comfortable farmers, some of which had been conducted by members of the middlemen gentry, were an illustration of close social contact with local life, and of much similarity between the mores of middlemen and of the tenants below them. In coastal districts, these small gentry or middlemen tenants were in close contact with the country people through the smuggling trade as well. Increasingly the distribution of smuggled goods was in the hands of numerous small importers, conducted therefore not on the account of a few large individuals but of a large number of local individuals who made petty speculations in spirits and tobacco. A central figure was necessary not only to co-ordinate the landing of the goods but above all to collect and to transmit the payment for the goods to the suppliers overseas. For this a local figure of repute and means was essential. The Hutchins at Bantry, small middlemen tenants, were smugglers throughout much of the eighteenth century, promising their head landlord — disapproving, as most head landlords did, of contraband activity — to desist but continuing at least as late as 1778. Many other instances can be cited, for instance at the outset of the nineteenth century, John Hodnett at Crookhaven, James Walmsley at Newcastle, co. Down, or Duke Ormsby at Ballycastle, co. Mayo. While smuggling or abductions were disapproved of by the upper classes, they were part and parcel of everyday life. Lacking in popular discouragement, they are a testimony to the tight net of social and economic interests which bound tenant and middle tenant together. The predominantly dark picture of middlemen was painted either by head landlords whose rustic manners of an earlier age the middleman tenant often perpetuated or by outside commentators aware that middlemen who had a vested interest in an unchanged society were instinctively opponents of reform or modernisation. For the smallholder, the middleman prepared to let land in small parcels at a high rent was much less menacing than the successful tenant farmer anxious to maintain or enlarge the amount of land managed by himself. One of the contemporary accusations, as also that of later historians, against middlemen was that they were prepared to acquiesce in subdivision, a practice which, while disowned by the best opinion of the age, was often a godsend for the desperate small man anxious to have a permanent stake, however small, in the land system. The large tenant farmer on the other hand was increasingly reluctant to subdivide land, letting plots at ever more prohibitive rents for a single season to labourers where it suited him on the farm. In fact, it was in large measure the readiness of middlemen to subdivide that contributed to their ultimate undoing: the occupiers of smallholdings were particularly vulnerable when prices collapsed in 1814, the resulting arrears, more than any other single factor, giving the impetus to the last stages of the downfall of the middlemen. As a consequence, throughout the rural Ireland of the late eighteenth and early nineteenth century, the middlemen were much less resented by the lower classes in the countryside than were the large graziers and mixed farmers. Rural unrest was much more endemic in the grazing districts of Tipperary and Limerick or in the region of large mixed farms in Kilkenny than in the locations where middlemen succeeded in holding out into the post-1815 period. Middlemen were important social brokers in the countryside, who, however archaic and conservative they were, contributed powerfully to the cohesion of social life. As they disappeared, the conflicting social interests of rural Ireland confronted one another much more directly.

Middlemen were a striking proof of the backwardness of Irish rural society. Just as some of the problems facing them lay in the relationship between them and the landowners from whom they rented land, even more of their emerging problems derived from what was happening below them. The more sedentary pattern — now long-established — of rural life and its progressively commercialized character were stages in the emergence of self-sufficient, comfortable farmers. Hence while at one level middlemen were being ousted, willingly or unwillingly, by their own class, at another level they were becoming redundant because of what was taking place below them. The dramatic increase in cow ownership by tenants in the dairying districts, the most archaic of Irish rural areas, is an instance of the change which was undermining the central function which they had played in financing the cattle stocks of the dairying regions. The parliamentary report on the butter trade in 1826 is based throughout on the premise that the farmer was owner of his own herd, and the dairyman, relying on a rented herd, was now a figure of the more remote parts of Kerry and Cork, not as he had been at one stage, of the entire south Munster region. With access to land much more difficult, except quite literally on barren and waste land along the coast or on the fringes of mountains, an increasing number of the smaller men were reduced in status from smallholder to labourer. In this dual process of stronger farmer and increasingly marginalized labourer lay the seeds of growing rural conflict which characterized the early decades of the nineteenth century. Conacre holdings were much more common: land for a single season usually for potato growing, let by a farmer not by way of a middle-term commitment to provide land for a labourer but because he was anxious to have a root crop in his own crop rotations. The relationship was highly exploitive. The rents were high, determined every year by the forces of competition among labourers, and if the manure was provided by the farmer, were very high indeed. The labourer relied on selling his labour on the open market, which took up all the labour available only in the haymaking and harvesting seasons. Many, though a decreasing proportion, were tied labourers. Their rents were somewhat lower, but they were tied to work for the farmer if required at rates which were in effect book entries credited as payments against the rent, and as such the rates showed none of the buoyancy of open market wage rates. In the eighteenth century, their lot was made easier by the fact that the grazing of a cow was often a feature of the agreement, but this had ceased to be general by the early nineteenth century. The conacre tenant was likely to default on rent payment if his crop failed: increasingly the rent was exacted in advance, so that if his crop failed he had neither cash nor food, and it was this precariousness which made him the most miserable and vulnerable of all the members of rural society. It is hardly surprising therefore that labourer-farmer conflict became more common and that increasingly conacre rents loomed as a major grievance. Even at an early stage in relatively advanced areas, rural conflict had acquired a savagery which had no parallel elsewhere. By the 1770s in county Kilkenny, agriculturally one of the most advanced counties in Ireland, it had taken on the form of a vendetta between the poor and the richer members of tenant society. It is not of course possible to describe this conflict in exclusive terms. As smallholders had been more prevalent in the past, populist aspirations to hold land rather than to hold a plot were quite general, and the unrest of the countryside had a complex background which should not be oversimplified. Again, many labourers were a product of downward social mobility by the sons of small farmers, and were seeking to reestablish their place in rural society. In consequence the range of rural grievances was in fact quite large. The populist tendencies were reflected too in the uneasy relationship of the Land League, in effect an association of farmers, with labourers in the 1880s. Farmers were not sympathetic to labourers' direct demands but were quite happy to head them off by support for the more nebulous aims of facilitating the access of small men to land.

Irish rural society was highly fluid in the late eighteenth and early nineteenth centuries. The middlemen stood between their own class and the farmers, and if unsuccessful were increasingly likely to slip into the latter class. The circumstances in which they surrendered advantageous leases and became déclassé occasioned the advance of the better-off farmers. While often holding on to the lands they had managed directly, middlemen were surrendering the acres they had sublet which head landlords in turn then let directly to occupying farmers. The rising farming class reflected the pronounced advance of stratification below the level of middleman. It was thus increasingly a stratified society with its landlord class isolated, as the middleman class who had overlapped between landlord and tenant disappeared, and the occupancy of land became more sharply divided than ever between a powerful farming group and the more marginalized members of rural society. Yet while much more stratified than previously, it was still a much more classless society than those rural societies where a high degree of economic development had left stratification entrenched for generations. Because so many sons of landowners had become gentleman farmers and because so many gentleman farmers in turn had been reduced to the level of large working farmers, a vague identification with the upper classes reached far down the scale in the countryside. Likewise, because the marginalised members of the farming class sank to cottier status and because many cottiers aspired to a higher status, the conflict between labourer and farmer, however bitter it was, was softened by overlapping ties and by the deep underlying aspiration of smallholders to acquire tenant status. In a quite unique way, given its fluidity combined with the abruptness of change, Irish society at all levels below that of the landed class (who in a more rarefied atmosphere were even more obsessed with their standing) was as deeply concerned with status as with its economic interests. One of the most interesting features of the accelerating decay of the middleman world after 1800 was that it greatly weakened the Protestant interest in the countryside. Except where there was a strong Protestant farming group spread through an area, as there was in north-east Ulster and in north Wexford and Wicklow, many of the Protestants in the countryside were poor Protestants: smallholders, cottiers and artisans. They depended heavily on the succour or support of a local occupier of gentry status, who could favour them in the allocation of leases, employ them on the demesne farm or give them preference as artisans. Protestants were disproportionately well represented among the middlemen, not only because of landlord preference but because of the tenurial advantages which they could enjoy under the penal laws. As they disappeared, the central support of pockets of rural Protestants fell apart. The decline of the rural middleman inexorably meant the decline of the smaller rural Protestant communities. Decline of middleman and small community alike both foreshadowed the more general decline of the Protestant community which set in later in the nineteenth century.

Thus the changes in Irish society in the seventeenth and eighteenth centuries were not simply demographic but more general social changes on a scale unparalleled in the more settled and stratified rural societies of England, France or lowland Scotland. More profoundly still, the intimate detail of everyday life in Ireland, because more backward to start with, underwent a continuing process of evolution. The bulk of the housing was still chimneyless in the early seventeenth century, families lived without privacy in one or two rooms, and subsisted on a butter-based diet, long abandoned in more crowded societies. In other words, just as its demography was archaic so was the style of everyday living, by a century or two. Even for a sixteenth century Englishman, that is for a visitor from a country much less evolved at the time than western Europe at large, it seemed far removed from the pattern of advanced society. Borde even headed his account of Ireland by a woodcut of a woman, picking lice out of the hair of her companion [23]. In anthropological terms, sixteenth century Ireland had affinities with Europe two centuries previously. Equally, Captain de Cuellar spoke of the natives as 'savages', using the term in its anthropological sense, to distinguish them from more advanced peoples [24]. The fact of sustained transition occasioned a wide range of contrasts. Diet for instance was varied, not so much in the sense of a great variety of foods being consumed by the same family as in the existence of a wide range of balances of foodstuffs in various social or geographical contexts. Likewise, the decline of the Irish language was a continuing phenomenon. It took place with overwhelming speed, even within the seventeenth century, in much of the midlands and the east, while at the same time it declined scarcely at all in much of the west and south of the island before the end of the eighteenth century. Within a few miles of Cork, Irish was an active language of large rural communities in the eighteenth century, and the countryside in the vicinity of both Limerick and Waterford cities was still largely Irish-speaking into the early nineteenth century. There was indeed more Irish spoken in the Pale than to the west and south of it. Even the character of the English language varied widely, depending on the history of its advent in a region. John Millington Synge, the most sensitive of all observers of Irish linguistic cadences, noted of the remote valleys of Wicklow that the people 'have retained a peculiar simplicity, and speak a language in some ways more Elizabethan than the English of Connaught, where Irish was used till a much later date' [25]. Yet even in such regions some knowledge of Irish lingered on for long. On the western slopes of the Wicklow mountains, less intensively overwhelmed by English influences than the eastern valleys which opened on to the lower lands impregnated with English settlement, Irish was still spoken at the end of the eighteenth century, or at any rate in the view of the traveller, Coquebert de Montbret, more Irish was spoken there than on the rich, undisturbed Kildare plain below [26]. In the Fingall district of north Dublin and in south Wexford, among the regions least touched by later outside settlement, local dialects, bastard languages with words of French, Flemish, Irish and English origin, survived into the eighteenth century.

6
Social and cultural frontiers

Social and cultural contrasts imply geographical or physical barriers between regions. Such contrasts are sharpest in the case of backward regions where the transition to modern conditions often operated very swiftly. By contrast, changes were less sweeping in the economically richer and culturally more self-sufficient regions: there was considerable in-built opposition, social and cultural, to outside forces, and changes were adopted slowly rather than imposed by necessity, as in poorer or more remote regions. At the outset of the period there was a frontier between Ulster and the rest of the island, the cultural backwardness of the north being originally the main constituent of the contrast. It was this region, the most backward to start with, which experienced the most profound transformation of all. The backwardness and low population density of the north provided the main attraction for the hordes of British settlers who flooded into the province in the course of the seventeenth century, the intensity of British settlement transforming much of the province, and creating in turn a new contrast between the north and the rest of the island. Relatively mobile people like the Scots were not likely to be content with a single move; and the high degree of mobility of the Scots, reflected in movement within Ulster and in the eighteenth century in emigration to America, was reflected also in a drift by Scots from Ulster into north Leinster and Connaught both in the seventeenth and eighteenth centuries. Thus there was a somewhat unstable frontier between Ulster and the regions beyond, and at the end of the eighteenth century social tensions were evident all along this frontier, their character being determined, on much evidence, by influence radiating out from the north.

The meeting point for all these forces radiating outwards through Ulster and the frontier counties of Connaught and Leinster was Armagh. It was the county most densely settled of all by English settlers, and in the pre-1641 period the numbers were impressively large, even allowing for some exaggeration by victims of the numbers said to have been stricken by the outbreak of the 1641 rebellion [1]. Moreover, Armagh was not only the county in which English settlement was greatest but the sole one in which it was not later overwhelmed by the massive Scottish influx. The existence of a uniquely large number of pre-1641 villages points to the success of Armagh in attracting small entrepreneurs who were the main source of support for sponsored English settlement. The frequency of relatively small landed estates, the wide scatter of demesnes, and residence on their lands by landowners continued to provide succour for the Anglican communities throughout the eighteenth century, and even in the southern half of the county the penetration of Scots was counterbalanced in the first half of the eighteenth century by the colonist figure of the landlord-rector Hill. In co. Derry, where English settlers predominated originally, they lost ground rapidly to the Scottish Presbyterians well before the century was over. It was the dramatic advance of the Presbyterians in the county which accounts for the almost hysterical fears in the 1690s of the diocese's great bishop, William King, that the Anglican community in the island would be swamped by Presbyterians.

Armagh county was a cockpit of colonization. There was a frontier within it between British and Irish. Many Scots, not finding church and landlord dominance to their liking, either passed through the county or moved towards its south, creating a three-fold division of English, Scots and Irish settlement respectively. Within the county's most important town, Armagh itself, the three-fold division was repeated in the names of three principal streets. The same pattern was quite distinct in the county at large, massive Anglican ascendancy in the northern districts of the county, Presbyterian predominance in the middle reaches, and a Catholic majority in the more remote and poorer south. The county was the centre of the Oakboy movement in the 1760s, an agrarian movement sparked off by complaints about road building and local taxation. Though sometimes anti-establishment, it was much less so than the Steelboys, an agrarian movement a decade later in more staunchly Presbyterian districts, which often wreaked vengeance on the homes of landlord and parson. The Anglican countryman's loyalty to his landlord was partly a consequence of the old-established order of the countryside and of the presence of numerous small resident gentry. Cohesion with the establishment in church and state was promoted also by the competition which rural Anglicans experienced from

Presbyterians and Catholics alike. Significantly in this county of dense population, small farms and the most intense religious divides in Ireland, Presbyterians themselves failed to display the radicalism of their brethren in Down and Antrim. Presbyterians in Armagh, unlike their prosperous rural brethern in south Antrim and co. Down who had few Catholics to contend with, did not provide membership for the United Irishmen in the 1790s: in Armagh there was no armed rebellion in 1798. The fact that the troubles which culminated in the formation of the Orange Order were contemporaneously attributed to journeymen, i.e. dependent textile craftsmen [2], a very high proportion of whom were Anglican, as opposed to independent farmers or master manufacturers, among whom the Presbyterians were well represented, illustrates how the impetus to form the Order came from the ranks of the Anglicans. This is supported also by the fact that all the decisive early events in its history took place in parishes with a large excess of Anglicans over Presbyterians. However, the fact that the main thrust of Presbyterians in this county, avoiding the Anglicised, densely-populated and high-rented north, carried them further south in the county, meant that they were in direct competition with Catholics. Presbyterian hatred of Catholics in this region, where unlike Antrim or Down they were in competition with them, was a by-word by the early 1790s. Moreover, Presbyterians in Armagh were poorer than in adjoining areas of Ulster. Even in modern times its Presbyterian congregation was socially beneath that of the Presbyterians of neighbouring Down and Antrim. Significantly, however, reflecting their greater economic standing and political independence as compared to either Catholics or Anglicans, many Presbyterians held out against the emerging violence. A minister in 1788, denying that Presbyterians were the sole culprits, pointed on the one hand to 'the old leaven of Tory and High Church principles among many' and on the other to 'men of midling rank among us, and the Presbyterian ministers particularly, (who) have used all their influence to suppress the spirit of riot' [3]. In other words, the Presbyterians of middling rank, clearly more cautious, were slow to abandon their independence of mind, and did so only as the raging civil unrest threatened to overwhelm their modest prosperity.

Frontiers existed within the south as well, although none as striking or as long as the one which quite literally straddled the northern half of the island. But while the changes in landownership were sweeping almost everywhere, new settlers in the south were evident in large numbers only in the woodland areas. Old-settled areas, whether those of the Pale or of the Ormond palatinate, received few settlers. There were in fact more English settlers far afield in counties where there was no revolution in landownership than in these densely populated, highly cultivated counties. The large number of castles here (400 in Limerick, 250 in Tipperary, for instance) points to the presence of a middle interest between the landowning families and the humble occupiers, which was quite likely with its entrenched local business and family ramifications to provide a daunting challenge to any colonist weighing up the cost of investment in a colonizing project. In woodland society, things were quite different. The population was less dense, and though castles were numerous for defensive purposes, there was not quite the same intense network of fortified tower houses which bespoke rich agricultural settlement. Settlement of outsiders was largest in areas where there was woodland to clear, whether for agricultural purposes or for iron mining. In Carlow, north Wexford and south Wicklow, and in the lands below the north-eastern and south-eastern slopes of Slieve Bloom, the purpose was dual; there agricultural settlers and mining populations were established simultaneously. In the river valleys of Munster with their rich woodlands and good transport, mining was the focal point, though by no means the exclusive one, of settlement. In Wicklow or in co. Limerick, settlement was mainly agricultural and both in Wicklow and in the valley of the Maigue it followed rich woodland. Everywhere the new settlements were overwhelmed by the 1641 rebellion, and even where settlers returned to Ireland afterwards, they did not necessarily return to the same districts. Settlement in the Munster river valleys never quite regained its pre-1641 dynamic, because the iron industry did not recover its vitality. Midland and east Leinster settlement fared better, because, less geared to the iron industry except at Mountrath, it had from the start attracted a more independent type of settler. It continued to do so in the second half of the century; the Protestant farming class spread out across the countryside in Wicklow and north Wexford and in a belt to the south of the Slieve Bloom mountains in south Leix and north Tipperary, constituting in these four locations both the largest Protestant populations of southern Ireland, and the most durable. Significantly this post-1660 population was largely rural: few villages were created after 1660 in this region and none of them flourished, the characteristics of pre-1641 settlement surviving well precisely because the villages were slow to lose their rural character. Much of the pre-1641 settlement was concentrated in or around village sites. Offaly was the scene of a large network of villages all sited at a discreet distance from the only partly subdued Slieve Bloom mountains. After 1652, with rebellion crushed, settlers could not only fan out more readily in the countryside, but could settle on the rising ground directly below the Slieve Bloom mountains. The most striking illustration of this is the tiny village of Rosenallis at the heart of intensive post-1660 Quaker settlement in the midlands. The Slieve Bloom mountains are ringed in fact with a chain of relatively late houses high up on their slopes, illustrating the new-found colonist dominance of the very mountainside. Roundwood, an isolated, undefended house, built around 1730, the finest of its period in the region, is a good illustration of this characteristic. Only a few isolated outlaw bands in the 1730s and 1740s provided an echo of more lawless times, and with their suppression, the region had been firmly modernized.

By contrast, the large pre-1641 settlement in Limerick, although not mining-oriented as in Cork and West Waterford, succeeded less well in recovering from the effects of 1641. Pre-1641 colonisation was widespread across all of Limerick, even if it was only extensive in the middle reaches of the county. To some extent, this was a consequence of the fact that the downfall of the Desmond Principality, much of it in Limerick, provided the occasion for the Munster plantation; to some extent the success of the settlement was the consequence of active sponsors like the Courtenays and Southwells. But after 1652, it never recovered in the western or eastern parts of the county; it fell off at Newcastle, and while it prospered in the Maigue valley in the long term through the accident of the support of four strongly Protestant families, the Protestant settlers there never revealed the dynamism of the native families, and settler farm families were rarely the largest or most prosperous in a parish. Ultimately, Limerick settlement was doomed to failure because of the density and strength of the native population. Even before 1600 Limerick was the second largest city in Ireland, a reflection of a comparatively rich hinterland. The fact that the number of tower houses in co. Limerick runs to a remarkable 400 [4] is a pointer to a deeply-entrenched local middle interest whose hold was only marginally shaken by the overthrow of their landlords.

The contrast between dependent communities and independent ones is well illustrated even within the limits of a narrow region by the differences within north Kilkenny. Castlecomer, though remote, poor and upland, was the main centre of settlement in co. Kilkenny. The colony was continuously renewed through the demands of iron and coal successively. Moreover, its landed family, the Wandesfordes, continued to hold land in Yorkshire as well, and it was from Yorkshire that many of the immigrants, all apparently with skills developed or rejected in their home district, came. But despite these advantages, the immigrants never fared well, sinking to the level of the poorest around them, proving more boisterous and violent than the natives, and never replacing or even attempting to replace the Catholic native middlemen and large farmers [5]. The only way in which their presence decisively altered the cultural pattern of the region was in introducing the English language which precociously ousted Irish. In the adjacent poor parish of Mothill, on the other hand, Protestant upland farmers, probably with landlord support, created an expanding community at the outset of the nineteenth century. While their holdings were middle-sized, and the indifferent quality of the land meant that they were comparatively poor, the success of the community was a contrast with the larger community in Castlecomer. Even the relatively equal size of the holdings points to artificial creation under landlord sponsorship, the surnames suggesting that the migrants had come from crowded northern Wexford or South Wicklow where there were strong, successful Protestant communities.

Middlemen and gentry, it has been argued, were originally difficult to distinguish in their social origins: they were essentially the same class with individual members distanced from one another over one or two generations by the normal process of mobility in a society where primogeniture held. This is no less true of Catholics than of Protestants. The fact that so many Catholics, dispossessed as landowners, were able successfully to maintain their gentry status or pretensions is paralleled by the fact that younger Protestant sons of landowners, inheriting no land, faced precisely the same problem. Both Catholics and Protestants faced similar dilemmas in maintaining their status; this helps to explain the intense social rivalry in parts of Ireland, made intense precisely because these pretenders to social status, both slightly on the downgrade, were of roughly equal standing. The conflict between Morris and Arthur O'Leary is an instance immortalized in verse in west Cork; the Miles Byrne-Hunter Gowan conflict in north Wexford and south Wicklow is a similar example of less literary but more practical consequence. There must have been hundreds of lesser known cases: these two were recorded in the poem attributed to the wife of one, and in the memoirs of another [6]. Nicholas Sheehy's cousin, Edmond Sheehy, executed in 1766, was nicknamed 'Buck Sheehy': a man of property and of sporting disposition: it is quite likely that similar circumstances singled him out for attention [7]. Such accounts written from the viewpoint of the defeated tell only one side of the tale. The problem of a place for the sons was a crucial one in this status-conscious society, because success or failure determined the standing of the family, both in the case of cadet branches of Protestant families and in the case of Catholic families who had failed to hold onto acres in fee. The renting of land on advantageous long leases was one path to success: if the rents were sufficient to enable the renter to live off the income from subletting, they served to maintain a gentry status or even, somewhat more ambiguously, to establish one. Careers in the army, law or the Church likewise were consistent with gentry status. Careers in law were particularly significant. Many of the prominent Irish gentry of the seventeenth century had been educated for the bar. It was very common for the eldest son to have a legal education, — more often in fact than a university education — even if he never afterwards practised. It was younger sons who practised the profession, and the high earnings from careers in law made it possible for a successful lawyer to purchase land and to establish a landed family. The ancestor of the Quins of Adare, or the father of Fitzgibbon (i.e. of Lord Clare) are instances of spectacular success at different dates; the father of Edmund Burke is another though more modest instance. Such rising families not only conformed outwardly to the Established Church, but identified themselves wholly with its aims: Burke is an exception, and his liberal outlook can be explained in part by his absenteeism which freed him from the stresses and strains imposed on ambitious families in the competitive conditions of a highly mobile society.

Families who remained Catholic in the eighteenth century sought to emulate precisely the same pattern as other families of their milieu. They were either imitating the practice of Irish families in the seventeenth century, or that of Protestant landed families. The only difference was that if they did not conform, as some did in order to pursue their aims with success, they were dependent on the continent for career outlets. Sons went into continental armies; careers in the Church were pursued on the continent; and openings in trade existed in every port in western Europe. Family links by blood and marriage created a Europe-wide network of influence for Catholics on the continent. Commissions in Irish regiments were reserved for Irishmen: the regiments bore the names of their proprietors and young men related to the proprietor or recommended by his relatives predominated. The Irish colleges had a definite place in the Church, and helped to launch sons into ecclesiastical careers. Except in the 1690s, after the Jacobite defeat, the migration to the continent was largely an upper-class affair. The rank and file in the Irish regiments ceased to be Irish, and after mid-century only the officers were Irish. The Irish colleges trained small numbers of students, emphasising the fact that education for the priesthood, like the army, was reserved for younger sons of comfortable families. Moreover, only half of the clergy trained in them returned to Ireland: the rest pursued more lucrative careers as parish clergy in France. In Bordeaux, for instance, where there was an Irish college, they were a small but conspicuous element in the diocesan clergy. In Paris, there was even an Irish rector of the university, and some pursued successful careers up to the level of archbishop. The same families had outlets in army, church and trade for their sons and nephews. There was an overlapping interest between all three outlets. The correspondence of officers and merchants tells us much about relatives in the other careers. The Galway families who dominated Irish merchant communities in the West Indies were equally prominent in the Catholic Church there. The prominent role of nephews in the maintenance of family influence and the bequests of a few hundred pounds made to them in wills tells us another aspect of the social history of these families: the ability of successful families to look after the sons of less successful brothers and sisters, and to stave off downward social mobility.

All this reminds us that the patterns followed by Catholic families should not be attributed simply to persecution or the penal laws. Inevitably, more of their careers would have been pursued at home than abroad but for these obstacles, but it should be remembered too that there were too few careers for all the younger sons of socially ambitious families in a poor country like Ireland. Hence in Ireland as in Scotland, for want of sufficient domestic outlets, many of the careers had to be pursued abroad, especially by the socially weaker or smaller families who could not command preference or support. The very fact of their religion in a Europe divided by Reformation and Counter Reformation determined the direction of some of these paths, and an emerging gentry pattern of careers in the church, army and trade abroad cannot be attributed solely to discrimination. The pattern of Scottish careers abroad at the same time is a reminder of this, and there are arresting similarities between the career prospects and pursuits of younger sons in the poorer and more peripheral parts of the British Isles.

In seventeenth century Ireland, before the upheaval in landownership, there were very close-knit regional patterns in the Irish gentry, and when Irish families emigrated or sent sons abroad these patterns were repeated. Two family groups were comparatively undisturbed by the land upheaval in the seventeenth century — the powerful Catholic landowning group within the Pale, and the very extensive family grouping within Connaught revolving around the famous Galway tribes. Both groups were very similar in some respects, and in fact the Galway group provided some of the most distinguished lawyers and spokesmen for Old-English claims in pre- 1641 parliaments. Both held on to much of their land. The Pale families, somewhat richer and less numerous than the Galway families, provided a smaller stream of emigrants than the Galway group, but it was well-defined and of long-standing, reflecting the mobility and ambition of younger sons. These qualities were still more evident in the case of the younger sons of the families in the Galway group. These families, centuries previously, had been of merchant origin in Galway town: subsequently they acquired land across Galway and Mayo, and a large and highly intermarried network of families intimately involved in trade and land at the same time gradually came into being. This pattern, already long-established, continued into the eighteenth century. It is not necessary to argue that the Penal Laws drove younger sons into trade. Indeed they had already for generations been going into trade, and it was the fact that the Galway families had held onto their lands that explains their comparative success abroad [8]. Of the other groupings the most successful were those of Limerick and Waterford. Limerick, second largest city in sixteenth century Ireland, had a relatively rich hinterland;

the large number of fortified houses in Limerick and Clare is one measure of this, and Kerry, Clare, Limerick and north Tipperary families created a compact group of marriage alliances producing in turn a well-defined group engaged in overseas trade.

An equally, if not more powerful group revolved around Waterford and the inland town, Kilkenny; it brought together families from Waterford, Kilkenny, south Tipperary and Wexford. These families, with a powerful foothold in trade and the professions as well as in land, dominated the region. Like the Limerick group, they lost most of their land, but their tightly woven interests made it possible for them to preserve a strong family presence overseas. The Limerick one was the more archaic group. Its early leadership is evident in that it threw up the Trants, Arthurs, Stapletons and Cantillons all of whom had a very prominent role in the seventeenth and the early eighteenth centuries, but the follow-through was not quite on the same scale. With the sudden deaths in quick succession in the mid-1720s of the Macnamara brothers, at the time the richest firm in Nantes (then the major port of France) and correspondents of the Cantillons, the grouping took a secondary place in the overseas trade network. The Waterford grouping on the other hand was not only immensely powerful, but became more so in the eighteenth century. Its overseas ramifications equalled those of Galway, although more concentrated on Europe, whereas Galway families, coming from a declining port, had to identify more closely with colonial plantation and settlement. In fact, originating in a hinterland which rivalled the Pale as the richest agricultural region of Ireland, the Waterford grouping's composition was unique. The upward mobility of families was more marked in this region than elsewhere; the number of families entering trade, for instance, continued to grow and even to widen in the eighteenth century, and included members of comparatively modest families who could not draw on the wide kinship networks at home and abroad of Limerick and Galway families. The region produced two of the greatest Irish mercantile families abroad: the Walshes and the Fitzgeralds. The Walshes, moving from Saint-Malo to Nantes, piled up colonial plantations as well as land and titles in France. The importance of Antoine-Vincent Walsh in the trade of Nantes has in more recent writing been reduced but not his innovative role: as instigator of the *Compagnie d'Angola* his initiative is of a piece with other Irish initiatives in the organisation of joint-stock companies on the pattern of the English East Indies Company. The Fitzgeralds in London, uncle and nephew, successively, were among the greatest of Irish houses, and through their monopoly of the French Farmers General tobacco contract, played a key role in the tobacco trade of the Scottish ports until the final collapse of the house in 1759.

Not only did new houses from the south-east continue to be established but some of them were of major importance. Thomas Sutton for instance was married in Castletown, near the Wicklow border of co. Wexford, to Phyllis Masterson in 1742 before emigrating to France. He rose to dramatic prominence. Along with another Wexford family, the Wexford branch of the Rothe family, the Suttons dominated the East India Company until its disestablishment in 1769. The Suttons and Rothes were partners too in mining ventures in France and Spain, in which many of the peers of France invested funds. Sutton owned plantations in the West Indies, traded from Cadiz and acquired large tracts of wasteland along the Garonne for reclamation, a fashionable exercise in which another Irish family, the Galweys, made a name in Brittany. The marriage strategy of the family was interesting: it combined alliance with both trade and blood. One daughter was married to a marquis of suitably ancient lineage in the aristocratic fastnesses of the Perigord; another married a MacCarthy of Bordeaux, one of the city's most prominent merchants, and a third married Andrew French of London. One of the MacCarthys married at the same time Edward Byrne of Dublin whose business success was destined to make him the richest Dublin merchant of the closing decades of the century. French's rapid rise as a financier flows from the Sutton marriage, and from London, he, with the Tobins, a Tipperary family in Nantes, helped to finance the East Indian ventures that the Suttons pursued after the disestablishment of the East India Company [9]. Byrne in Dublin, the MacCarthys in Bordeaux — one of whom had been consul of the bourse at the end of the 1760s — French in London, and Sutton in Paris constituted an impressive financing network [10].

The Cork region was surprisingly backward compared with Galway, Limerick, Waterford and Dublin, more particularly in the early stages. Cork was a smaller port than the others at the end of the sixteenth century: it started off the period therefore with a more limited interpenetration of mercantile and landed life in its hinterland. With originally a poorer hinterland as well, it was not able to compensate for the comparative lack of landed interest in trade by a sufficiently strong upward mobility of yeomen or rich tenant families. Despite Cork's rapid growth in the eighteenth century, when it became the second port of Ireland and one of the main centres of trade along the Atlantic seaboard of Europe, relatively few of its families entered trade. Some of those that did so first, Sarsfields, Galweys, Roches and Meades, had Limerick origins or attachments. Overseas, colonies of Corkmen were small, the Roches being almost alone at the outset of the eighteenth century. Even in Bordeaux, the largest Irish colony whose rise corresponded closely in timing with Cork's ascent, only the Roches, Coppingers and Galweys were prominent merchants of Cork origin. The MacCarthys and Kearneys, whose names could suggest a Cork background, were in fact Tipperary families, and their interest lay with the south-eastern group, as the marriage alliances of the MacCarthys with the Byrnes and Suttons illustrate. The relative backwardness of Cork's hinterland initially compared with other regions may explain this contrast. Another reason is of course the fact that the intense growth of dairying, financed largely by middlemen, provided a greater opportunity for younger sons to make a gentry style living than in other regions, where a middlemen-financed dairy system was not so entrenched or as in Waterford's hinterland scarcely existed at all. Certainly, this may account for the fact that a large number of younger sons remained behind, and provided the nucleus of the numerous truculent young gentry who gave the hinterland its somewhat turbulent character. Their success itself was of course a function of the backward or archaic condition of the region: the absence of non-gentry farmers of substance facilitated access by them to holdings which were sufficiently large and low-rented to sustain a gentry-style of life. In other words the source which provided a good deal of the entrants into foreign trade in Waterford's hinterland, especially in later years, was absent.

The fact that so many families could remain in Ireland as gentry suggests that a source of social conflict existed quite independently of purely agrarian quarrels, whose underlying significance has taken up so many pages in innumerable accounts. In the west and in the Pale, much of the land remained in Catholic hands so that its gentry either remained Catholic or conformed with varying degrees of conviction. Common ties of blood and marriage, however, made it impossible to make any clear division between Catholic and

Protestant gentry. Few of the gentry who conformed identified themselves with modernization in the sense in which it was understood in the eighteenth century: the introduction of outside tenants, and the cause of the Established Church. In both regions the gentry at large remained liberal on the Catholic question. The crucial centres of conflict between gentry of different origins lay in Cork and Tipperary. In most other areas, either some of the old gentry remained as in Wexford, south Carlow/Kilkenny, Kerry, or more unevenly, Limerick and created a more tolerant society, or the new gentry were totally dominant, as in the midlands, Wicklow or the north. In fact, there was scarcely any Catholic gentry in the north: the only exception was south Armagh. The consequence was that the Protestant upper classes had no occasion to contend with actual or potential equals at all. This comes across graphically in the statement by Wakefield that 'the Protestant gentry of the north, in estimating the character of Roman Catholics, are frequently disposed to form a general opinion from the habits and manners of the wealthier class in Ulster, whose occupations seldom rise higher than that of a grocer or retailer of spirits' [11]. The situation was similar in Wicklow where in 1812 there was only a single Catholic with the property qualifications which would warrant appointment to the grand jury. In such an exclusively Protestant atmosphere, comfortable Catholics had difficulty in maintaining any preference for leases especially for the larger or more favourable ones. Protestant dominance is reflected also in the fewness of Catholic acts of conformity in the eighteenth century: both in the north and, in Wicklow, only some twenty. It also illustrates how limited the interests of the Byrnes, descendants of one of the two former dominant Wicklow families, were. Between Wicklow and Wexford, not more than four members of the Byrne family conformed [12]. In the more mixed society of north Wexford, however, a social rivalry existed which could in certain conditions be quite explosive. In Cork, though Protestants were relatively less numerous than in these counties, the change in land was not only complete in the sense of its transfer to Protestant hands, but the possibility of tension was exacerbated by the fact that a high proportion of the Catholics remained in the form of gentry-tenants. In all there were between 100 and 200 gentry families in Cork [13], a larger Protestant gentry than in any other county in Ireland and a source, especially once allowance is made for the spread of younger sons into local trade and middleman landholding, of entrenched power. Thus social conflict was inevitable, an underlying gentry-based tension being more evident than in any other southern county, highlighted moreover by several celebrated incidents almost without parallel in the rest of the island in the eighteenth century.

Tipperary, close at hand, presented a similar tension although for quite the opposite reasons. Tipperary and Kilkenny represented a situation in which a large portion of the land remained in Catholic hands. This was mainly because of the large acres of the Butler family. Quite the largest landowners in Kilkenny, intermarried into local Protestant families and thus restraining its politics, they also held much land in Tipperary, especially in the hands of the Cahir branch who remained Catholic and did not even conform nominally. Tipperary had other Catholic landowners as well, a fact reflected for instance in the comparatively large number of esquires among Catholics who took the acceptable oath of loyalty devised by parliament in 1774. Quite apart for the 'gents', numerous in Tipperary as elsewhere and signifying gentlemen tenants, there were no less than 26 esquires, a far larger number than in any other county where the oath was taken extensively. This strong Catholic interest was faced by an active Protestant interest which was concentrated in two areas of the county, respectively in the north-west and in the south along the lower reaches of the Suir. The conformity of the Callaghans at Clogheen, one of the rare instances in which a family after conformity identified itself wholeheartedly with the Establishment, seems to have swung the balance towards the Protestant group. The county had an almost physical frontier between the largely Butler lands stretching from a centre in Kilkenny across Tipperary though Cashel to Cahir, and flanking regions of predominant Protestant landowning on either side. The flashpoint was the contested 1761 election in which two of the contestants were the Evangelical Maude at Dundrum and his neighbour Mathew of Thomastown and Annfield whose conformity to the Established Church was in doubt. The starting point was thus in the north of the county, with two neighbouring families, the Maudes and Mathews confronting each other. But the tension quickly set the upper classes aflame along the lower reaches of the Suir, where the Catholic landed families of the Cahir Butlers and the Mandevilles were close at hand to the Callaghans — who at Clogheen were engaged in social engineering of the sort that occupied the Maudes at Dundrum

— and more significantly to the quite rabid Protestant congerie around Clonmel. A sign of the zeal of the Protestant landed class was the establishment of no less than three charter schools: Newport, Cashel and Clonmel, and the projection of a fourth at Fethard. The underlying bitterness erupted in the early sixties into the notorious support by the Tipperary Protestant gentry of the charge of a 'popish plot' against the Catholic landowners and minor gentry: the whole episode can be viewed as a consequence of tension between two rival groups within the county's landed class, and as having the purpose of totally undermining the social position of the Catholic group. Given the Butler interest across the counties, it affected Kilkenny as well, and because many families, Catholic and Protestant, had relatives by blood or marriage across the borders in Limerick, Cork or west Waterford, the 'plot' spread into those counties as well. It had enthusiastic backing in Cork, where the Protestant party was militant from a position of strength just as it was from one of weakness in Tipperary. Father Sheehy, for instance, who was executed in 1766 had relatives living in Limerick. While the ferocity of this witch-hunt was striking, its anti-gentry bias has been underestimated because it concided with purely agrarian unrest which ironically started on the Catholic Cahir lands, and because Sheehy was involved at two levels, both through some association with the agrarian rebels which remains obscure and through his comfortable family background. The purely regional basis of the furore is very evident. The gentry outside Munster never joined in, even in bastions of Protestant landed interest farther afield. Its regional nature is also reflected in the patterns evident in the taking of the new oath of loyalty for Catholics in 1774. It gave rise to a national controversy about the propriety of taking it: the division being broadly between the counties experiencing the furies of the 1760s which were in favour of it, and the rest of Ireland which was against it. The numbers taking the oath were large in the southern counties: 368 in Tipperary, 189 in Kilkenny, 174 in Waterford, and 139 in Cork, some 63 per cent of the total taking the oath in the entire country[14]. The sectarian tension of the 1760s must thus be regarded as in the main one within the upper classes of the time. It was quite different from the sectarian tension of the 1790s which was evident outside Munster (apart from Limerick which was not heavily involved in the 1760s incident), especially in Armagh and Wicklow and Wexford.

Although the gentry were homogeneous in some respects,

there were regional contrasts within it, which of course were influenced also by the tendency of the smaller families (but not the greater ones) to intermarry within their own region with their neighbours. One of the most striking contrasts is in the different attitudes of the gentry towards Catholic emancipation in and after 1800: strongly opposed in the Protestant bastions of the north, Sligo, Wicklow and Cork, liberal or mixed in most other counties. The needs of political life, regular social intercourse, intermarriage facilitated by Catholic conformity, nominal or convinced, all created a fluid situation, and remind us constantly of the dangers of engaging too readily in broad national generalizations. That allowed for, there are also some striking contrasts between the older gentry, of Anglo-Norman or even Gaelic origin, and the newer gentry of English origin. The contrast between the two should not be encapsulated too readily in the framework of a backward older gentry and an innovating new gentry. This contrast can sometimes be made, especially in the case of agrarian changes where it was easier for an outsider, perhaps foolishly, to make light of local interests. But in fact the older gentry often espoused change. The Butlers, for instance, or the O'Briens became early patrons of the iron industry by leasing lands to industrial entrepreneurs. Many old landowners were quite content to let lands to English immigrants whose large resources were a guarantee of rent payment. In fact, some of the old gentry after conforming identified themselves completely with the new order. This is most striking in the case of the O'Haras in Sligo who conformed at a very early date, and in the eighteenth century are scarcely distinguishable from the county's Cromwellian families. Other striking examples are the Frenches of Monivea, co. Galway, strongly associated with the Protestant Church, the O'Callaghans at Clogheen, co. Tipperary, and symbolically the most striking of all, the Cotters whose family head had been executed in 1720 and whose subsequent identification with the Protestant establishment was total. In the 1760s the son's proposal to establish a Charter School at Cottersborough near Mallow was accepted by the Society. Such instances in the eighteenth century are however rare among long-established landed families, and more common among ambitious families rising from modest or professional backgrounds — for example the Quins — among whom on occasion the urge to identify with the establishment was deeper. Some families only toyed fleetingly with the ideas of the Protestant establishment, an example being the shortlived Daly sponsorship in the 1740s of a Charter School at Mountshannon, and became strongly identified with the Protestant interest only in the nineteenth century. But by that stage, the landed class was on the defensive, no longer committed to the wide and confident goals of colonization and modernization which had characterised it almost to the end of the eighteenth century. Families of recent origin were more likely to identify themselves with the new order. Illustrious families like the Butlers, the O'Briens and the Clanrickardes always remained somewhat ambivalent in their commitment, drawn into it by their family interests but never giving it a support equal to the weight that their wealth and prestige could have carried. Full commitment was more commonly associated with a rising family of non-gentry origin eager to establish its social standing. The Quins at Adare are a good example. They conformed only in 1739 but their subsequent identification with the Protestant landed families of mid-Limerick was firm and they brought the Palatines to Adare. They were by no means the only family which attemped to alter the social and racial composition of the countryside — Robert French at Monivea was even more committed — but they were one of the rare families not of English origin to preside over a successful experiment of this sort. The Fitzgibbons illustrated the same tendency for the upstarts to be wholehearted in their identification with the new order. The father's success at the bar left the son a rich man, but John Fitzgibbon more than any other individual was the articulate voice of Protestant extremism in the late eighteenth century: in the 1780s, when the Protestant gentry was more complacent than at any other time in the eighteenth century, it was he who sternly reminded them that the origins of their property lay in confiscation and that their actions should be guided by unfailing awareness of that fact.

One of the clearest marks of modernity is usually considered to be the readiness of families to retain an interest in business or to send their sons into it. On this criterion, surprisingly, the older families emerged as much more involved than the newer families of English origin. This is true even of plantations in the West Indies. None of the Anglo-Irish families with the exception of the La Touches became plantation owners. The situation was if anything the reverse. Englishmen or Scotsmen who had made a fortune in the East Indies sometimes bought estates in Ireland, set up as landed families, and set out singlemindedly to forget their origins. The older families remained identified with the colonies and plantations to a greater degree. Sir James Cotter in Cork had held colonial office in the 1680s; the Stapletons held colonies in both the English and French islands, the Trants held lands in the West Indies, and members of the Daly, Browne and Nugent families became plantation owners also. The precise relationship of the head of the family to colonial ventures is not always clear, because colonial wealth was often in the hands of cadet branches who became wholly expatriate. But even as late as 1791, Coquebert de Montbret noted of the Browne family, which had sent many younger sons into trade and colonies, that 'the present lord (Lord Altamont), having vast estates in the West Indies, is at least as wealthy as the Marquis of Clanricarde' [15]. Many of the families remained intimately identified with trade. In the case of the Blakes, the head of the family, Thomas Blake of Menlough, had spent a period as a merchant in Bordeaux in the mid-eighteenth century. This was less true on the whole of the larger families, such as the Butlers. There were many Butlers in trade in the early eighteenth century, but many must have come from remote branches of the family, like the Butlers of New Ross. The movement of younger sons into trade is a striking feature, similar in nature to what took place in contemporary Scotland. But equally striking is the fact that the range of families in foreign trade was comparatively narrow, and the relative absence of new names suggests a restricted range of mobility within Irish society as a whole. Mobility on any scale is evident only in the southeast, and here it may be largely related to a non-gentry element not found in the other regions: the upward ascent of tenant families both in land occupation and in trade. The fact that some of these families, like the Rices of Callan, or many of the families engaged in the Newfoundland trade [16], were modest tenants illustrates quite exceptional mobility for Ireland. It is almost certainly no accident either that at a lower social level the south-east at large provided the manpower for the seasonal emigration to Newfoundland which at its peak accounted for 5,000 individuals every season. It was the only large regular stream of emigration from southern Ireland in the eighteenth century, and suggests that in this, the most prosperous agricultural region of Ireland, a combination of social pressures and aspirations predisposed even the lower classes to mobility on a scale unequalled elsewhere outside the ranks of non-conformists and Presbyterians. In other words at all levels below the gentry, who as elsewhere were mobile in the interests of the careers of their sons, a mobility existed in the south-east which was rare in traditional Ireland. Emigrants from the region sometimes pioneered patterns of emigration: a colony of emigrants from Wexford was prominent in Savannah at the outset of the nineteenth century [17]. In the nineteenth century farmers' sons struck out for the frontiers of colonisation in North America or for the Argentine rather than crowd into the big cities of the north-east like so many immigrants from Ireland. This mobility, social as well as geographical, was already evident before the end of the eighteenth century: Wexford men from the north of the county moved into trades in Dublin, or from its coastline into seafaring. These included individuals as varied as John Connor, the Rush smuggler of the 1760s, or John Barry in the 1770s, first commodore of the American navy. The scale of the mobility may be illustrated c.1850 in the occupational pattern of the Barrys at Poulrane, Kilmore, co. Wexford, descendants of the family from which John Barry had ventured forth to the New World. Significantly, the eldest son was lost at sea, the second inheriting the farm. Other sons included a priest, medical doctor and coastguard. Yet another emigrated to Britain, becoming an M.P. for a British constituency and eventually founding a manufacturing business at Kirkaldy. A good deal of mobility between land and business and the professions existed in Protestant Ireland as well. But it was on the whole not remarkably pronounced, and it is quite clear that many of the sons chose either to go into the church or to remain in the countryside as rural gentry. The impressive stream of immigration from Britain into business in the Irish cities, especially Dublin, helps to confirm this. The immigrants set up in a wide variety of activities, including commerce and industry: the influx of Scots into Irish wholesale trade and industry in the late eighteenth and early nineteenth centuries is a particularly striking instance of this. Considering their numbers and wealth, members of the Church of Ireland made a comparatively poor impression compared with the Scots of recent or remote origin, non-conformists such as Quakers, or even to a degree Catholic members of the old families. Anglo-Irish families tended to identify closely with land, and to seek careers outside trade. A striking case is that of the Bartons of Bordeaux who, although about to emerge as the largest merchant family in Bordeaux, purchased an estate in Ireland. Although William, the son of Thomas Barton of Bordeaux, was to return to Bordeaux it was only because the commercial crisis of 1778 there imperilled the fortunes of the family. The career patterns of the Barton's sons illustrate the family tendency towards gentry-careers and marriages. Only a few of the family married in Bordeaux and only into other northern Irish families, Boyds and Johnstons, and what makes the Bartons so unusual is their success in keeping a foot in both camps [18]. Most families moved over decisively into land. The social values of the gentry were already dominated by those of the larger landed families, especially those in eastern Ireland who had the least links with trade. The Irish parliament, dominated by the gentry, showed itself unsympathetic to banking. The slowness with which a chartered bank was established is one proof of this. More striking still was the act of 1756 which prohibited merchants from engaging in banking. It illustrated the urge of parliament to restrict banking to social groups closely identified with the landed class and to penalize bankers in the more risky but socially more useful business of discounting trade bills [19]. The largest of the banks which failed had been Catholic or Quaker, and the banking experiment of 1758 conducted by Malone, Clements and Gore, a partnership of the chancellor of the exchequer and two privy councillors, points to the interests which lay behind the obscure politics of the 1756 act. The dominance of gentry values was so complete that by 1800 it began to affect the older families who had retained links with trade. As such families became more finely attuned to the social ambitions of their age, the close association with trade began to break down and involvement, even in the wholesale branch of it, was consciously frowned on.

Paradoxically, the high point reached by the gentry families in these opening years of the nineteenth century also represented the onset of crisis. Landed incomes had risen dramatically in the eighteenth century, a fact which added to the dazzling prestige conferred by land even more than did the example of the social patterns of like families in England. The abandonment of trade illustrates the universal acceptance for the first time of gentry social values by the landed class at large. After 1815 the economic situation of the gentry began to change, so rapidly in fact that contemporaries did not at first appreciate what was happening. Rents were no longer rising rapidly, and the aggregate rent roll of 1815 was not to be greatly exceeded at any time in the nineteenth century. If the rent rolls of individual head landlords rose somewhat, and in the case of some landlords who had lands set out extensively to middlemen quite sharply, it was of course simply through the process of transfer of rents from intermediate tenants to the head landlord. But that was a process of transferral of income within the landed class. While the transfer of income seemed to assure the fortunes of the head landlord, the contraction of intermediate rents doomed a part of the upper class to extinction in rural Ireland. This did not seem disastrous to landed families themselves because in the nineteenth century, thanks to mobility and to the expanding frontiers of the empire, careers abroad especially in the army seemed to open up. For the individual son this was immensely better than the frustrating frontiers of an ambiguous social position or the narrow horizons of the hunting field. But it meant that local leadership in rural Protestant society was beginning to contract abruptly at the very time when the Protestant birth rate in individual parishes was in many instances rising. In other words, a vital section in the support of local Protestant society fell into rapid decline. The minor gentry or large farmers represented by the middlemen were much more closely identified both by residence and economic interests with the welfare of the parish and the support of its humbler Protestant families than were the landed families whose heads were constantly distracted by their responsibilities across many parishes or by social or political life. In retrospect, it can be seen as the first step in the decline of the Protestant community in rural Ireland, as significant if not more so than the disestablishment of the Church of Ireland two generations later. If for the sons of gentry middle tenures no longer offered an easy path into the pains and pleasures of landed society, and if entry into trade was increasingly disregarded by this time, the pursuit of alternative careers became an inevitable necessity. Some existed in Ireland: the emergence of professional land agents, for instance, helped to compensate for the loss of outlets as middlemen, although agents of landed background were probably much less practical than the agents of yeoman background who predominated in Scotland. But for numerous sons, careers abroad were necessary. The army became much more common as a career for the sons of gentry. University education was little prized in the eighteenth century, many of the students of Trinity College in the eighteenth century being destined for the Church: at one stage, two thirds of the students graduating were intended for holy orders [20]. University education now acquired a new value. The number of students admitted at Trinity reached a peak of 460 in 1824[21], a significant date, because coinciding as it did with a crisis in middle tenures, it reflected a turning to new horizons. But increasingly the university was geared to training young men for the frontiers of the empire. A large number of its graduates went into foreign careers, and Trinity at a later date even provided special courses for the Indian civil service examinations. The sons of landed families were sucked into the colonial world in many ways. Sir Horace Plunket spent many years abroad managing lands his father had purchased speculatively in north America; he returned to Ireland to launch the cooperative movement, but he could just as easily have remained in America, and had he been a more typical younger son this would have been the more likely outcome. The management of gentry estates was much better in the nineteenth century than in the past. The gentry who inherited estates were much better educated than their predecessors, they were consciously aware of the deficiencees of their estates, and with interests in industry or politics which were often more peripheral than in the past, gave the management of their estates much more single-minded and professional attention than in the preceding century. This, however, while intended to add to the fortunes of the families, often brought them new headaches. It was inevitably destined to create differences with their tenantry who were more traditional in outlook and unlikely to be the direct or immediate beneficiaries of change to the same extent. Management measures did not always lead to conflict, but they frequently led to alienation, and estate rules, while justifiable objectively, were actively resented by tenantry. Indeed the very concept of 'estate rules' was a novelty, no less than attempted enforcement. The brisk and impersonal action of a reforming landlord or of the relatively impersonal agent of gentry status on a large estate was positively resented. The widening gulf was evident in several ways: landlord subsidization of emigration of broken tenants on poorer estates, while expensive and having a very justifiable economic and social rationale, stood for totally different things to landowner and tenantry respectively.

The greatly improved estate management of the nineteenth century and the objectives it held before landlord and estate, while intended to strengthen the position of the landlord, in fact positively weakened it. It had replaced the more paternalistic relationship of the past. It was much more likely to lead to conficit. The new landlord interest in education from

1800 onwards in a divided society was much more damaging to the landlord's relationship with his tenantry than the lack of interest which preceded it; the relationship would have been far more harmonious if the landlord, like most of his eighteenth century counterparts, had not strayed into the administration of education at all. The breakdown of a paternalistic tie between landlord and tenant was in part a consequence of the conscious change of stance by the landlord, but that was of course only part of the picture: the landlord's predicament lay precisely in the fact that other factors had emerged as well. Just as landlords had increasingly put paternalism behind them as a result of changes in aims, or simply through their own better education and higher aspirations for their class or their estate, the tenant was quite independently of this laying his deference aside, even if very uncertainly at first. The conflict outside Ulster, where it already existed between Presbyterian tenants and their landlords in the eighteenth century, is really one dating from post-Famine times, and even as it grew, a generation gap existed in the attitude of local people to the landlords; the older tenants deferential, the younger positively hostile. This itself underlines the need not to see anti-landlord feeling as simply one induced by memories of oppression. Synge, with his unique perception, noted this in 1905: 'The older people in co. Wicklow, as in the rest of Ireland, still show a curious affection for the landed classes wherever they have lived for a generation or two upon their property . . . The younger people feel differently . . .' [22] .

Ireland was becoming a literate society in the nineteenth century, a change whose rapid advent, entailing a transition from an oral culture to a written one, had itself profound consequences. The efforts to explain the decline of Irish as a result of oppression, associations with poverty, or middle class abandonment of the language are all inadequate. The essential problem is that the amount of Irish in printed form had been very limited. Most of the writing in Irish was in the manuscripts written in the countryside, often by people of quite simple social position. The circle which the written word in Irish reached in this form was quite limited. Although the teachers were often themselves transcribers of manuscripts, the education they imparted was largely in English. Poets who did not come to the language through practice in transcribing manuscripts frequently had no knowledge of the written language, and when they put their verses or the prose of everyday life into written form for some purpose they were reduced to doing so in a phonetic rendering of their own based on English. In other words, their literacy had been acquired through English. This was the problem facing the Irish language. Literacy and the written word had acquired a real value in the more mobile world of the early nineteenth century, and what led to the rapid abandonment of Irish was the prestige of written over oral culture, and the fact that for most Irishmen in the absence of printed texts, English was perforce their introduction to literacy in a nation which within one generation between 1790 and 1820 had moved from selective, though haphazard education, to virtual mass instruction. The decline in Irish, rather gradual before the 1820s, acquired a dramatic abruptness after that date: essentially its decline, given its oral character, is related to the prestige of written above oral culture, and the explosive growth in the demand for literacy.

The relatively late spread of literacy is reflected in the absence of highly developed bureaucratic traditions and in haphazard respect for records or their preservation. Even the systematic keeping of Church of Ireland records, though as a practice imported from a more developed England, often withered in the relaxed colonial climate. If the indigenous population were profoundly influenced by settlers, settlers in a mixed society also showed many signs of absorbing native influences. This is understandable in a thinly populated diocese like Ossory [23]— although hardly so in a cathedral parish like Kilkenny itself with a substantial Protestant population — but record keeping sometimes disintegrated in more favourable conditions. In the parish union of Wicklow for instance, despite a large Protestant population the parish registers went silent in 1665 after beginning in 1655, and only resumed in 1698. Burials and marriages, recorded only from 1729, lapsed between 1733 and 1746 [24]. The absence of Catholic registers is usually explained by the Penal Laws. Irish Catholics on the continent, faced with the bureaucratic demand to produce certificates of baptism and having difficulty in accounting for their inability to do so to officials in countries where bureaucratic practice in church and state was highly organized and efficient and where the tradition usually went back to the sixteenth century, often took refuge in this explanation. In reality however the Counter Reformation, which like the Reformation imposed literacy on the Church, was slowly, painfully and incompletely introduced to Ireland in the course of the seventeenth century: tight parish organization and the record keeping that went with it was an index of modernization. The Penal Laws have little to do with it, as is illustrated in the fact that many of the urban parishes in cities like Dublin and Waterford have parish registers from the middle of the eighteenth century. On the other hand, the keeping of parish registers was practised in Ireland at large only from the 1820s and 1830s. There is a contrast between the towns with their relatively early record keeping, the eastern rural parishes (often with diocesan records from the late eighteenth century) and the remaining parishes where the process is later. In other words the lags in perfecting church organization in Ireland are if anything more cultural than otherwise and stem from the difficulty of imposing on a primitive country and church the tight administrative standards devised by the Tridentine Church for the Counter Reformation in more literate and educated parts of Europe.

Even morals, long a sensitive subject in modern Ireland, had been slow to change. The relatively free Irish sexual morals had shocked the Normans [25], particularly the tolerance of concubinage which survived long in Ireland. The process of securing observance for the strict marriage rules imposed by the Council of Trent was inevitably destined to be a long-drawn-out one, especially as the introduction of tight parish organization, the great vehicle of all reform, itself met a prolonged resistance. The practices relating to marriage rules were one of the two main concerns of the Irish Church in the enforcement of the Tridentine decrees in Ireland [26]. Moreover, a degree of licence or libertinage reflected in sexual freedom quite out of character with the more conventional restraints of English and western society at large, still lingered on. When Cuffe, landlord of Ballinrobe, and his friends crossed the Corrib, they were entertained by the chieftain of the region who when he 'began to grow mellow, called his favourite girl to sing, which she did very well, and was a neat handsome jolly girl. Before he called her in etc. he told his guests that they were very welcome to any liberties with her from the girdle upwards, but would not permit any underhand doings' [27]. Not only were the morals somewhat freer than the conventionally stricter Anglo-Irish ones, but there was generally an element of licence or libertinage, at times involving the use of force. In a barely post-medieval society with a church disorganized into the eighteenth century, a whole range of misdemeanours which were becoming uncommon in western Europe existed, ranging from irregular marriage to libertine conduct in which sexual favours were sought at a lower social level. While abductions — socially the most archaic of these practices — in some cases represented an arrangement between suitor and girl in defiance of family opposition, they covered a wide gamut in the exercise of force.

The protagonists in many of these incidents frequently had some standing, however modest or ambiguous, pointing to a tolerance which they no longer enjoyed in western society. The decline in the acceptability of abductions was not dissimilar to that of the faction fights in which the rural upper classes were once the leaders. Finally abandoned by the upper classes, faction fights lost social approval, making it much easier for the clergy to denounce and isolate them in the early nineteenth century. The fact that sexual excesses existed and that in contrast to faction fights, social disapproval was often lacking in rural society, accounts for the heavy emphasis in the early nineteenth century on the imposition of strict canons of sexual morality. There is no need to seek refuge in an innate puritanism or in the transmission of French jansenism to Ireland through links in the education of the Irish priesthood. A church, freshly organized to Tridentine standards with a lag of over two centuries, confronted an ambiguous attitude towards archaic excesses which no longer enjoyed public countenance in Europe. Because they were blatant and because they were often committed by individuals of at least some social standing, they were particularly obnoxious to clergymen. The Church had long waged a similar campaign against faction fights although with mixed success into the eighteenth century: its stand against them was eventually somewhat simplified by the fact that the rural upper classes abandoned participation or approval from the middle of the eighteenth century. It was slower change in the case of sexual morals that forced the Church into its vigorous efforts to purify them. If viewed narrowly from a sexual perspective, the Church's zeal might seem excessive: illegitimacy in rural Ireland was, and remained, low. But the Church's concern can be fully appreciated only if placed in the context of a long-drawn-out effort from Tridentine times to root out unseemly practices and of the fact that the belated attainment of organization inevitably heightened the emphasis on moral reform, given the survival of archaic practices. Change was of course also taking place independently of the Church, but as in the case of faction fights, the Church's reforming policy was far ahead of popular outlook. But moral reform especially when exacerbated by the fact that it represented an organizational as well as a moral challenge, could easily become an obsessive commitment to sexual purification. When combined with the fashionable moral preoccupations of the nineteenth century and the religious fervour of the second half of the century, neither of which was particularly Irish in themselves, the emphasis on sexual morals assumed a distinctive intensity in Ireland.

The belated achievement of Catholic emancipation, taking place in 1829 in the form of a democratic victory greatly admired by continental liberals, played little part in the re-organization of the Church which was the culmination of a momentum which was quite independent. But the victory put the Church in the forefront of Irish nationalism, and emancipation, coinciding with the achievement of Tridentine standards of organization and education inevitably gave the Church and its churchmen their peculiar triumphalist character. The Irish Church's distinctive character — as opposed to the much more easily explained fact of its survival — was more the product of contemporary events than of preceding centuries, although its heady position now led many of its protagonists to give it an all-embracing role in Irish social or cultural history.

If the Church's role in Irish cultural development is less deep than often believed, the cultural pattern of modern Ireland becomes even more arresting, because the institutional underpinning for it is quite weak. This serves to underline the fact that Irish cultural history is in some respects paradoxical: given the belated, and in consequence rapid, transition of recent centuries, it combines a confused mix both of archaic beliefs and more recent traditions. The overall consequence however is that, compared with societies which experienced much of this cultural transition in medieval times, the country seems both to have fewer real traditions and less attachment to tradition. If the survival of old practices gives an impression of conservatism, the real position is quite the reverse: the country has been exceptionally open to and receptive of change to the detriment of its more traditional character. Modern Ireland has some parallels with Italy which has absorbed modernization to the detriment of much of its character, whereas a much more robust culture like that of France has provided an arresting combination of modernization and cultural conservatism, able to embrace novelty while protecting its own distinctiveness. Ireland has surrendered its language more rapidly than any other society in western Europe, including its sister societies in Scotland, Wales and Brittany: while their languages have also declined and in Scotland Gaelic is now spoken only by a few thousand, the linguistic change in no case matched the astonishing one in Ireland between 1810 and 1840. At another level, Irish food traditions, because they are archaic or combined with later ones, are complex and even rich, but the popular food sense is probably the poorest in western Europe, and in comfortable rural homes two decades ago was in some respects much poorer than a century and a half earlier.

Ireland's architectural heritage is also quite disappointing. The appearance of the countryside and of the villages is often a curiously unfinished one. More recent building of the eighteenth and the first half of the nineteenth centuries has often been overtaken by later building, with the result that the core of Irish towns and villages consists of a variety of styles, all of them comparatively recent, none of which has come to predominate. So unstable has the position been that even thatch has disappeared with considerable rapidity. A century and a half ago, Ireland was a country in the main of thatched houses. But since 1800 they have disappeared at an astonishing rate. In more recent times, in perfect consistency with the pattern of Irish social change, they have disappeared more rapidly in the poorer districts than in the richer districts. There are some 50,000 thatched houses in Britain [28]: this is many times the number surviving in Ireland. The heritage of older buildings looks deceptively rich because ruined medieval and early modern buildings create a more haunting impression of the past in Ireland than in many other parts: neglect or lack of occupation on a scale unattained elsewhere is itself however a singular index of the absence of continuity. In fact, if exception is made of the ruined tower houses, which were simply the dwellings of comfortable families in the countryside, the number of structures even in ruins is comparatively small if related to particular regions or to specific chronological periods. This poverty of artifacts has often been attributed to destruction, but in reality destruction and war have done little more damage than in other countries. The survival of the tower houses is proof of this because their defensive properties were very limited, and they reflected local insecurity rather than military resistance: they survived the military campaigns of the seventeenth century in great numbers. Many Anglo-Irish gentry lived in them into the mid-eighteenth century, and lesser families until much later.

Their use was often prolonged by the addition of living quarters in the form of more modern and commodious wings, and many tower houses still stand in close proximity to later houses. The disproportion of population between medieval Ireland and England was not great, perhaps three to one, but the disproportion in early buildings is overwhelming. A single prosperous county like Suffolk has no less than 500 medieval churches. There is nothing remotely comparable in Ireland, and while a more warlike condition contributed to the contrast, other factors were present as well. The poverty of ecclesiastical building reflects primitive parish organization — the surviving stone buildings are usually monastic rather than parochial in origin — and the use of flimsy and primitive structures for many purposes. The slowness of churches to appear in the eighteenth century is attributable not only the the Penal Laws but to the slowness with which Tridentine standards of regular mass attendance developed, and the belated arrival of effective parish organization, which, when attained, was immediately reflected in a great wave of church building from around 1830. The coincidence of these changes with Catholic Emancipation in 1829 has inevitably led to far too much consequence being attached to that measure.

In the last analysis the relative dearth of building is a reflection of poor economic conditions. Incomes were low, with the partial regional exception of the rich grain lands of mid-Kilkenny, and even the upper classes, with individual exceptions, had smaller resources than overseas. Material possessions were equally scant. If seventeenth century painting is sparser in Ireland than in Scotland [29], a society itself relatively retarded, this must be attributed, as the tower houses which would have housed them survived very well into the eighteenth century or later, to its absence to start with. The dearth was not solely one of valuable objects but of even more modest objects in popular culture. As Synge observed: 'it is part of the misfortune of Ireland that nearly all the characteristics which give colour and attractiveness to Irish life are bound up with a social condition that is near to penury. While in countries like Brittany the best external features of the local life — the rich embroidered dresses, for instance, or the carved furniture — are connected with a decent and comfortable life' [30].

This society suffered acute problems of identity precisely because of the limitations of its traditions. Protestants had to adapt the pattern of their home culture to that around them. Catholics, while they surrendered their language and archaic traditions to the forces of modernization, retained a marked racial awareness. The relative absence of traditions explains why the Church, one of the few institutions rooted in the past and identified with the Irish side of the conflict, was able to obtain such a hold over Irish life in the early nineteenth century. It did so in a period of growing nationalism when institutions were increasingly important and when its own institutional organization, long defective, improved very rapidly. Catholicism thus coloured nationalism strongly, and the fact that Emancipation, promised in 1800, was witheld till 1829, inevitably made Catholicism more radical than it would have been in other circumstances. But because of its own late acquisition of an organized structure, the Church was itself poor in traditions by European standards. Significant though the new organization was and impressive the feat in building, neither churchmen nor people were strongly attached to the buildings. The continuity that existed around the actual church, whether the parish churches of France or England or the equally old wooden churches of Norway, is unknown in Ireland. No tradition has stood in the way of their replacement in more modern times, the expressive buildings of the first half of the nineteenth century being in many instances thoughtlessly and needlessly replaced. The very physical location of the buildings reflects their limited relationship to their environment: in villages, partly because of their late erection, they are frequently on the fringe or even outside the village boundaries altogether.

With few traditions and the weakening of surviving ones, the separate identities which existed in nineteenth century Ireland necessarily attached an importance to symbols. Commemorative occasions and events also acquired an increased importance. The uncertain nature of national identity is reflected in attitudes towards the Irish language and the possibility of a distinctive Irish culture. Protestants, faced with isolation as the institutions of the old order broke down, even went so far as to interest themselves in the Irish language as a means of creating a cultural identity, and although the linguistic interest was short-lived, the support for a distinctive literary culture was more lasting. Equally, politicised Catholics seized on the language, turning a broader cultural movement into a bleak linguistic crusade which provided a new identifying badge for nationalists, and a further divisive element in an already divided community. A colonial past necessarily left Ireland divided between the colonizer and the colonized. The crisis of identity was doubly great because colonization speeded up modernization which in turn directly affected the colonized. The archaic traditions of the old society were replaced by more modern values, of which the abandonment of the language is a symptom. Few things illustrate more strikingly the weaknesses of Irish traditions that the linguistic issue: the readiness with which the language was abandoned, and the fact that the strength of the linguistic revival in the pre-1914 decade, and the ultimate reason for its failure, lay not in an attachment to traditions but merely in a seeking for the symbols of identity.

7
Diet in a changing society

Ireland was, on the evidence of its social and demographic evolution, a society in rapid transition. Marriage ages remained relatively low, the growth of its population was exceptionally sustained, and its social structure changed in a complex fashion. One of the most significant of these changes was the shift in the relative importance of middlemen and middle-sized farmers in favour of the latter. All these changes could hardly have taken place without interaction with the food supply and with diet. In fact, the evolution of diet corresponds closely to the general profile of transition in Irish society. Food supply altered strikingly over time, and the evolution of diet was hardly less marked than the general social transition. In most societies fundamental changes in diet in recent centuries have been limited in the main to the 1880s and later. The preceding pattern was one of comparative stability over centuries. It is in this general context of the conservatism of continental and English diet and sustained transition in Irish diet that the potato itself has to be sited: its diffusion in Ireland was far more precocious than in the rest of Europe.

Demographic growth in association with the archaic base of food supply to start with and the precocious and unrelenting commercialization of agriculture meant that the transition in Irish diet took the form of a series of adjustments in subsistence more complex and protracted than in western society at large. Any explanation of Irish diet must also not only explain the general character of the evolution of diet but also how, while it temporarily put society beyond the threshold of famine, it failed to do so in the long term. Both the occurrence of the Great Famine, and the arresting regional and social contrasts in its incidence, are comprehensible only within the general transformation of Irish society over the preceding three centuries.

Irish cooking traditions, though at their best sound, are relatively unsophisticated, and the belief is almost general that Irish cooking was still simpler in the early nineteenth century, the potato banishing most foods from the table and the process impoverishing Irish *cuisine* to a rudimentary art. Post-famine cooking, it has been argued, rested neither on old traditions nor on the rediscovery of lost traditions or methods. Irish diet and cooking have thus been represented in what is on reflection a paradoxical position — a poverty of repertory and skills in a food exporting country. Such a combination of factors would be unusual, as would the apparent lack of a conservatism seeking to retain traditional foods or of an ability to innovate and vary diet in the midst of difficulty. Elsewhere, peoples have, though reluctantly, varied their diets under external pressures, and there is no parallel at least in western Europe for the reduction of the diet above the lower social classes to a single foodstuff. Indeed, so universal is the assumption of an impoverishment of the Irish diet by the outset of the nineteenth century that the sole historical investigation of Irish diet — a remarkably thorough one — is entitled simply 'Irish food before the potato'. It refers to a 'quite abnormal truncation of many aspects of Irish diet in the eighteenth and nineteenth centuries' and even refers to 'the dark reign of the potato' [1]. Professor Evans had likewise regarded the dietary consequences of the potato as disastrous [2], and the most recent writer on Irish food has regarded the division of the subject into two periods as the main though not sole generalization about Irish diet [3].

In fact, while Irish diet and cooking are relatively simple compared with French (which is hardly a fair comparison as the same would apply to a comparison between French and all north European cuisines), it is one of the most interesting culinary traditions in Europe. Irish diet, reduced to crude statistical terms, has several significant comparative features. The per capita consumption of butter is the highest in the world. Meat consumption per capita is also relatively high — even without taking into account the fact that incomes in most major meat-eating countries are substantially higher — and the range of meats consumed is also uniquely wide, spread across beef, pork and mutton in almost equal proportions. The fact that at one and the same time Irish consumption of meat and butter is very high and per capita consumption of the potato the highest in the world, points to the unusual and complex character of Irish diet. The present high butter consumption was even greatly exceeded in the past in rural Ireland: as late as 1600 Irish diet was based primarily on milk, both liquid and in its many solid and semi-solid forms, a dependence at that time already uncommon as a general pattern in Europe. The Norman invasion in the twelfth century had also introduced a quite different dietary pattern. As the conquest was incomplete and the colony even receded in the fourteenth and fifteenth centuries, the two patterns overlapped and in the march or frontier lands even fused — the butter-based tradition of Gaelic Ireland and the tradition in the Norman areas of gruels based on cereals, peas and beans and of bread often of mixed cereals and sometimes even incorporating beans.

Unlike other European societies which from early medieval times have been remarkably free from the intrusion of outsiders in large numbers, Ireland experienced a large inflow of Scots and English from the late sixteenth to the end of the seventeenth century. Relatively and absolutely it was the largest immigration seen within Europe within the last eight hundred years, profoundly influencing indigenous traditions and often fusing them into a new and distinctive pattern which represented a mix of influence from both sides of the Irish Sea. Scottish and English diet was more cereal-based than the Irish or Norman ones, and within cereals a higher proportion was consumed in the form of bread than of porridge or stirabout. In Ireland, probably more than half the oats was consumed in the form of porridge [4]. Oats were also combined with the large surplus of butter in various ways as for instance in the roasting of both together into cakes before the fire as late as the early eighteenth century [5]. In the old Anglo-Norman areas peas and beans loomed large in the diet, and in these areas as in the Gaelic areas the scant evidence seems to suggest a greater prominence of gruels than of bread in the diet as late as the early seventeenth century. The relative absence of bread struck outsiders. Even in the Pale, the four or five counties surrounding Dublin, the author of *Advertisements for Ireland* in 1623 observed that all their corn was 'eaten up by their peasants that attend their tillage and husbandry before half the year be spent' [6]. By contrast with England and lowland Scotland, the wetter Irish climate favoured dairying. As early as the twelfth century the chronicler Geraldus Cambrensis who accompanied the Normans to Ireland observed that the unceasing rain made the reaping of the harvest difficult [7], and Boate in 1652 reflected the attitude of the new English settlers in observing that the danger to the Irish harvest was not from scorching dryness but from excessive rain [8].

It is not surprising therefore that diet especially among the Gaelic population should have depended on milk and milk products. Butter, whey, curds, constituted the main items in their summer diet, and the autumn harvest of oats supplemented by butter constituted the winter food supply. Butter was regarded as a winter food, and the practice of burying tubs of butter was a means of saving food for the lean days before the supply of milk resumed with the fresh pastures of late spring. As late as 1802 in county Tyrone, many parts of which were remote and comparatively unchanged, the 'maxim of the common people is, to live on buttermilk in summer, and reserve the butter for winter' [9]. The main consumption of the inadequate supply of grain was restricted to the winter and early spring before the supply of milk resumed. Thus, given the seasonal pattern, important though milk was in the diet, its universality could easily be overstated. For the same reason in reverse, the absence of grain could be overestimated, because if little was consumed from April onwards, it was widely consumed from Autumn to spring. Moreover, even if most of it was eaten in the form of porridge, bread was by no means unknown. The comment of foreign observers was that bread was little used, not that it was unknown. In fact, bread, easily portable, was essential for the military hosting, for the ambulant worker or for the traveller, a fact no less evident to the largely potato-eating poor of the rural countryside in the early nineteenth century. For the Limerick region Gerald Griffin's novel *The collegians* refers to 'a griddle bread done in the morning before you, an' you goin' a long road' [10], a fact recalled more prosaically by William Tighe in 1802 for the ordinary people of the barony of Iverk in co. Kilkenny where 'oaten cake is taken by workmen going to a distance where potatoes could not be brought hot' [11].

A milk and butter diet presupposes essentially an abundance of cattle, general access to the possession or the ownership of a herd of dairy cattle, and little commercialization which would otherwise transfer much of the output to the towns or overseas. A general dependence on milk and butter as the main constituents of diet is characteristic of a thinly populated country with little foreign trade. A larger population limits access to land and cattle for many of the poorer members of a community, and at the same time the growth of trade in butter gives it a commercial value and transfers it from the countryside. The impressive growth of population and trade in Ireland in the seventeenth century, quite independently of other factors, was bound to alter Irish diet. The growth of a trade in butter necessitated the introduction of other foods to replace the once lavish consumption of milk and dairy products, especially in the winter months. The shift in food supply was even more marked for the very poor, now reduced even in favourable circumstances to the possession of one or two cows, and increasingly over time to none.

All accounts from the second half of the century seem to have a much greater emphasis on bread whether it is in the form of oatcakes or, in the counties of strong Anglo-Norman settlement, of mixed cereals in bread. There was of course no novelty in the bread itself whether it was the mounds of oatcakes piled up on the table of a rural chieftain beside the meat [12] or 'the course unsavoury bread' to be found in the Anglo-Norman region of Kildare [13]. The greater emphasis on bread was independent of the influx of Scots and English. But the influx of people from regions with a longer bread-making tradition and a greater variety of cereals in everyday breadmaking, was bound to reinforce the trend already under way for more compelling economic and demographic reasons. The compact small settlements of English colonists in the early seventeenth century sometimes had a baker with his oven, as in co. Carlow in 1641, the first evidence of professional breadbaking in Ireland outside the walled towns [14]. The greater emphasis on porridge as opposed to bread in much lower-class diet in eighteenth century rural Ireland seems to be a reflection of unchanged attitudes inherited from earlier times. But bread itself, whether oaten, barley, wheaten, or mixed, in lower-class diet in many regions, reflects complex internal patterns or frontiers in breadbaking of native, Anglo-Norman or more recent origin. Even in lower-class diet wheaten bread could be found in places as for instance in the diet of miners in the colliery districts around Castlecomer where much of the mining population was of English origin and had brought their attachment to wheaten bread with them. Strikingly too the first flour mills in Ireland ground for urban markets, especially for the Dublin one; none of the Ulster flour mills were erected to cater for the Dublin market, suggesting as Ulster towns were small, that there was some demand in the 1760s for flour, outside the towns and the houses of the great.

The decline in butter and milk, especially in the diets of the poor, accounts for the greater reliance on bread and porridge as a replacement of butter, increasingly out of reach of the rural poor, and the emerging prominence of the potato. The early potato did not keep well: its main value was as a supplement to the butter or winter food. As grain supply was too small to stretch out over the entire year, the potato made it possible to economize the consumption of oats in winter and to spare it for the lean days of late spring. There are two dietary changes in the seventeenth century, greater consumption of grain, and increased use of the potato. Both are closely inter-related, the potato replacing grain in winter, and grain becoming the main spring food. These changes were especially crucial for the poor among whom butter was now becoming scarce. The process was not the one of contraction of food supply seen by Salaman[15] but of evolution to a more varied diet and from simple forms like porridge to bread. As the transition was so rapid, it is likely that some countrymen advanced from porridge to the potato without ever relying on bread in their diet. A Danish soldier recorded in 1691 lying in quarters in Cork with an old man who said to him that he had eaten no bread other than potatoes for sixteen years[16]. From what we know of eating habits and the keeping qualities of the potato, this seems impossible at this period. It does not imply an exclusively potato diet in the way that the quotation has usually been interpreted, but a diet in which there were seasonally other constituents, but none of the bread which to a lowland Scot, Englishman or Dane was the staff of life and for whom a diet without bread was scarcely comprehensible. A poem by the Gaelic poet Seán O Neachtain shows how a diet characterized by the consumption of potatoes was not as restricted as it might look at first sight: the poem, incidentally to its main purpose, contrasts the diet of the lowland people of the Dublin and Kildare plain, consisting of grain, peas and beans in the form of pottage and to a less extent bread, with the upland people of the Dublin and Wicklow mountains beyond Tallaght, who had a potato diet. The contrast did not lie in poverty; the upland people's potatoes which were said to last from the first of August till St Patrick's day were accompanied by 'ever-lasting happiness and roast meat'[17]. It also implies reliance on other foods, presumably grain, very probably oats more suitable to upland soils, for the remainder of the calendar. The potato's importance, undeniably of course, increased in the eighteenth century, no longer supplementing but even replacing bread or porridge in the diet of the poor, and becoming prominent even in regions where it had made little headway before 1700. Arthur Young was adamant in the notes made on many of the districts that he visited in 1776-8 that the potato had made rapid advances in the quarter-century before 1776, and indeed on his evidence the potato had become the main item in the diet of the poor for up to 9 or 10 months of the year. In these closing years of the eighteenth century, the potato began to spread very rapidly throughout Europe, but with initial greater reliance on it at the outset, dependence on it remained more marked in Ireland. Hence, for the Irish poor, the 'hungry 1840s', difficult everywhere in Europe, were more catastrophic than elsewhere because the potato blight which swept Europe made greater inroads into their food supply.

It is misleading to see the evolution of Irish diet as divided into two periods separated by the Famine. In fact Irish diet had been in a continuing evolution during the two preceding centuries. The diet was characterized both by change, in the form of increased emphasis on grain and the potato, and continuity in the persistent consumption of meat and butter in quantities. Much of the misunderstanding about Irish diet and the exaggerated emphasis on the poverty of the diet is based on the assumption that the bulk of the population had been degraded to the lowest social level, an assumption which overlooks the complexity of rural society outside the fringe of poverty-stricken regions along the west and south-west coasts. Moreover, the change in diet in the nineteenth century is not as closely linked as generally believed to the Great Famine. Admittedly in the poorer regions, immediate post-Famine change is evident with maize supplementing the potato, a change whose scale can be exaggerated because maize replaced oats as much as it did potatoes. In comfortable families or in areas whose very survival had not been threatened by the Famine, conservatism slowed change. It came only two or three decades later, and the reaction against the prominent place of the potato in the diet was set in motion by visits by members of the family who had settled abroad and whose pretensions and aspirations were those of the outside world [18]. A general change in diet thus comes late in the century in the 1870s and 1880s, and is therefore simultaneous with changes for largely the same reasons in rural France. Moreover, the changes in Ireland as elsewhere at that time were not so much a once for all change as the beginning of an ongoing process in which rural classes gradually adopted the foods and eating habits of the towns [19]. The process was accelerated by the heady rural prosperity during and immediately after the first world war (the Irish parallel with rural France is again close), and was assisted by the emergence before 1900 of the horse-drawn baker's van, and the greater literacy and mobility of the country population.

If the changes in Ireland from the 1880s are only part of a widespread revolution in rural Europe, the sustained evolution in Irish diet in the preceding three centuries had been without contemporary *parallel*. The dependence on butter as opposed to cereals, and within cereal consumption the reliance on porridge as opposed to bread, shows the limited evolution attained by Irish diet at the outset of the seventeenth century. The sustained evolution of diet in the subsequent centuries led to the presence to a remarkable degree of archaic and modern elements simultaneously. The Irishman of the middle decades of the nineteenth century was likely to be familiar with potatoes, oaten or wheaten bread, maize and butter in substantial quantities. The belated evolution of the Irish diet gave it a fossilized character with the survival of heavy consumption of milk and butter. As late as the 1830s butter was the substitute for meat in the household of Humphrey O'Sullivan in the small rural town of Callan, and among the labourers dieted by the Kettle family farming in north co.Dublin [20]. Butter and milk made the Irish diet a rich one in both a practical sense and a dietetic (i.e. protein) sense. The lack of variety in Irish diet has tended to be exaggerated because of a very general tendency to think that traditional diets in Europe were richer and more varied than they actually were. The rich diet and elaborate cooking reputed in France for centuries were the prerogative of its townspeople. French country people relied heavily on cereals — even as late as the second half of the nineteenth century per capita consumption of wheat in France was 60 per cent higher than in England. In the countryside in previous centuries it was often black bread in the poorest regions and mixed bread in other regions, and the meat consumption varied from little to moderate; the meat typically consumed in rural families was pork and largely on festive occasions. Moreover, as Ireland was a livestock economy more than a cereal one, meat was relatively abundant. Meat loomed large in the diet of the well-off rural large farmers; middle-sized farmers consumed it three times a week, and more frequently in festive seasons. A total absence of meat was a sign of destitution, and while the destitute were a significant element of the population (larger than in France, and much larger than in England), the rest of the population, its majority in absolute terms, in varying degree enjoyed security and comfort. Even in the Callan region in co. Kilkenny, where the contrast was sharp between its modestly comfortable farming class and numerous labouring population, the poorest of the rural population, the occupants of rural hovels (*lucht botháin tuaithe*) enjoyed meat on three days in the year — Christmas day, Shrove Tuesday and Easter Sunday. By contrast the farmers of the region purchased or killed their own meat several times a year, and had it in abundance over the festive seasons. As late as 4 January, ten days after Christmas, O'Sullivan noted 'now is the festive season, for there is not a farmer nor yet a small farmer who has not pork or mutton or beef, and "biped meat", that is the flesh of fowl, abundantly' [21]. Moreover, during the festive season, it was customary for farmers to have more than one kind of meat, the choice of several meats, a modest reflection of upper-class comfort, being the evidence of their own status and comfort [22].

Diet is conditioned by several underlying influences, a factor of special relevance to Ireland, because of its comparatively belated transition. The first one is the evolution from primitive to more modern diets, effectively the replacement of 'moist' diets based on butter, and porridges by more solid diets based on bread. A butter-based diet was the diet of a relatively primitive people. Survival on the milk of the dairy herd was more economical than reliance on meat which entailed the large costs of rearing replacement animals to maturity. Frugal in its approach to livestock husbandry and implying summer abundance and winter penury, it was therefore easily associated with poverty. In England, as early as the late medieval period, such a diet, already in decline there, was regarded as a poor diet [23], and in rural France milk products remained as late as 1936 the very symbol of the food of the poor [24]. In Ireland, butter and milk were consumed prodigally into the eighteenth century, even if the evidence for a decisive evolution was already sharpening in the second half of the previous century. Dunton was offered in a poor cabin in Iar-Connacht as late as the 1690s in addition to oat cakes ' a greate roll of fresh butter of three pound at least, and a wodden vessell ful of milk and water', and 'a hare swimming in a wodden boul ful of oyl of butter' [25]. Beans and peas as a pottage in place of bread were still widespread in 1700 in districts settled centuries before by the Anglo-Normans even where they were later gaelicized. They were already disappearing in 1776 although Young, the source for this observation, understates their role at that date. As late as 1783 in the aftermath of the terrible harvest of 1782, Francis Harvey of Bargie Castle in south Wexford provided relief to hundreds with a mixture of boiled beans and milk [26]. Changes in diet involved social changes in which upper-class styles of living were imitated further down the social scale. The consumption of bread and of meat was based on upper-class standards, dietary aspirations to improvement being a powerful lever in promoting change. Potatoes, widely consumed across social classes, were less significant in denoting status than meat or in the nineteenth century white baker's bread.

The second factor in the evolution of diet was commercialization: foods once widely consumed, were often abandoned by necessity or choice as they acquired an enhanced price. Rents and taxes had to be paid, or cash acquired to buy conventional necessities that entered into popular budgets like tobacco after 1650, after 1750 whiskey or the tea, shop meat and baker's bread that entered increasingly into popular diets in the second half of the nineteenth century. By the early nineteenth century butter had totally disappeared from the diet of labourers and milk was disappearing as well, as cottiers and labourers could no longer afford to rent land for a cow and both butter and milk were too dear to buy. In the great boom in agricultural prices after 1793 butter and pork began to disappear from the diet of small farmers in Cavan and Monaghan [27]. In 1687 Sir William Petty thought the growing exports of butter the produce of dairies maintained by English settlers in Ireland [28]. By implication the native diet remained heavily dependent on butter for which there was as yet no market. Subsequent growth made inroads into domestic consumption: Samuel Madden in 1738 related how formerly butter was sold 'by night and as privately as possible, thinking it disgraceful to make a profit of the industry of their wives', indicating the acceptance of commercialization by that time [29]. Significantly in the Cork and Kerry region which had experienced a sustained growth in dairying from 1720 to 1775, Young thought the conditions of labourers worse than elsewhere in the kingdom, many or most of the labourers having no cow and having to buy milk [30]. The situation worsened subsequently in the dairying regions of Cork and Waterford, and at the outset of the nineteenth century while milk was already rare in the diet of labourers the diet even of the middle-sized-farmers seemed sparing.

Observers had too little knowledge of social classes in the countryside to make subtle distinctions between social classes and geographical regions. Just as thatched housing was invariably described with contempt in early nineteenth-century literature (comfortable homes and hovels being dismissed alike), popular diets were described with a total lack of intimate knowledge. In consequence where contrasts between regions were made explicitly by contemporary writers the divides seem more absolute than is possible in the subtle configuration of dietary patterns. Likewise, where novelty is evident to the writer, its prominence is exaggerated if not by the author, by later readers. An interesting instance is the consumption of wheaten bread by the miners of Castlecomer, mentioned with some emphasis by Tighe in 1802. A tradition of wheaten bread is certain in one of the inland parts most heavily and successfully settled with English colonists in the seventeenth century. But in bleak limestone upland where only part of the population was of English origin consumption was in fact, at the level of the parish, sparing. At an early date, in Bishop Tenison's report on his diocese in 1731, the parish of Castlecomer was already singled out by comparison with the rest of the diocese of Ossory for its heavy consumption of potatoes: 'the advantage of potatoes in this parish being the ordinary food of the coal carries(sic) and their families is so great that the tithe of potatoes amount to between 47 and 50 pounds a year. Half the tithes of this parish must consist of potatoes . . .'[31]. Another instance of the tendency of novelty to attract attention is contemporary comment on meat consumption among weavers in the north. Weavers were more likely to spend money on tea than meat, and, tea apart, their diet was if anything rather bleak. In reverse, the basically sparing and monotonous nature of popular diets led contemporaries to underestimate the variety of items in the diets of strong farmers, which while not akin to upper-class diets, had a richness and variety which decisively differentiates them from poorer diets. Upper-class accounts, even those by well-informed parsons, and country gentlemen, fail to make allowances for the subtle distinctions in diet. It is unlikely, for instance, that the diets of middle-sized farmers were quite as sparing as Townsend's statistical account of co. Cork suggests[32]. Another case in point is the sparing diet suggested by Tighe for the large dairy farmers like the Aylwards in south Kilkenny[33] or by the well-informed author of the memoir on Tullaroan parish in 1819 in Shaw Mason's *Statistical Account* for the comfortable farmers of that parish many with 'their division of rooms, plastered walls, built up fire places and grates'[34]. Near at hand, for the parish of

Callan, the account by Humphrey O'Sullivan gives an impression of a much more varied, even if fundamentally simple diet.

Meat also reflected (even more powerfully) the impact of commercialization. For the poorest it was the symbol of comfort, the son of a poor family about to emigrate to America 'boasting to the maids of the amount of beef he would eat on the other side of the water'[35]. As far as the poor were concerned their range of purchases, in O'Sullivan's Callan on Christmas Eve was:

Many a pork steak, and pig's head; many 'a little market joint' of lean, tough beef; many a large fat junk of an old sow's groin; many a remnant bit of a little old ram being bought by poor people; for the wealthy prosperous folk have already bought choice meat[36].

The large farmers killed their own beef; this was done at Martinmas[37]. As farmers, even prosperous farmers, could scarcely afford to kill more than a single cow (and many retained only a side for their own consumption) the bulk of beef consumed by the population at large, even by the large farmers, was salted. The fact of a substantial consumption of beef in this manner explains the prominent position of salt beef, and of 'hung beef', beef more lightly salted and cured by hanging from the kitchen rafters above the large fire place. In other countries, either less meat was eaten or as in England with large fresh meat markets reflecting the greater purchasing power of its rural population[38], more of it may have been acquired by small regular purchases. Large gentry households, killing a cow or ox regularly — in the case of the Martins of Ross for example every month[39] — enjoyed fresh beef fairly regularly but even in such families it was frequently supplemented in the intervals between killings by salt beef. Families like the Martins dieted their labourers on beef, whereas large farmers universally in pre-Famine Ireland did so on pork.

The high monetary value of beef and the importance of cattle in inland trade is reflected in the fact that throughout rural Ireland, pork and mutton were the meats most widely consumed, below the level of gentleman farmer. The wide availability of pork is in part explained by the growing importance of potatoes and the fact that potatoes as a largely non-commercial crop made easier the fattening of a pig. Pigmeat was invariably cheapest in the season after potatoes had become available, and when potatoes were particularly abundant, the pig population rose sharply. The feeding of pigs on potatoes developed only in the eighteenth century after potatoes had ceased to be a garden crop and had become a field one. As late as 1729 the writer Arthur Dobbs clearly envisaged pigs as fed simply on 'thrash'[40]. Pigs fed on grain or beech mast were necessarily something of a luxury, although a prized one, as the numerous references to them in the source material for early historic and medieval Ireland show [41]. In consequence, even as late as the 1670s the traveller Dinely regarded the consumption of pork as confined to 'people of condition'[42]. The spread of potatoes brought about a dramatic change: pork was transformed from a relative luxury fed on the surplus grain of rich households into the most universal and cheapest meat. Pork exports themselves rose — although the pork trade was slow to become commercialized, only becoming so extensively from the last three decades of the eighteenth century. The cheapness of potatoes ensured that the supply of pigmeat kept ahead of export trade. No doubt commercialization did lead to the withdrawal of pork from the consumption of households. Moreover, in pre-Famine Ireland the number of the labourers and cottiers not keeping a pig also increased. But the majority of rural households kept a pig for their own consumption at the end of the eighteenth century and the practice was so general that pork or bacon had become the popular form of meat. In a prosperous region like Kilkenny and Waterford in 1790, at a time when the pig trade was still only in the early stages of commercialization and when labourers still had access to sufficient land for potatoes, Coquebert de Montbret wrote that he had not seen a cabin with less than two or three pigs [43]. Mutton by contrast showed no signs of commercialization. It did not salt well, which meat that it did not enter into the export trade, and sheep themselves were kept for their wool rather than meat. No market price series for mutton exist, and we are dependent on private account books, which confirm the regularity of purchases, for prices. However, the reason for mutton consumption was not exclusively its availability but the fact that it was the only fresh meat in regular supply. It entered into the diets of the upper classes even more regularly than into the popular diet, and good mutton was appreciated as Mary Tighe's letter in 1801 from Woodstock House at Inistioge to her husband in Dublin, shows [44]. Fresh meat was always sought after. One of the reasons why pork steaks, pig's head and feet were prized was that unlike the rest of the animal they were not salted and were consumed immediately. With a fall in sheep numbers by the end of the eighteenth century and a rise in pig numbers, mutton became less freely available than in the past, and gave way to pork. One of the consequences was a sharp rise in the proportion of salted meat in total meat consumption. Another striking result of market forces was the fall in consumption of home-cured bacon in the second half of the nineteenth century as bacon factories opened in the major dairying regions across the country and guided a rising proportion of home-fed pork into the export trade. It was replaced increasingly in the farmer's diet by cheap fat imported American bacon purchased in shops. By 1904 as much bacon was imported to Ireland as was exported, one of the most striking instances available of the interplay of market demand, the spread of shop facilities and rising American food supply.

Fish, fowl and eggs were very important in the diet, more important in the eighteenth century than later because export markets were then few. Fowl and eggs were widely consumed: in the absence of export demand or large urban markets, consumption was local and prices low. Arthur Young had been struck by the abundance of fowl: 'poultry in many parts of the kingdom, especially Leinster, are in such quantities as amazed me, not only cocks and hens, but also geese and turkeys'[45]. A concomitant was the abundance of eggs, especially for breakfast, Sir John Carr after his Irish visit regarding their breakfast-time abundance as a distinctively Irish feature[46].

Fish were a significant supplement in diet, much more important in fact than in later times, especially as external markets were frequently small or non-existant. Pilchards and herrings had of course been important in export trade at one time or other, pilchards in the seventeenth century, herrings intermittently at several points along the coast over the centuries. But as the shoals deserted Ireland, the commercial fleets departed, leaving the seas to local fishermen. Moreover, commercialized fishing on a large scale was almost confined to co. Dublin and to a much lesser extent counties Cork and Waterford and the few highly commercialized ventures elsewhere were in the hands of businessmen or speculators, some of them landlords like Lord Conyngham in the great herring boom off the coasts of Donegal in the 1770s and 1780s. Less commercialized ventures in the hands of local fishermen existed side by side with these ambitious and transient enterprises. With no market except a local one, seafish, herring in particular, were the food of the poor. In 1784 at the end of a year of near-famine they relieved want dramatically in co. Sligo, as the correspondence between members of the O'Hara family, one of the Sligo landowning families shows:

I learn with great satisfaction that last August my worthy countrymen about Sligo were able to purchase an horse load of herrings for 3p — many a nak'd back was comforted by a full belly — and the parson will make his fortune next year by christenings....[47]

Fish, being cheap were consumed not only along the coast but up to 30 or even 40 miles inland. Willes noted in Galway that 'the herrings they dry are generally sent into inland parts, and the turbots and soles etc are generally sent the same way'[48]. Such fish were usually salted, and the inland epicure like Humphrey O'Sullivan liked fresh fish: 'I do not like salt fish, and fresh fish was not to be had, except too dear and seldom'[49]. Fresh fish in county Kilkenny came from Dungarvan. O'Sullivan on occasion had hake, and the Frenchman, Coquebert de Montbret, recorded enjoying it also, 'a fish little appreciated in England'[50]. For O'Sullivan, herring was 'poor food'[51]. Fresh hake, sole and turbot were all highly prized delicacies, appearing on the tables of the well-off and often celebrated, especially the turbot, in literary references. When the Duke of Rutland as Lord Lieutenant visited Killala, he was presented with 38 enormous turbot, each donor bringing along his own fish[52]. Fresh water fish were widely consumed as well, not only the salmon and trout but perch, eel and pike. The poorer people in the countryside ate pike across much of Ireland from Mayo[53] to Kilkenny, where ponds were drained to catch the eel and pike[54]. At the eel weir on the O'Brien farm at Lough Gur eels were sent direct to Limerick market or taken by Meggy-the-eels, an itinerant vendor who came from Bruff to buy 'the take', which she peddled from house to house[55]. In fact in eighteenth and early nineteenth century Ireland, the widespread consumption of fish contrasted with England, Arthur Young for instance being provoked by the consumption of fish (in France) to declaim against the situation in England with 'a lake, a river or the sea within view of the windows, and a dinner everyday without fish, which is so common in England'[56]. Coquebert de Montbret was sometimes provoked into similar comments as at Cong, or around Enniskrone[57], but in fact fish was often extensively caught and eaten by the poor. It was precisely its consumption by the poor that may have caused some prejudices against it by others only above the poverty line in some regions. De Montbret noted that ray salted by the people of Skerries, co. Dublin, with its highly developed sea fishing, were thrown out by the fishermen at Kinsale [58]. Salmon were caught in enormous quantities especially in the estuaries where they often numbered hundreds in a single draft. Salted salmon were exported in significant quantities from both Coleraine and Galway for modest markets such as the lenten market for fish in Italy and in France where it was in demand in the early eighteenth century in monasteries. In a highly commercialized fishery like Coleraine salted salmon reached the poor consumers near the coast, but the fresh salmon was regarded by all as a delicacy. Much of the fresh salmon was taken by the towns. The price of salmon in Thomastown was more than halved when the cholera raging in Kilkenny made people afraid to eat it. O'Sullivan had salmon for his dinner the day after making this entry in his diary [59]. With fresh fish so abundantly available, there was no need to feed fish artificially as in the case of carp in France. The fact that Wesley mentioned the fishpond at Eyrecourt (which is still to be seen in overgrown weed-choked condition beside the ruined house at Eyrecourt) is a suggestion that it was a rare sight in Ireland [60].

Shell-fish were everywhere prized by the country people as were crabs and lobsters. Contemporary accounts often give a picture of their abundance and profusion and of their place in the diet. An account of the Rosses in co. Donegal from the eighteenth century is one good instance [61], as is the description by Maxwell from the poorer Mayo coast over a generation later. Maxwell related how he 'frequently saw more than would load a donkey, collected during one tide by the children of a single cabin' [62]. De Montbret in the region of Westport, co. Mayo, saw heaps of shells outside the fronts of houses, showing the nourishment that the inhabitants derived from shellfish [63]. If crabs and lobster were relatively little consumed by the Mayo peasantry, it was only because they could get what was procurable at low spring tides and lacked the equipment to catch them in deeper waters. In fact, the peasant taste for shell-fish even exceeded that of the upper-classes, Maxwell observing that besides the wealth of cockles, scallops and so forth 'there are . . . other shell-fishes greatly prized by the peasantry but which I never had the curiosity to eat, such as razor-fish, clams, and various kinds of muscles' [64]. In the towns shell-fish, as contemporary price quotations confirm, were abundant and cheap. Hawked around the streets, they reached appetites far down the social scale. But the oyster, like the salmon, was highly prized. In consequence though cheap on the spot or in urban fish markets, they were both expensive and sought after farther afield. The oyster boats from Carlingford were almost as familiar as the potato boats along Dublin quays. Even from the Burren in Clare oysters were sent to Dublin [65]. A barrel of oysters sent from a friend on the coast or in the towns to an inland family was a much appreciated gift. Oyster beds were sometimes seeded by local gentry who wanted to expand both employment and the food supply. To cater for the upper-class taste for them salmon and oysters were pickled for consumption at a later date or for carriage to a distance: they were the sole exception to the epicure dislike for preserved fish.

The abundance of fish in the diet, where they were available along rivers and on the coasts, was a consequence of limited commercialization of fishing, organized for export or urban markets only where rich shoals of sea fish came or in the estuarine salmon fisheries. Cheese did not experience the impact of commercialization directly because significant quantities were never exported. It did, however, indirectly, because the rising price of milk for liquid consumption, soaring butter production and the feeding of the expanding pig population of the late decades of the eighteenth century, all served to reduce the supply available for cheese-making. In fact, some cheese was exported, an average of 5000 cwt p.a. in 1719-1726, a level which was not maintained in later decades as butter exports soared. Given the importance of the demands for milk and butter in the Irish diet, there was a limit to the expansion of cheese production which required large quantities of milk in relation to the size of the output. Because of butter production, cream was scarce. The residual skim-milk which could be converted into non-cream cheeses, if not consumed in liquid form, was increasingly absorbed as an animal feed by the growing calf population and, especially from the 1780s, rising pig numbers. Cheese production was largely of simple cream cheeses for home consumption. The fact that hard cheeses made from skim-milk, whey, and curds, were less important and declined more rapidly is a reflection of the abiding demand for liquid milk for human consumption and for liquid and semi-solids for animal feeding. Some tradition of cheese making was in fact widespread, lingering on into the nineteenth century. Visitors who commented on the absence of cheese exaggerated the position somewhat, because production and consumption alike took place in the home. As late as the 1840s, Charles Lever's novel *Charles O'Malley*, which is remarkably authentic in its incidental detail, could still record the sale of 'soapy cheese' at fairs in Philipstown [66]. A little was made for home consumption in county Tyrone as late as 1802 [67], and a farm inventory in co. Armagh at an earlier date includes a cheese press [68]. In co. Kilkenny O'Sullivan mentions on one occasion 'fragrant cheese' [69], and some was even exported from Kilkenny through Waterford [70]. Cream cheese is mentioned in Griffin's *Collegians* in the 1820s [71], and the making of cream cheese at least in homes lingered on in co. Limerick into the second half of the century, described in nostalgic detail in Mary Carbery's *The farm by Lough Gur* [72].

The changes in Irish diet were thus in no small measure determined by the forces of commercialization. The major exporter in Europe of beef and butter in the eighteenth century, Ireland very rapidly became an exporter of grain and flour in enormous quantities to Britain in the early nineteenth century. Exports, already a million quarters by 1810, soared to three million quarters at their peak in the 1830s. Such a vast and rapid change taking place within a comparatively short period implied significant reorganization in Irish agriculture, notably the increased importance of root crops, in Ireland almost invariably the potato, in crop rotations if soil fertility was not to be undermined. The country was even more highly commercialized in the second half of the nineteenth century: fifty per cent of agricultural output was exported; per capita exports were very high, exceeded only by those of New Zealand and Australia among non-industrial countries, and were much higher than those of Denmark. Such a high degree of commercialization, associated with the rapid changes that commercialization entailed, was bound to have a major impact even in the short run on diet as either opportunity enticed farmers to produce for the market or pressures drove them in the same direction. The soaring exports of grain in the early decades of the nineteenth century made the production of grain attractive for the farmer, especially as trends in livestock trade were uncertain. As output could be maintained only by increased reliance on root crops, grain and potatoes were in effect in joint supply, and short-term cash gains were maximized by increased sales of grain and growing home consumption of potatoes. High grain prices raised living standards; as a farmer poet in co. Galway put it; 'féadaidh tú bheith ag ól seal ó d'éirigh an t-arbhar daor'[73]. Low grain prices in the years intervening between good seasons made the process of substitution all the more irresistible, as an increased volume of sales was then necessary to attempt to maintain the level of cash income attained in the years of high prices.

Commercialization was still more intense in the second half of the century as maize, imported wheat and even baker's bread were substituted for home-grown oats and ultimately even for the potato, and farmers' high-priced bacon was sold and replaced in their diets by cheap, American bacon. As early as 1834 the cumulative change in the preceding thirty years was already very evident in a parish such as Dungiven in co. Tyrone, more vulnerable under the full-blast of commercialization than more prosperous areas:

the potato crops were very limited in the parish up to the above period ... the entire crop of oats, barley, and potatoes were consumed within the farmer's home and his cottiers' ... seldom was potatoes used at the farmers' or cottiers' table unless during the winter and close season of the year and this at dinner only [74].

But the change in the diet in the early decades of the nineteenth century merits particular attention because of the stress placed on the potato in the Irish context and because of the scholarly controversy surrounding its place, timing and role in diet and society alike [75]. The spread of the potato diet is a complex phenomenon. Even in south Munster where the potato had made most progress, a diet exclusively of potatoes and buttermilk was a target of social ridicule in the poetry of Eoghan Rua O'Súilleabháin as late as the 1770s, emphasizing the fact that such a diet was associated with poverty [76]. In the century and a half preceding the 1770s some use of the potato was made by all, even if in the case of the poor increasingly it became the staple of life. The more general dependence on the potato in the early decades of the nineteenth century is related to commercialization as much as to poverty, and for the classes above the level of the cottier and labourer must be seen as a process of substitution between grain and potatoes rather than between potatoes and non-grain items in the diet. It is not at all evident that meat consumption was altered. Indeed the growing supply of potatoes, cheap in good years because their market was local, promoted a rapid expansion in pig production, bacon compensating in the diet for the decline in mutton.

In families above the labourer/cottier level, heavy potato

consumption thus came late. Moreover, the early stage in the spread of the potato is not closely linked to the native population. It was grown by immigrant English in their first generation in Ireland in the early seventeenth century, as incidental references in the 1641 depositions show [77]: in the case of a large farm in co. Wicklow, the quantity of potatoes — in the ground and in store — amounted to about 100 barrels which would represent the produce of between one and two acres [78]. In fact, it may well have been the progressive and relatively advanced English farmers, coping with unfamiliar Irish conditions who introduced it as a crop which did well in the wet Irish summer. Its consumption was then adopted by native families in the same regions especially during the rapid commercialization of the 1650s and 1660s which saw a sharp rise in the market disposal of grain, butter and cattle. A familiarity with and fondness for potatoes pervaded all classes in Ireland. An Irish Quaker, born in co. Kildare in 1685, who had emigrated to the Americas — and Quakers typically had settled in Ireland in the 1660s and 1670s — advised a co-religionist about to leave Ireland to bring:

Good potatoes abord with him . . . as to some particulars I had I would have given them all for potatoes, I haveing good butter on board. It would have been more serviceable with potatoes to me than anything I had. Beside I longed so much for them that I dreamed night after night that I left the ship and got home and there I was sacking them in barrell sacks [79].

The potato was prominent in the diets of the highest families, as the comments of the most distinguished visitors to Ireland show. Consignments of potatoes were frequently advertised in colonial newspapers [80], and Irish merchants in France, where the potato was not yet extensively grown, were regularly the happy recipients of presents which they shared with their intimates in the Irish colonies in the French ports. In the case of the Hennessys the largest recorded quantity was 2 hundredweight, although a fellow-Irish merchant, John Saule, wrote to Richard Hennessy in 1769 of the arrival of a Dungarvan vessel at La Rochelle with 70 barrels of potatoes: 'this you'l perhaps think a fable, but I do assure you its true' [81]. James Delamain, born of Huguenot ancestry in Ireland, settling at Jarnac near Cognac in 1760, shared this liking. In April 1768 he thanked the captain of an Irish vessel for the offer of potatoes, asking him to send from Rochefort to Jarnac 'a small quantity between this and Tuesday, as that day we have Messrs Saule and Hennessys families to dine with us, we heartily wish you could be of the party'[82]. The continued reliance of the Irish merchants in the south-west of France on presents of hampers of potatoes from Ireland, prized as much if not more than the occasional barrel of tongues, Irish cheese or a piece of hung beef, suggests how little-known the potato was in this part of France right up to the revolution. Delamain may in fact have been the first man to plant potatoes in the Cognac region, as in February of the same year he had asked the master of another Irish vessel: 'Pray have you a few potatoes to spare. We should be much obliged to send them up here, they are to plant and we shall return you the compliment in some old brandy'[83]. On one other occasion he thanked Hennessy in an undated letter for potatoes: 'they shall please God be in the ground tomorrow and taken greater care of in hope you will help me destroy their produce'[84]. As late as 1791, as an old man, he nostalgically referred to Ireland, when his close friend, Richard Hennessy, was proposing to visit Ireland, as 'the land of potatoes'[85].

The belief that the potato debased Irish diet is subject to much qualification. Complex changes were afoot. Beans and peas had virtually disappeared as field crops. Maize meal was already making its appearance in Irish diet ahead of the rest of the British Isles and in particular ahead of the Great Famine with which its use as a food in Ireland is popularly associated. Its first recorded use as a food in Ireland is in co. Wicklow in the hard season of 1800-1[86], and it was extensively consumed in Callan in co. Kilkenny in the bad years at the end of the 1820s and early 1830s[87]. Contemporaries certainly thought that the potato was driving or already had driven field crops such as beans, peas and vegetables out of popular diets[88]. But while they believed that potatoes had driven out beans, the decline in beans had in fact been a progressive and long-drawn-out process in its final stages by 1800. There were other reasons affecting the decline in beans as a field crop. They were thought as a field crop to encourage weeds and in consequence to leave the ground dirty; they were also, it was said, disliked by females for more intimate personal reasons 'to escape a mark, which they are said to impress on the person'[89]. The argument that potatoes reduced the consumption of vegetables as opposed to pulses appears at first sight more plausible. Vegetables had been widely cultivated among the upper classes. Samuel Faulkner regularly sent seeds to his steward at Castletown in

Carlow, and it is possible to trace from the correspondence some planting of lettuce by the steward for his own use [90]. Just as the planting of orchards was evident as late as midcentury, large kitchen gardens were at the same time erected beside the big houses. Young's comment in fact was that the kitchen gardens were if anything too large:

gardens were (formerly) equally bad; but now they are running into the contrary extreme, and wall in five, six, and even twenty Irish acres for a garden, but generally double or treble what is necessary [91].

The decline in the use of vegetables around or after 1800 is however not a simple or straightforward phenomenon. The decline affected orchards as well as vegetables. Even in Down orchards were already said to be declining, and in north Armagh, which had the most intense concentration of orchards in Ireland, they were said to have been uprooted by 2000 farmers in the course of the 1790s [92]. Nor was the change confined to the ordinary people: the emphasis on the kitchen garden and orchard was declining even among the inferior gentry [93]. Among the poor only the cabbage held its ground, and in July 1830 towards the end of the difficult harvest year of 1829-30, O'Sullivan in Callan thought that the poor were subsisting on cabbage [94].

The universality of change at this time, affecting Armagh in its most prosperous decade as well as the rural population at large, and having an impact on orchards as well as pulses and vegetables, suggests wider influences at work. Vegetable growing and orchards were both poorly commercialized; produce was intended for home consumption; most farmers were remote from middle- or large-size towns, and successful disposal of vegetables required weekly attendance at markets at a season of haymaking or harvesting when the labour demand in farming was itself at a peak. Apples presented not dissimilar problems in marketing. The difficulty of disposal almost certainly accounts for the emphasis on cider-making. The decline in cider consumption, as whiskey made inroads on cider first in the north, more slowly in the south, must have reduced the attractions of orchards still further. For the Armagh farmers, with orchards looming large in their relatively small acreages, the attractions of conversion of orchards for crop production or for renting at high prices during the linen boom to the county's teeming weaver population must have been irresistible.

The availability of vegetables was not, however, reduced as sharply as that of apples. Even in a small town like Callan there was on the evidence of Humphrey O'Sullivan's diary a fairly wide availability of vegetables. Dutton, highly critical of county Clare agriculturally, commented very favourably on the supply of vegetables at the Ennis market [95], no doubt in part a consequence of Ennis's proximity to the relatively sophisticated farming region of the Newmarket area. Almost certainly one of the reasons for the decline in popular vegetable growing was the growth of specialist market gardening, which took some of the residual profitability out of vegetable growing by part-timers. Tighe, who had commented on the decline in vegetables in popular consumption, elsewhere noted that 'the cultivation of vegetables by market gardeners, had encreased three or four-fold, within these twenty years' [96]. The lesser gentry, less able to maintain a prodigal house and garden staff than the large gentry and peers whose walled gardens remained in intense use, but sophisticated enough to wish to retain vegetables in their diet, were increasingly content to supplement their supply by purchases, like townspeople, at markets or from specialist gardeners.

It should be clear by now that diet was not as narrow as has often been suggested: the factors making for change did not all spring from poverty or even from the availability of the potato. In fact, while the potato bulked large in early nineteenth-century diet, the diet at the level of farming families, was impressively rich in protein-content and to a degree varied. In the admittedly relatively prosperous milieu of north Dublin, from the resources of a 30 acre (or 45 statute acre) farm, the diet of both family and dieted labourers on the eve of the Famine seemed rich:

The food was nearly all home made: wholemeal bread; oaten meal grown on the farm made into stirabout; potatoes, generally all floury; first quality butter; bacon, raised, killed and cured on the premises; milk unadultered 'ad libitum' for everyone and everything and honey bees in almost every garden. I often held the scales for my paternal grandmother to weigh a pound of bacon for each workman's dinner three days a week, with a quarter of fresh butter and four duck eggs on the other days. No tea, not much butcher's meat unless at Christmas or Easter, but plenty of pork steaks at the pig-killing periods, and the best of pig's pudding or sausages [97].

The profusion of butter, milk and potatoes make this a relatively simple diet, but for variety and especially for the quantity of meat, the diet would be hard to surpass in contemporary rural France or Britain. Even among the small farmers in the foothills of the Dublin mountains there was variety including wheaten meal and a little meat [98]. In the baronies of Forth and Bargy, families had meat twice or three times a week; a diet like the North Dublin one but richer than appears at first sight because on the meatless days butter or herrings were consumed. Humphrey O'Sullivan's diary suggests a good deal of meat consumption by the farming classes at all levels, at least spread over festive seasons. The south-east like co. Dublin was, of course, a well-off region. The migrant for the Newfoundland fishery, in Donnachadh Rua Mac Conmara's poem, *The adventure of a hapless fellow*, which was based on personal experience, brought on his journey across the Atlantic oatmeal, potatoes, butter, eggs, fowl [99].

While the poor had meat, which they purchased only on festive occasions, both strong and small farmers had it more often, strong farmers killing a cow in addition to the pig or pigs universally killed for home consumption. As for the minimum size of farms at which cattle slaughter for home consumption took place the evidence is necessarily imprecise. At Shaen's Castle in co. Antrim, according to Young, farmers of 20 acres and upwards (30 statute acres) had a side of beef for the winter [100]; in Clonmore, co. Louth, farmers of 30 to 80 acres (45 to 120 statute acres) killed a cow in addition to the pigs they cured for family consumption [101]. At a lower level it is probable that the only meat cured for home consumption was pigmeat. But even among the families on larger farms, pork was more common than beef. The comfortable farmer, Mr Power, in the neighbourhood of Callan, who entertained Humphrey O'Sullivan and two priest friends to dinner on a July afternoon in 1827 and who possessed a fine dwelling house, a barn, byre with 40 milch cows and 'a splendid vegetable garden . . . amid trees and effectually sheltering hedgerows . . . and a fruitful sheltered orchard', regaled them with the comparatively modest, though ample, fare of 'fat smoked swine flesh, that is, bacon, white cabbage, magnificent potatoes and hot-mixed whiskey' [102]. Little if any beef, and only of the inferior sort, entered into the modest festive purchases of the poor. At Gloster in co. Offaly, according to Young, cottiers bought meat for ten Sundays in the year; even as late as 1802 the family of every cottier in the barony of Kilcoursey was said to consume a bacon pig annually [103]. In co. Armagh, at the end of its booming 1790s, the lower classes were said to consume meat more regularly than in any other county in Ireland, bacon in summer and beef in winter [104]. But Coote's evidence for Armagh is ambiguous as to the precise social categories involved, and it is doubtful in fact whether the consumption of the weavers was as extensive as has been suggested. Across the borders in co. Antrim the weaver-small farmer poet, James Orr, 'the bard of Ballycarry', while he confirms the heavy weaver consumption of tea commented on by other sources, seems to give a picture of what is otherwise a rather bleak diet of potatoes and maslin bread [105].

The rural classes tended to suffer from the process of commercialization of their production which carried it to the towns; the reverse side of the coin was a more extensive, regular and varied consumption of meat by townsmen far down the social scale and even at a lower level than the farmers who produced much of it. Humphrey O'Sullivan at Callan on Shrove Tuesday 1831 purchased 5 pieces of beef and a half hogshead of neats tongues; he killed a pig of his own regularly, so that one has a crude idea of the family consumption. His supply the following year was no less ample as he recorded at Easter 1832 that he did not require to purchase meat for the festive season as he had ample bacon and smoked beef hung [106]. Of course, O'Sullivan, as a smalltown notable, although a very modest one in a very depressed little rural town, represents a degree of comfort and sufficiency that is hardly representative of town dwellers at large. The little Franciscan community in Cork city is a better example. Although their gross income per capita in the 1760s and 1770s in a community of about six persons was about half that of an artisan in regular employment, they seem to have purchased about a half cwt of beef, the same amount of mutton, and about a cwt of pork (more pork in later decades). This would give a modest but still sizeable consumption of about 38 lb per annum, and was supplemented by some purchases of veal, fowl and especially fish, in particular dried ling (44 lb in January — April 1765) and herrings. They also appear to have consumed 10 to 20 lb of butter per person, in addition to potatoes and bread [107].

Irish diet originally had a marked regional character. The most fundamental contrast was between the regions with a diet heavily dependent on butter and milk in all their forms, and the old Anglo-Norman regions which relied more on peas, beans and grain. The latter regions included the Pale, the entire south-east and much of the Shannon estuary especially the rich lands along the Fergus on the Clare side where beans were still cultivated extensively as late as 1808. They had at least in stable conditions little need to adopt new foods: in a culinary sense they were the most conservative regions in Ireland, the conservatism being proportionate to their agricultural wealth. Dried peas and beans preserved well, and supplemented the grain supply. This diet, buttressed with milk and butter from May, was sufficient to provide an all-year round supply of food. In the cereal and pulse region the period of scarcity was the late spring and early summer before the new crops arrived. This accounted for the emphasis on peas and beans which because they ripened early helped to ensure that the food supply could be eked out over the critical months before the next year's grain harvest. It also explains the importance of bere or winter barley which ripened as early as July, well ahead of the other cereals, in traditional diets. Except in the intensely conservative diets of south Wexford, barley bread was no longer of importance in the diets of comfortable rural families, though significantly, in the relatively poor and archaic west, de Montbret in 1791 was received in a castle at Roslee by a Mr Brown, and the visitors given 'round cakes of coarse unleavened barley meal cooked before the fire'[108]. In some parts of Ireland it still featured in the diets of crisis years into the early nineteenth century. The fact that in Callan barley bread was regarded by O'Sullivan as a poor food of 'long ago' and that it had been one of the traditional foods of the penitential day of Good Friday, illustrates its established association with food shortage or seasons of relative deprivation[109].

In contrast to the cereal-pulse regions where scarcity was a feature of the summer, winter was the season of scarcity in milk regions: cows went dry in the autumn, and the widespread practice of burying butter in wicker baskets in bogs is testimony to the necessity of storing food for the winter and spring before the resumption of grass growth in April when the cows calved and the milk supply began again. The dairying regions were coming out of crisis therefore at a time when in cereal/pulse districts the supply of cereals and pulses was beginning to run out. The potato, before varieties which kept longer began to appear towards the end of the eighteenth century, was consumed in the winter and spring: in early accounts it was regarded as a food from August to March, St Patrick's day being the traditional divide. For the dairying districts with their winter food shortage, the potato was particularly attractive. It is hardly accidental that the bulk of the regions where the potato was tithed were in Munster much of whose economy was based on dairying from an early date. Kilkenny, the only Leinster county where dairying loomed large in the economy and where resistance to the tithe proved longest and fiercest in the dairying south of the county, was the only Leinster county where the potato paid tithes. It is tempting to assume that tithe was imposed on the potato in those areas where the potato first became prominent and that growing lay resistance halted the spread of tithe to potatoes in areas where it become important only later. The results of this resistance have usually been seen as selfish, as reflected in the celebrated resolution by the Commons in 1735 against the levying of the tithe on dry cattle. One of the indirect results of the resolution may however have been of more popular benefit — to halt the spread of a tithe on potatoes to other counties. Potato tithe was still a local issue in some areas in the middle decades of the eighteenth century, emphasising the fact that the tuber was only late acquiring significance. The fact that outside Munster and Kilkenny the potato was untithed, while cereals and pulses were, must itself have enhanced the attractions of the potato for people on the margin of subsistence with no real surplus to pay taxes or tithes.

In the early eighteenth century, after a century of transition and before dietary patterns began to fuse under the impact of the intense commercial development of the third quarter of the century, the dietary frontier was sometimes dramatically evident to contemporaries. O'Neachtain's poem, incidentally to its main task of burlesquing a traditional faction fight at Tallaght between hills people and plainsmen, points to the contrast between the cereal-poor diets of the south Dublin and north Wicklow uplands and to the cereal- and pulse-rich diets of the Meath, Dublin and Kildare plain below them. The Gaelic poet Uilliam O Maoil Chiaráin who passed his life between the northern-most extension in county Meath of this cereal-pulse region and the poorer lands of Monaghan, provides in his poetry an even more specific instance of the contrast a generation later. Living in co. Monaghan, away from his Meath homeland, he contrasted nostalgically the absence of 'parsnips, roots or new items coming to the fore except rubbish dug with a spade at the coming of August' with the wealth and variety of food by the Boyne: shoulders of meat for sale at stalls, barley, wheat, peas, beans, and stacks of corn still awaiting threshing as late as St John's feast in June [110]. The significance of the last

Diet in a changing society

point is self-evident: it implied surplus at the time when food traditionally became scarce in the countryside, unthreshed stacks in mid-June being the visible symbol of a rich district.

Another geographical contrast, even more sharp and more lasting, lay in the distribution of orchards. The most intense concentration of orchards was to be found in regions of strong pre-1641 colonization of English settlers, where landowners and tenants introduced their homeland-style of agriculture, largely in the case of pre-1641 colonists, that of the cider-rich south of England. Leases often bound tenants to plant orchards, and early tenants and their descendants, often themselves from the south of England, were eager to reproduce the farming patterns of their home regions. Where English settlement was strong, the number of orchards continued to rise well into the eighteenth century, a parliamentary report in 1730 observing the increased consumption of cider, 'of late years more drunk than ever, especially in the southern parts' [111]. The most intensive concentration of orchards was to be found in north Armagh which witnessed the most sustained early immigration of English tenants of any region in Ireland: it became and has remained the orchard region par excellence, despite the massive uprooting of apple trees in the 1790s. A similar pattern was to be found extensively in regions of strong English settlement elsewhere: in south-east Antrim, the western fringe of Down, and Fermanagh in the north; and in the south, in parts of Cork, mid-Limerick, south-east Clare, west Waterford, and north Wexford. In the rich farming district around Dromoland in co. Clare (where bean cultivation also survived into the early nineteenth century on the rich lands near the Fergus), Young commented that 'this country is famous for cyder-orchards, the cakage especially, which is incomparably fine. An acre of trees yields from four to ten hogheads per annum, average six, and, what is very uncommon in the cyder counties of England, yield a crop every year. I never beheld trees so loaden with apples as in Sir Lucius O'Brien's orchard: it amazed me that they did not break under the immense load which bowed down the branches. He expected a hogshead a tree from several' [112]. The surveyor Wight in the diary of his travels in the course of his survey work in the more anglicised areas of co. Limerick in the 1750s dilated on the quality of the cider [113]. By contrast, orchards were relatively few in the Scottish regions of co. Down, or in the rich Anglo-Norman regions of the Pale, south Wexford, or of Kilkenny. The local frontier between orchard-districts and non-orchard districts

167

was sometimes as abrupt as if it were a physical divide. While orchards were by no means unknown elsewhere, they were far fewer on the homesteads of families below the rather ambiguous status of minor gentry or gentlemen farmers. The contrast between south Wexford and many other regions was that they were unevenly present on farmsteads in the former. In other regions, even in counties as prosperous as Kilkenny or east Waterford, they were frequently remarkably absent from the larger farms.

Whatever its regional distinctions, Irish diet in its way was rich. While the Danish soldiers in Ireland were struck by the comparative absence of bread, they were clearly impressed by the availability of other foods, and by the possibilities of substitution between foods [114]. Such observations in the middle of a military campaign are in their own way remarkable. Contrasting too with the less fulsome comments of English commentators during and after the Elizabethan campaigns, they may suggest something of the strength of the evolution of Irish diet in the seventeenth century. The emphasis in the literature has exaggerated the poverty of Irish diet, because in the seventeenth century it had become more rather than less varied and while the potato was the dominant new element it was not the sole one. Thus, to take one illustration, while beans and peas declined in their traditional locations, they actually spread in the poorer regions of mid-Ulster, almost certainly in consequence of imitation of the diet of English settlers in Armagh who brought a more varied diet to Ulster to supplement the narrow existing one of the region. Sir Charles Coote who had studied both southern and northern counties contrasted the absence of beans in King's county with their presence in the north where they came into the diet early in the season 'boiled and mashed with pepper, salt, milk, butter and a little oat or bere meal . . . much liked, and is also introduced in season at the tables of the wealthy' [115]. In Armagh, which was the centre of bean cultivation in the north, beans were mixed with potatoes as a variant of colcannon called *stulk* or *sthik* [116]. The same dish survived as late as Carleton's day farther afield in the co. Tyrone [117].

With its extensive use of beans, grain, potatoes and butter, Irish diet had a variety of products to help it over the difficult months of early summer. Ireland escaped famine entirely in the 1690s and in the first decade of the eighteenth century, although both Scotland and Denmark were stricken in the 1690s and France in the 1690s and again in 1708. Famine remained a feature of relatively backward societies which failed to advance quickly beyond a secure threshold of sufficiency in food supply, but later Irish food difficulties should not be assessed without taking into account the fact that Scandinavia experienced severe famine as late as the early 1740s, France nearly experienced it in 1788 and Finland, at the time still a relatively backward country, as late as 1867.

The fact that famine was experienced in Ireland twice in the eighteenth century — in 1728-9 and 1740-1 — and near famine in three years — 1745, 1757 and 1783 — reminds us, however, of the countryman's continuing need or interest in varying and supplementing his food supply. The years of famine occurred almost invariably in the second of two years of harvest failure. After a harsh season all reserves of both food and cash were exhausted, and the ordinary people were ill-equipped in a second bad season to survive or in default of food to borrow against survival. In fact, so significant was the attrition of successive seasons of hardship that in comparatively prosperous communities such as the largely rural Church of Ireland communities in Wicklow parish or in Tullow or Rathkeale, to take only three instances, the highest level of mortality came in the season in the winter and spring following the first good harvest after the year or two of failure. The highest mortality in these parishes in the 1750s did not follow the bad harvests in 1755 and 1756, but in the first half of 1758, despite the good harvest of 1757. In poorer parishes with less food surplus or cash savings high mortality appeared earlier. A country with a wet climate was particularly vulnerable to harvest failure, and in fact the one near-famine, which took place without an immediately preceding year with a bad harvest, came in the wake of the torrential rains of the summer of 1744, which both ruined the grain and destroyed the hay that would help to carry livestock over the winter in good condition. There is some evidence, impressionistic because the seventeenth century sources are poor, that near-famine in the eighteenth century was more common in Ireland than in the seventeenth century. If this is correct, one of the reasons for it may have been the decline in a butter diet. A larger population increased the number of families with access to few if any dairy cattle. While until the middle of the century many of these families were able to rent grazing for a single cow or two, the milk supply from one or two cows was not sufficient to provide a very large surplus of butter for the winter. After the middle of the century, the number of families not possessing a cow also began to increase significantly. The critical period of shortage for a primitive dairying community was the winter; in May, on the other hand, when the food supply of cereal districts was running out, the resumption of grass growth ensured an abundant supply of food. If the ownership of dairy cattle became less general, however, the proportion of the population at risk in the spring rose sharply, and a short grain or potato supply after the harvest could herald a critical food shortage in the following spring.

It is true of course that a shortage of hay could imperil the survival of livestock or delay by a critical period of several weeks the resumption of milk supply from the debilitated herds, but on the other hand hay saving took place in June/July compared with the harvest in September/October, and unfavourable seasons within the same year for both hay-saving and harvesting required an abnormally prolonged rainfall even by Irish standards. Moreover, a shortage of hay was itself totally disastrous only if the following winter was severe and the animals which had survived the winter with difficulty had then to face a prolonged delay in the recovery of grass growth in the spring. On the whole, on the evidence of food shortages, food supply deteriorated somewhat in Ireland after the relatively halcyon decades of the 1690s and 1700s whereas in both Scotland and France the community successfully put famine behind it after 1699 and 1708 respectively. Survival remained more critical in Ireland because as cow ownership, more significant in Ireland than in drier France or colder Scotland, ceased to be universal, milk and butter were no longer as readily available as in the past to compensate for the traditional shortages of grain and potatoes in the late spring. The fact of an emerging milk and butter shortage among poor families added greatly to their interest in having potatoes, because the earliest potatoes were available at the beginning of August, two months ahead of the staple cereal of the poor districts, the late ripening oats. With its cloudy summer, ripening of all cereal crops tended to be later than in the drier climates of lowland Scotland, England and France. The habit of late harvesting was thus well-established and persisted even in the years when sunshine could guarantee an earlier one. This attachment of the Irish countryman to a late harvest was commented on by many contemporaries, and is attributable to the habits created by the uncertain harvests more than to the insouciance which observers also noted. It was of course also promoted by the fact that many smallholders could save their own only after working on the harvests of large farmers or gentry or after their return from migrant harvest work to the south or east. The potato thus had a double advantage in Irish climatic conditions; for the cereal regions, the new potatoes filled in the traditionally hungry months before the new cereal crops ripened; for the dairying districts, they helped to replace the disappearing milk surplus of smaller rural dwellers for whom dairy cows were increasingly inaccessible. Even the potato was not sufficient to lift Irish diet at the base of rural society above the threat of famine; indeed the reverse, the condition of the bottom strata of Irish society became more precarious. It was thus a very complex situation because the changes in Irish diet and farming had proved sufficient to put the farmer beyond the threat of starvation: the famine of 1740-1 was the last one in which the farmer and the rich farming districts were faced with the threat of famine. On the other hand, the condition of the labourer and cottier deteriorated progressively: first in the fall in the proportion possessing a milch cow between the 1670s and 1730s; secondly in the progressive disappearance of milk altogether from the diet of many of them towards the end of the century. Their potato dependence was by then near total: in the rich Dromoland district of co. Clare, Young commented that 'the poor live upon potatoes ten months of the year; but, if a mild winter, and a good crop, all the year on them' [118].

The diffusion of the potato in Ireland, more precocious than in Europe at large, must be studied in the context of the transition in Irish diet, rather than, as is generally done, as an isolated phenomenon. Moreover, the most arresting feature of Irish dietary innovation is that, though it was a response to commercial and demographic pressures, its beneficial results, though real, were incomplete. While life was much less precarious than previously, the innovation failed to put Irish society securely beyond the threshold of starvation. Famine could still occur, although one of the beneficial results was that its incidence had changed quite dramatically. The famine of 1845-8 was far less general than preceding ones; the farming class was not directly at risk, and regions where the farming community was very strong, escaped lightly. This underlines still further the complexity of the transition in rural Ireland. Economic and social changes had not been sufficient to lift rural society beyond the threshold of crisis, but in the altered social structure the incidence of famine was more uneven and less general both regionally and socially than in the past.

8
Hospitality and menu

Transition in food supply and commercialization were inevitably reflected in the ways of life which revolved around food: the foods sought in menus, the time of meals, and the spirit of hospitality. The openness of Ireland to innovation, for instance, is reflected in the changes in meal times: the upper-class dinner hour in Ireland as in England becoming progressively later, whereas in more conservative France dinner remained a mid-day meal. Hospitality reflected the changes more profoundly, although as it corresponded to the life style of the better-off or to festive occasions on which no expense was spared, it was much more conservative or archaic than the general pattern of food consumption. This itself, however, made for sharp contrasts between older conventions of hospitality, closely identified with a profusion of food and drink, which obstinately lingered on, and less archaic hospitality. Contemporaries were well aware of the contrast, and after 1800 of the fact that the more celebrated excesses of old-fashioned hospitality were firmly in the past.

Fashion and commercialization both had a striking impact on Irish food. The role of fashion is predictable, but that of commercialization is more complicated. The most startling instance of all is that of whiskey. Whiskey had in the past been an almost totally non-commercial beverage, distilled by comfortable families for festive occasions or for a lavish table. It was not the regular beverage of any class and certainly not of the lower classes. In the middle of the eighteenth century a commercialized whiskey industry began to emerge. Irish countrymen were quick to spend some of the money that cash wages, rising food prices or the sale of textiles brought their way on the commercial product, and by the end of the century in the form of punch it was becoming the habitual upper-class drink as well. It is in particular striking to see the upper-class beverage change so rapidly. It reflects something of the social prestige of the product, and like the general upper-class interest a generation earlier in harp music, it was one of the comparatively rare instances in which native civilization seduced Anglo-Irish attitudes. Ale and cider at popular level and wine and brandy at higher levels were thus largely replaced within two generations by what was for most a hitherto inaccessible product. Where food is concerned, commercialization had a still more complex role. But one aspect is worth stressing. In a highly commercial society, poor foods, that is, foods which were free or almost free, stood out, and quickly acquired a social stigma. The social pressure to avoid them, or replace them with purchased foods, was real, especially at the foot of the social ladder.

Hospitality is one of the basic characteristics of society, its nature mirroring the degree of social development, and the presence or absence of the integrating bonds between host and dependents which unstinted hospitality repeatedly given and received denoted. Hospitality was originally unsparing, and, as costs rose, increasingly expensive: for that reason, it is not surprising that the tradition lasted longest among the most archaic gentry, insecure rising families, or in remote regions, and longest of all among the rural poor, whereas the upper classes became more cautious or exclusive in their hospitality. Visitors to Ireland in the eighteenth century and even later were impressed by the profusion on the tables of the great, just as travellers were greatly taken by the generosity of the ordinary people in the countryside. If well-off families spent less prodigally on habitual hospitality, as they became more cost-conscious, they repeated its established pattern calculatingly for a smaller number of persons or more intimate occasions. As social imitation has always spread downwards, upper-class menus influenced meal-styles in the comfortable farming families. Thus, hospitality, menu and everyday food are closely related. Even the hours of eating are part of the dynamic. As old-style hospitality went out of fashion, entertainment was increasingly deferred to a later hour to leave time for work or more restrained pleasures.

Thus, food has to be seen in terms of the character of meals as well as of the spirit in which hospitality is imparted. In primitive times in Ireland as elsewhere meal times were erratic, a fact said to be true as late as 1814 of the remote parish of Dungiven in co. Tyrone: 'a general inattention however and carelessness with respect both to the matter and the manner of their hourly meals still mark an immature state of society' [1]. Such a pattern still existed, as outside observers noted, in the congested districts along the west coast of Ireland as late as the 1890s. However, in most of Ireland a regular pattern of times for meals was long-established, although it could vary seasonally and could conform to the pattern of farm work. In co. Down, comfortable though the county was and profoundly influenced by Scottish patterns, vestiges of older patterns still existed as late as 1800: breakfast was taken in the course of the morning's work and was not followed by another meal till dinner was taken at 6 p.m. or in the winter earlier at dusk [2]. However, a main meal at mid-day was becoming well-established throughout the farming regions, in imitation of the well-established upper-class pattern of a mid-day dinner. But upper-class dinner times were themselves changing; by the middle of the eighteenth century dinner was already taken at 2 or 3 in the afternoon, becoming still later by the end of the century with an almost stereotyped hour of 7 emerging in the course of the nineteenth century. Arthur Young, travelling in France at the end of the 1780s was astonished that even in the best society a mid-day time was still almost invariable. The advantage of the later time was that it enabled the day's duties to be completed before dinner and that guests did not have to return afterwards to more mundane tasks. The later the dinner time, the more effective it was in dividing the day into two sections reserved for work and pleasure respectively. Such a division was feasible only for persons with a good deal of leisure: for ordinary families, the practical advantages of a mid-day meal remained paramount at least until the age of commuting. In very comfortable farming families an interesting division sometimes operated in the nineteenth century: labourers and maids dined at 12.30, parents and children at 4 p.m. [3]. As dinner became later, it was necessary to interpose a mid-day meal in its place — with dinner as late as 7 p.m., luncheon was a well-established meal in the early decades of the nineteenth century — usually lighter, simpler and more informal than the main meal. Dinner had usurped supper as the evening meal in upper-class circles but supper continued as the main evening meal in farming families, in summer taken at about 7.30 when the day's farming tasks, including the important evening milking of the cows, were completed. With the human tendency to overeat, when incomes or abundance admitted it, supper as a late-night snack made its appearance in upper-class families, and at all levels, where a degree of comfort existed, afternoon tea made its appearance; in well-off farming families it was well-established by the middle of the nineteenth century and tea and bread were brought to the work force in the fields.

Breakfast was a vitally important meal, especially if meals

were irregular or as in farming areas work started as early as 6 a.m. and it was taken two or usually three hours later. A mainly or exclusively potato breakfast was a sign of poverty, and outside very poor regions, such a meal for adults cannot be regarded as traditional. Stirabout made of oatmeal was the established basic morning food in town and countryside well into the nineteenth century, made on milk rather than water except among poor families. Barley bread was sometimes an alternative as in Carne in Wexford [4]. Stirabout was not a standard or regular constituent of upper-class breakfast by the late eighteenth century, although, judging by a comment by Sir John Carr on his Irish visit in 1805, it could in fact be met within the upper-class breakfast on occasion. In more fashionable circles it was probably already an anachronism. Carleton's tale of the young man destined for the priesthood typifies the class distinction that had emerged with the young man, in contrast to the rest of the family, being supplied with 'a *tay* breakfast instead of stirabout, which, in polite society, is designated *porridge*' [5]. The basis of a comfortable breakfast in a middle level of society, however, was boiled eggs. Sir John Carr thought the profusion of eggs at breakfast — as opposed to the bacon and eggs already known in Britain — a distinctively Irish feature. But even in a well-off family the eggs were the prerogative of the grown members. In Griffin's *Collegians*, at breakfast at the Dalys, comfortable middlemen in the Shannon region, the children were served with milk and potatoes at a separate table [6], and in the second half of the century in the O'Briens' prosperous farm home at Lough Gur, servants and children had stirabout and only the parents ate eggs [7]. The eggs were of course not consumed on their own, but were supplemented by other food, stirabout or bread, and where available, honey. In the richest families cold meats and fowl were also served as part of the breakfast, 'fare that spoke satisfactorily', as Griffin observed, 'for the circumstances of the proprietor' [8]. The rashers and eggs breakfast, which was not distinctively Irish, was beginning to make its widespread appearance. It merits a mention as a breakfast in Irish literature in Carleton's *The Squanders of Castle Squander* [9], but its lower social standing is well-hinted at in the contrast at the pre-election breakfast at Castle O'Malley between 'some rubicond squire . . . deep in amalgamating the contents of a venison pasty' and 'his neighbour, less ambitious, and less erudite in such matters . . . devouring rashers of bacon' [10]. Tea and coffee had already made their appearance at fashionable breakfasts, and were beginning to make an uneven appearance elsewhere. With tea consumption having become universal in the twenty years after 1850 the popular Irish rural breakfast had evolved into boiled eggs, bread, butter and tea.

For other meals, the menu has been heavily influenced by the fare of festive occasions. The profusion of meat dishes marked such occasions at all social levels and was at all times the hallmark of the tables of the well-off. But if we know a good deal about the food of festive occasions, because it impressed — and was intended to impress — and is recalled in letters and in literature, we know much less about the food of other occasions. All we can be sure of is that it was simpler at all social levels, and was served with informality. The greatest problem is determining not what was the food of festive occasions but how frequently the fare on other days approximated to it. The English traveller, Dunton, entertained in Iarconnaught in 1699 at the home of 'one O'Flaghertie the most considerable man in this territorye', observed at dinner 'no less than a whole beef boyl'd and roasted, and what mutton I know not so profewsly did they lay it on the table. At the upper end where the lady sat was placed an heap of oaten cakes above a foot high, such another in the middle and the like at the lower end'. The previous night at supper, when mutton was the only meat served, it was provided both boiled and roasted [11]. Sixty years later, Mr Cuffe of Ballinrobe related to Baron Willes his experience of having being entertained on the far side of Lough Corrib by the occupant of 'two long cabbins thatch'd opposite to one another, the one was the kitchen and appartments for the family, the other was his entertaining room'. The profusion was obviously as great as Dunton had experienced:

The entertainment was half a boil'd sheep at top, half a roasted sheep at bottom, broil'd fish on one side, a great wooden bowl of potatos on the other side, and a heap'd plate of salt in the middle, after dinner some pritty good claret, and an enormous wooden bowl of brandy [12].

On the same side of the Corrib, as late as the early nineteenth century the quantities were still truly enormous at the Martins of Ross; a sheep every week and a bullock once a month were killed, all that could not be eaten fresh being salted down in huge stone pickling troughs [13].

Such hospitality was the successor of that of Tudor times, described with a combination of awe and condescension by Tudor visitors to Ireland. Andrew Borde had described how 'in those partyes they will eate theyr meat in a beastes skin.

And the skyn shall be set in many stakes of wood, and than they wyl put in the water and the fleshe and than they wyl make a great fyre and the skyn betwixt the stakes and skyne wyl not greatly bren. And whan the meate is eaten, they for theyr drynke, wil drinke up the brothe' [14]. Another Tudor has left an artist's impression of an almost identical scene [15]. The large consumption of meat was the main dietary distinction between the upper classes and the ordinary people, and festive occasions were therefore marked by the profusion of meat even more than by the abundance of drink. Such hospitality was repeatedly lauded in verse, nowhere more specifically than in Egan O'Rahilly's poem praising the hospitality of the planter Warner, an Englishman gone native:

Meat on spits, and wild fowl from the ocean;
Music and song, and drinking bouts;
Delicious roast beef and spotless honey,
Hounds and dogs and baying [16].

As the poem implies, the hunt was the occasion for much of the most lavish hospitality. Eibhlin Dubh Nï Chonaill's lament for the death of her husband in 1773 recalls vividly post-hunt entertainment, essentially that of a small gentleman farmer:

..... those rough horseman
That hunted in the valley,
Till you turned them homewards
and brought them to your hall,
Where knives were being sharpened,
Pork laid out for carving,
And countless ribs of mutton
..... slender, powerful horses
And stable-boys to care for them [17].

Piaras Mac Gearailt, himself a co. Cork gentleman farmer of a slightly earlier period, in his lament for Maire Paor conjures up a similar picture:

In your kitchen strong fat beef used to be hanging up;
In your dining room I recall your bounteous hospitality
In distributing food and drink without stint . . . [18]

In Ireland, closer to medieval traditions of hospitality than the more modern society of England, a prodigality existed unequalled in England. After the execution of Sir James Cotter in 1720, his wife had to put her son in the care of an English lady resident in Ireland, remarking that though she was kind 'English ladies think a meal's meat a great expense' [19].

But in fact, even if Anglo-Irish hospitality could be compared unfavourably with native hospitality at least by natives, it did impress visitors. Mrs Pendarves (the future Mrs Delany) was very impressed by as many as six different meats being served at a single meal [20]. As late as 1825 no less an epicure than Sir Walter Scott, commenting on his Irish visit, was able to say that 'I do not think even our Scottish hospitality can match that of Ireland' [21]. At the highest level, hospitality was not pressing: Bush commented that 'to do justice to their generosity, however, (the visitor) is free and right welcome to eat just as much as he pleases . . .' [22]. At a lower level of course, the honours of hospitality were more demanding. As Carleton put it, 'about forty, or even thirty years ago, it was an easy matter to get into an Irish gentleman's dining-room, but not quite as easy to get out of it, especially in the west' [23]. Gerald Griffin's *The Collegians* as late as the 1820s at a lower but still comfortable level observed that 'the time had not yet gone by when people imagined that they could not display their regard for a friend more effectually than by cramming him up to the throat with food and strong drink' [24].

At the level of the great landowning grandees and politically powerful aristocracy in both countries, food was more elaborate, in its own way reproducing in Ireland and England alike a pattern of profusion and abundance that seem almost barbaric to modern tastes. At such a level on formal occasions food was served in three courses, each course consisting of a series of dishes, cooked or cold, savoury and sweet. Guests did not attempt to eat everything. They picked and chose among the foods, and the discerning were careful to eat sparingly in order to savour the delicacies. What seems extravagant to modern tastes is not the gluttony because in their way guests exercised discrimination as much as modern diners in different circumstances, but the implication of waste. However, this is qualified by the fact that food left over found its way to the servant's hall, the big occasion thus providing in its way a feast for all [25].

Meals at inns stand somewhere between festive meals and simple meals on ordinary occasions at home. Fowl were very frequently part of the fare at Irish inns, usually served, at the turn of the century, with meat or fish. At the inn at Newrath Bridge, already highly reputed, fowl and trout were the fare served to Sir John Carr [26]. A somewhat jaundiced view of Irish inns was that of Weld in 1832: 'bacon and eggs, and chicken, are the current dishes of an Irish inn, during the summer season'[27]. Almost a century previously Mrs Delany noted that at a public house, there was no food for callers 'not even a little bacon'[28]. Because it was a small country with most journeys likely to be accomplished within the day, inns were very few. Young, who travelled extensively in France and who compared the fare at its inns more than favourably with Scotland or England, did not speak well of Irish inns, but in fact spent comparatively few nights of his Irish sojourn in them. Coquebert de Montbret, a sympathetic French visitor, leaves a more favourable impression. In an inn at Athy, he had an 'excellent supper of two chickens, ham, cabbage and potatoes'[29]. When no inns were available, he stayed at simpler lodgings, observing after staying in a miserable thatched cabin in the village of Buttevant, co. Cork, and having a supper of snipe, teal, and wild duck that 'this was not the first time when expecting nothing he was better served than elsewhere'[30]. There were of course good inns, some of them improved considerably by 1800, both those at Bray and Newrath bridge well-situated for the explorer of the beauties of the Dargle and of Wicklow respectively, often drawing the favourable comments of visitors. In 1825 Walter Scott, Scottish gourmet and patriot though he was, on the strength of a month's travels in Ireland, though Irish inns better than Scottish[31].

Humphrey O'Sullivan records meals with the parish priest of Callan, Father Hennebry[32]. Irish priests' incomes were modest although secure, the priests usually coming from strong farming families. Father Hennebry's dinners were sometimes intended for intimates among the modest Catholic notables of Callan which included O'Sullivan, sometimes for somewhat larger groups or more formal occasions in the public life of the town. They probably represent accurately the fare of the well-off rural Catholic farmer and modestly comfortable townsman for social occasions.

20 June, 1828	*An informal occasion* Two trout 'one of them as big as a small salmon' Hard boiled hen eggs and cooked asparagus 'soaked in melted butter on boiled new milk and salt' Port wine and punch
22 July, 1828	*An informal occasion* Boiled leg of mutton

Hospitality and menu

	Roast fowl with spiced stuffing Punch, tea
14 September, 1828	*Dinner for five* Boiled leg of mutton with carrots and turnips Roast goose with green peas and pudding Tripe 'swimming in new milk' Port and punch
28 September, 1828	*An informal occasion* Tripe 'smothered in butter and new milk' Bacon with cow's kidney and white cabbage Roast duck with green peas
8 October, 1828	*Dinner for eight* A leg of mutton Bacon Chickens and white cabbage Two roast duck and green peas Sherry, port wine and punch
17 March 1829	*'A jolly group' for 'our Patrick's pot'* Fresh cod's head Salt ling 'softened by steeping' Smoke-dried salmon and fresh trout 'Fragrant' cheese and green cabbage Sherry, port, gin, whiskey and punch

Another dinner of interest was that given by Father Simon Walsh and 'his people' near Waterford, on the occasion of O'Sullivan meeting a relative of the priest's, Mary Walsh, as a prospective bride:

A chine of beef new-salted and white cabbage
Roast goose with bread stuffing in it
A leg of mutton and turnips
Bacon and chickens and roast snipe
Port wine and punch

The novelist Carleton has recorded the fare of the comfortable farm houses of Tyrone of about the same period:

Neither is the rich smell of oaten or wheaten bread which the good wife is baking on the griddle, unpleasant to your nostrils; nor would the bubbling of a large pot, in which you might see, should you choose to enter, a prodigious square of fat, yellow, and almost transparent bacon tumbling about, be an unpleasant object . . . [33]

In the intimacy of his family, on Easter Sunday 1828, O'Sullivan had smoked bacon and fowl. On Easter Sunday a year earlier he had been entertained at Butlers 'where we got white baker's bread, fat pork, delicious mutton, whitish pudding, and a drop of whiskey'. He noted in his diary that on 4 January 1828 'there is not a farmer nor yet a small farmer who has not pork or mutton or beef, and "biped meat", that is the flesh of fowl abundantly'. On Christmas day itself the fare was roast goose stuffed with potatoes [34].

Humphrey O'Sullivan, whose diary bears testimony to a keen interest in food especially because details of meals on social occasions were frequently entered in the earlier although unfortunately not in the later years of the diary, affords some interesting details on diet. Meals at home were basically simple with a single joint at dinner, sometimes simply butter in place of it, and two joints were the feature of festive occasions. O'Sullivan was a successful shopkeeper, and his diary is evidence of the fare of moderately comfortable townspeople. His meals at hotels were usually simple affairs of a joint and bread or potatoes, although when he dined at the Rose Hotel on a Friday in July 1828 he had salmon, fresh hake, new potatoes and bread. When he visited with Father Hennebry the home of the parish priest's cousin, married to a Michael Hickey, the fare was fairly straightforward: 'juicy beef and tender mutton and merrily drinking sweet strong punch'. But these dinners are quite varied on more formal occasions: in the dinner [35] given by Father Simon Walsh profuse almost to the point of rivalling a gentry meal. Fish was usual on a Friday if entertainment for friends or visitors was provided on that day; in a comfortable milieu like that of O'Sullivan's friends almost invariably fresh — O'Sullivan himself did not like salt fish. It is interesting to note however that salt ling — considered a food for the poor — appeared on the St. Patrick's day menu in Father Hennebry's in 1829. The menu is of considerable interest because it provides an arresting instance of a fish menu — a varied one — of fresh, salted and smoked fish for a festive occasion. It illustrates the fact sometimes overlooked, that fish were in demand, in no way regarded as "penitential" foods. The vegetables are simple, but asparagus, once more common and still widely used in gentry houses featured in one menu. The one striking absence is that of desserts. Arthur Young, comparing inn fare in France and England, had of course remarked how inferior English desserts were. But their complete absence in Irish menus below gentry level is none the less striking. Even apple pie was recorded by O'Sullivan only as one of the Hallowe'en foods. Pies generally, whether sweet, or savoury — venison, pigeon, veal — were a feature of gentry diet. Even in the relatively modest society of Carrick-on-Shannon, the novelist Trollope had pigeon pies in the menu for the picnic luncheon after the races, and veal pies among the supper fare [36].

The beef consumed in Irish families was usually salted, and pork was usually consumed either salted, or cured as bacon. Only in large households was beef so profuse that much of it was consumed fresh. Hence beef steaks, well-known in the diet of the well-off, were a luxury among comfortable farming families, and the meal of 'whiskey, hot and cold, baker's bread, beef steak, crushed coltsfoot and tea' which O'Sullivan had at the home of the McCormacks after the burial of a member of the family was a meal of high luxury because it included both beef steak and baker's bread [37]. Pork steaks, which unlike the rest of the pig were not salted were a delicacy, and even seventy years later in the shop owned by the Brownes on the eastern slopes of Slievenamon, only some fifteen miles from Callan, 'customers, knowing that a pig was freshly killed, wanted pork steaks and cuts of fresh pork' [38]. Mutton was very common in the town as a purchased meat and in rural houses it was one of the festive foods. Its significance, however, lies not solely in its universality and in its comparative cheapness but in the fact that it was the only meat eaten exclusively in fresh form, and for the poor was virtually the only fresh meat they tasted. Significantly the meat in the boiling pot at Irish patterns (popular festivals) and fairs was usually mutton.

In the early stages of the Grand Canal the fare was varied in the passage boats of the 1780s, but just as with the growth in traffic the clientele inevitably changed to 'its never varying cargo of cattle-dealers, priests and peelers on their way to the west country' [39], so did the bill of fare. One of the Martins of Ross in recollection recalled that on the canal boat 'a baked leg of mutton was served for dinner everyday the whole year round with the greatest regularity' [40]. In a less kindly fashion the menu on the canal boat has been immortalized by Trollope: 'the eternal half-boiled leg of mutton, floating in a bloody sea of grease and gravy, which always comes on the table three hours after the departure from Porto Bello'[41]. Mutton was a basic meat at every social level. When Maxwell, arriving at the Mitre Inn in Tuam, required an impromptu meal in a hurry, 'a respectable quarter of cold lamb and a dish of exquisite potatoes' was produced[42].

But mutton and beef alike gave way to pigmeat. Moreover households like the O'Briens in co. Limerick where 'we never had mutton' existed[43]. Pigmeat provided the greatest outlet for the culinary skill of Irish families; fresh, it was consumed as pork, salted as bacon, and the entrails provided the filling for a variety of puddings. Collared head and pig's feet were a delicacy. Either or both of these delicacies, prized on any occasion, often appeared on the table over Christmas. In the late nineteenth century, Canon Sheehan observed of 'every Irish household' that 'the roast goose, stuffed with potatoes and onions, the pig's head, garlanded with curly cabbage, a piece of salt beef, and an abundance of potatoes, was, and is, the never-changing menu in these humble, Christian households'[44]. In the comfortable home of the O'Briens at Lough Gur in co. Limerick:

Six pigs of about two hundreweight were killed in the year for the use of the house; the curing and smoking were supervized by my mother whose secret recipe resulted in delicious ham and bacon. From pig's heads she made brawn or collared head, and from the cheeks came what we called French hams which, cured and smoked, were good to eat with chicken. We little girls helped — hindered — her as she went about her preparations. We — and mother — made collared head boiling part of the head almost to jelly, then chopped the meat very small and spiced it with pepper, allspice and finely ground nutmeg. After that we put it in a mould which opened on a hinge and was kept shut with a skewer. When it was set and turned out of the shape it made a dish fit for a king[45].

Two items whose place in the diet changed in the nineteenth century and which helped not only to reshape, but to revolutionize the menu in the ordinary house were tea and white bread. Bread was of course known from time immemorial in all households except the poorest, even if the dependence on it varied seasonally. Among poorer families, bread could be baked only on the griddle: in years when the harvest was bad and the glutin content deficient, the dough ran off the griddle[46]. The versatile wall-ovens, in which the temperature was first raised by putting in glowing embers and then after the oven was heated, the dough, with a leavening agent — usually barm — absent from griddle bread, were confined to well-off families [47]. They were universal among well-off families, whether gentry families, gentleman tenants — the imagery of Eibhlín Dubh Ní Chonaill's poem when it mentions 'bácús á dheargadh dhom' is referring to one [48] — or comfortable tenant farmers. Where such ovens existed, the variety, quality and quantity of bread was better, and their presence or absence accounts for regional variations in comments by contemporaries on bread. Travelling in a relatively poor region, de Montbret was prompted to remark that nowhere between Galway and Westport was wheaten bread to be seen except flat cakes [49]. In other words the oven was unknown in the countryside. By contrast, among comfortable families with ovens and stronger baking traditions, bread entered into the consumption at both breakfast and dinner of the labourers they dieted [50]. In comfortable areas, like Kilkenny, even in the countryside the variety of bread was quite extensive. In 1830 Humphrey O'Sullivan observed that 'country people have three kinds of bread, namely leavened bread, barmbrack fruit bread, that is, currants etc. and seed (i.e. unleavened) bread' [51]. Bread was made from most grains, and was sometimes mixed. Even as late as the 1780s rye bread lingered on in Wicklow, and in Meath, one of the centres of Anglo-Norman tradition, bread made of a mix of rye and wheat survived [52]. Barley bread was quite widespread as well, its consumption lingering on in O'Sullivan's Callan at least in seasons of hardship to the end of the 1820s. Unless mixed with other cereals, it made a coarse, hard bread. Coote in this statistical survey of co. Monaghan in 1801 stated that 'barley food is very weak and poor, too soon digested, and the peasants, when they are obliged to resort to this diet, can never work well or appear in good health' [53]. But he was confusing effect with cause. Peasants except in regions where it was traditional, resorted to it only in seasons when they were already suffering from undernourishment, and its life-sustaining power can scarcely be called in question. Although oatcakes were universal, wheat bread, i.e. wholemeal bread, was common in parts of the countryside. Bread made from wheaten flour was virtually unknown except in the towns and on the tables of the gentry. It was a luxury even for comfortable country families, and in a small town like Callan, 'white baker's bread' was a luxury as late as the 1820s because it is faithfully recorded in the details of the food O'Sullivan ate when he was entertained in other houses, and was apparently not regularly consumed in his own home. However, with its wheaten and barley breads, and its leavened as well as unleavened breads, Kilkenny represented the pattern of well-established Norman regions. It could be paralleled in Wexford, Wicklow and North Leinster. By contrast in co. Down, barm was not used in bread although, the absence of leavened bread aside, the varieties of bread in that region were otherwise numerous:

Baked into thin cakes on the griddle, with water and salt; I have never met it baked with barm; sometimes carraway seeds are mixed with it, and sometimes it is mixed with butter; however, it is mostly used, and, I believe, preferred simply, as already mentioned. There is a variety of it, called a bonaught, which is a thick round cake, baked on a clear turf coal, and often used on the first making of meal after harvest....

In Down, the smaller grain in the wheat harvest was made into a coarse bread for family use, baked in cakes on a griddle without barm [54].

Soda came into use in the first half of the nineteenth century as a leavening agent, and in the second half of the century soda bread was common in the farm households of Scotland, Ireland and England. Country soda bread has long been regarded as a traditional Irish form of baking. The fact that it is, is itself one of many illustrations, perhaps the most arresting one, of how recent many accepted food traditions are in the countryside everywhere and not just in Ireland. Another reason for the strength of the tradition is that Ireland, including even the north-east, avoided the intense urbanisation in the second half of the nineteenth century that occurred in England so that home baking could better survive than in a more urbanized society. Factory baking made enormous strides in the second half of the century. Ireland, including rural Ireland, itself experienced sweeping changes in the second half of the century as far as bread was concerned. The per capita consumption of flour doubled between 1860 and 1900 implying both increased reliance on shops and even in home baking the growing replacement of traditional cereals by white flour. The soda bread which was becoming popular was largely and increasingly not only wheaten but flour bread. A concomitant of white flour was the growth of the town bakery. The rural horse-drawn bread van was already well established by the end of the nineteenth century, bringing the fresh white loaves daily to the tiny rural shops, or direct to the farm house. Even in the youth of Sissy O'Brien who was born in co. Limerick in 1858, one of the regular callers was Peggy-the-caps, who 'went her round twice a week carrying on her back a large hamper of baker's bread from a neighbouring village'[55].

Home and shop baking made possible increased refinement in the afternoon tea, already well-established and well-garnished with baked tit-bits at least when visitors were expected. With the addition of cold meat, it made possible the high-tea which in many homes took the place of the evening meal and in all rural houses became the evening meal of an occasion when visitors or friends were entertained. If baking — home bread, shop cakes and apple pies — was one of the pillars of the high tea, the other was a beverage which itself from having a minor role in the diet of the typical family, became in the second half of the century both a frequent ritual and a necessity of life. In the eighteenth century tea was little known in the farming class at large, widespread only as a beverage in the more prosperous weaving areas in the north where the great boom in linen — at least in the centre of fine linen in Armagh — had provided enough cash for a little to be spent on tea at least as early as the 1770s. Among the workers in the Moravian settlement at Gracehill living a communal life, in 1794 tea was provided at three o'clock in the afternoon[56]. By the end of the century it had reached deep into the ritual of the rural classes of the north-east. James Orr, the riming bard of Ballycarry in Antrim, commemorated the jingle of the tea-cups at breakfast, and the numerous other occasions in everyday life for its consumption:

nae griddle's het, ane pratoe peel'd,
to mak' a bap o't;
nor weed nor head-ach tak's tje field
without a drap o't[57]

He described it as 'wealth-wastin' tea', appropriate words indeed because from his own description the normal fare of an Antrim household was very frugal. By contrast with the weaver rich in cash and poor in food, tea had made much less headway among the farming classes. In the Kilkenny of O'Sullivan's time, it was not consumed at breakfast times, and appeared rarely along with baker's bread on occasions when guests were entertained to a meal, and even then intermittently rather than regularly. Among the farmers at Listerling in the same county, not only bakers' white bread but tea was said to be a luxury, the priest being entertained with a breakfast of tea and white bread [58]. The practice of tea-drinking reached the servant-class in the big houses sooner than it did the farmers. At the home of Richard Martin in Ballynahinch, Maria Edgeworth recorded that the servants had to wait till after the family had their breakfast as there was only one tea pot [59]. Trollope's *The Kellys and the O'Kellys*, highly sensitive to the nuances and character of rural Ireland, in 1848, described one of the two female servants of Mrs Kelly who ran the inn and grocery in Dunmore, co. Galway as 'more devoted to her tea pot than ever was any bachanalian to his glass' [60]. The ease of access of servants to tea denoted changing times; even in very recent times tea had been kept firmly under lock and key to prevent its consumption by servants.

The growth in tea consumption in rural families was made inevitable too by the decline in traditional beverages — beer-making had virtually disappeared even from the homes of the great, much earlier from farming homes, and cider making too was becoming a thing of the past. While whiskey drinking rose, it was not a family drink in the way non-spirits were. In fact, while illicit spirit-making in the north and west was mainly a domestic affair, the spread of whiskey consumption in the south was closely related to factory production. In this way the decline of the domestic beverage traditions, no less than the nascent desire to emulate the social practices of the upper classes, prepared the way for the sweeping advance of tea within a generation. In the quarter century after 1850 tea drinking spread explosively first in the east and south. In the 1860s it was still little known in the congested districts of the west, but by the 1880s the rural community everywhere was engulfed by addiction. Among poorer families of the west, it was of course boiled several times to make it go a little further, but the addiction was at last general. With white bread and tea firmly established in the diet, the food pattern had become identifiable in relation to modern practices and meal times, and the pattern of fare had come close to that of our times. In being modernized diet and also become standardized, the wide contrasts which existed between region and region had diminished, and to a degree also the contrasts between social classes.

Irish cooking had similarities to English, which were commented upon by well-connected visitors with access to the best tables. But it had real differences. Fish, fresh and from the sea, were more abundant in Ireland. Even the cut of meat for a beef steak was different from the English, consisting as in France and Scotland of the sirloin, spare-rib or edge-bone in contrast to the middle of rump customary in England [61]. Above all was the presence of the potato, whose consumption everywhere is not evident in family cook-books but whose delights were sung both by natives and visitors. Even Bush whose upper-class contacts had led him to comment on the similarities between English and Irish cooking assured his readers that 'a good beef steak broiled on Irish turf, and served up with a dish of roasted potatoes, is excellent food for an English stomach . . . ' [62]. Even if made distinctive by the potato, upper-class diet was inevitably cosmopolitan. At exalted levels, it was not essentially different from Scottish, impressing even the greatest of literary gourmets, Walter Scott himself. In Scotland itself, Meg Dods' *Cook and housewife's manual* was a conscious effort to bring together the traditions of several countries and to fuse them, a process which was under way over generations at family level by word of mouth, and in family recipe books. In contrast to Irish cooking, Scottish had greater literary pretensions, hallowed by the appearance of books in the eighteenth century, whereas in Ireland no books on Irish cooking appeared at all. By contrast in colonial America, a single one appeared. Everywhere in Ireland the introduction to cooking was Hannah Glasse's book; Dutton in 1808 in his co. Clare volume mentioned it as one of the few books likely to be found on a gentleman's shelf [63].

There are of course, despite the cultural similarities, very real differences between cooking traditions. Irish cooking like English contrasted with French which offered a greater variety of dishes 'so that if you do not like some, there are others to please your palate' [64]. The contrast may be accounted for in part by the abundance of meat in Ireland or England whereas it was dear in France. The impact of Italian renaissance cooking is another factor. The fact that France was already the most densely populated country in Europe in the middle ages may also account for greater ingenuity especially in the light of scarce meat, just as its mild climate gave it more varied and finer vegetables and fruits than England or Ireland had. Scottish highland food was not particularly rich, but Scottish lowland food was. The 'Auld Alliance' with France was probably of limited impact, although it gave French terminology a lasting currency in Scottish cookery which illustrates the impact of the standards and usages of the court on the Scottish nobility at least. Lowland Scotland was an agriculturally rich region, and the fact that its wages and incomes were the highest in British agriculture at the end of the nineteenth century is not solely a consequence of the agricultural revolution in the nineteenth century: it reflects simple but relatively adequate food standards before the century began. Meg Dods' *The cook and housewife's manual* is an interesting reflection of the wealth of lowland Scotland. Not only does it assume Scottish cooking to be on a par with English or French, but it proceeds on the basis of seeing fowl as a sign of poverty as in Languedoc, patronisingly recommending a recipe for curing geese as 'useful in Ireland and remote parts of England and Scotland' and regarding butter and cheese making as a 'homely process' [65]. Also important were the strong town life which depended on the agricultural riches of the Lowlands, the numerous small gentry as opposed to the larger landed magnates of Ireland and England, and the close alliance between town and country constituted by the entry of younger sons of gentry into the professions and commerce. Cooking standards were the prerogative of the upper classes, and a strong and numerous class with comfortable living standards helped to advance a sophisticated interest in cooking. They were helped also by literacy; a literate milieu extolled its own interest in cooking and food. The incomparable prestige of Sir Walter Scott was also added to the emerging repute of Scottish cooking, and *Meg Dods* emerged from the milieu around him to the point that the authorship of the book has sometimes been ascribed to him. In Ireland by contrast, the literary circle was smaller; the amalgam of landed and urban society less complete, and the landowners, often richer though fewer than their counterparts in Scotland, more closely in touch with English lifestyles.

Entertainment emphasises the festive element in diet. Among the ordinary people profusion among the poor was confined to feast days, among the better-off to somewhat extended festive seasons. In upper-class circles, entertainment was related not to the calendar but to the requirement of entertaining friends, dictated by pretension, ambition or social occasions of which the hunt was the most frequent. But for all classes, a clear distinction must be made between the fare of every day and that of grand occasions. The sophistication of cooking is shown not in the daily fare but in the expectations of feasts. Even a rural feast will reflect this. In this context, Irish cooking emerges as relatively simple. In France by contrast, cooks from the neighbourhood or from adjacent towns were hired for the formal occasions of country life, [66], suggesting both the standard sought for such occasions and the presence, even if not often called on, of skills which had no parallel in Ireland.

Diet changed rapidly in the nineteenth century. As social aspirations rose, poorer foods were dropped, and continued reliance on them became an ever more distinctive badge of poverty. The consumption of coarse fish, pike, and several sea fish declined sharply. 'Thim's not company fish', remarked the R.M.'s housekeeper of pollock [67]. The pike likewise was abandoned. It might still be eaten in an upper-class home, although the fact that Violet Martin commenting on her menu for a meal alone described it as 'an excellent fish like haddock' [68] suggests that familiarity with it could no longer be taken for granted: it virtually disappeared from the upper-class diet as well. At all events, many food traditions died in the second half of the century, a reflection both of change in popular diet and of a simultaneous decline in the proportion of the population forced to eat what they could get, and in particular to consume the least commercialized products whose price was low or which were available simply for the asking.

Almost paradoxically, the comfortable family was less dependant on the shop for food for formal occasions. This reminds us rather strikingly of the changes in commercialization as a force influencing the character of hospitality and the very shape of the menu. Commercialization was much more intense in Ireland than in France, and became ever more intense as the century proceeded. By the end of the nineteenth century, fifty per cent of agricultural output was exported, a higher proportion than in France or even England or Scotland. The very fact that French farming population rose until the 1880s ensured that a high proportion of production continued to be consumed on the farm or within the locality, and that the process of switch-over from subsistence to market production, already far behind Ireland, continued to proceed slowly. At once less commercialized than Ireland and richer in its traditions, the French table and French agriculture remained relatively stable in the nineteenth century. In Ireland, by contrast, commercialization had advanced over centuries with little interruption. This entailed greater sales by the farmer on the market, emerging reliance on markets and shops for purchases, and all-round greater standardization. Some of the losses occasioned by standardization were no different than those in a richer and equally commercialized society, England, in both countries change being experienced precociously ahead of stable and conservative rural France. Some changes were subtler, representing simultaneously the ability to purchase food for cash, the tendency to imitate upper-class standards which were themselves simpler than those of France, and the urge to avoid certain foods whose social stigma emerged or worsened as access to cash gave people an increasing element of choice in their food.

The impact of change is reflected in both hospitality and menu. As food acquired a real price, hospitality became less profuse or at least was no longer distributed indiscriminately to a large retenue. The hospitality of Irish chieftans like the one visited by Cuffe and his friends from Ballinrobe is a lingering example of it, just as the generosity of poor families to strangers right through the nineteenth century into the twentieth remained a link with older traditions. But even where the spirit of hospitality survived, the menu itself changed, becoming less prodigal and less lavish, at the onset of the nineteenth century even in the most archaic circles, so that the memory of the hospitality of times gone by became a legend quite literally within a life span.

One of the purposes of looking at hospitality and food is to show that the situation in Ireland was infinitely richer and more complex than usually assumed, and that this was so both long before the Great Famine, and even in the decades immediately preceding it. This allowed for, the transition in Ireland was striking, and the lack of stability both in foods and the traditions of hospitality very evident. Even whiskey, an apparent cultural as well as commercial product, is more of an innovation than generally realised: commercial production and its diffusion were both very late. There are very few clear-cut continuities in Irish food traditions. One was of course prodigal and unstinted hospitality; but even this was commented on patronisingly by outsiders, and the Irish themselves had become apologetic about it by 1800. With so few long-standing traditions and so much change, there was little interest in a distinctive Irish cooking, or pride in its associations. Not a single book on Irish cooking was published in the entire period. Ireland thus contrasted with Scotland where national self-confidence extended to its food, and where the national cuisine was exalted as part of Scotland's cultural heritage in the early nineteenth century. The pattern of food and hospitality, a powerful day-to-day force whose cogency is often underestimated in English-speaking countries, was thus dominated by change. It was part of the wider framework of social change, and illustrated in its own context, devoid of the more self-conscious forces evident in other fields, both the lact of continuity and the crisis of identity in Ireland.

9
Settlers and natives: conflict

The interest in attracting settlers had been one of the outstanding features of the Irish land system. The urge was made all the more compelling by general underestimation of the actual population size and by the belief that population was stagnant in the first half of the eighteenth century. In 1693 Kean O'Hara thought that rents in Sligo would remain low 'till tenants come from the north or other places to inhabit this country for there is not half people enough at present in it to take half the land that is [waste?]' [1]. O'Hara's opinion was expressed in the midst of post-war devastation, but the same view coloured all thinking in Ireland into the second half of the eighteenth century, and is closely related to the sustained interest among landowners in attracting outsiders to their estates. Presbyterian settlement first evident before 1641, resumed significantly in Sligo in the 1750s, and the massive Catholic influx to Mayo followed an existing line of settlement pursued by Presbyterian tenants and encouraged by Connaught landlords. The outsiders sought were Protestant: they would at one stroke help to people underpopulated estates and make good the shortage of Protestant inhabitants. The motives were of course mixed; outsiders had prized skills in farming and in textiles as well as religious beliefs which would help to redress the imbalance of religions on most estates [2], and preference for Protestants was by no means the expression of a naked sectarian feeling. In seeking Protestant tenants for Downshire mountain lands in Wicklow in 1834 one of the aims was to break 'the bad idea that they have that the families that now are on them must for ever hold them in the same unimproved state' [3]. But the net effect was the same — the pursuit of a policy in which, whatever the nuances, the Protestant, other things being equal, was preferred to the Catholic. The policy is expressed frankly in a letter from O'Hara's agent in 1784: when the Catholic priest of the O'Hara parish of Leyney who in proposing for a farm had offered to build a house, and who had in his favour the consideration that 'I should like Mr MacNamara better than anyone else of his persuasion — as priests are generally deemed *good tenants*' [4], was to have his proposal accepted only if no equally good proposal was forthcoming from a Protestant. Thus, the preference for the individual Protestant tenant was a logical extension of the interest in attracting English immigrants in the seventeenth century or settling northern Presbyterians, French Protestants, or Palatines on estates in the eighteenth century. The tenant belief that Protestants were preferred was wellfounded. On the Downshire estates, there appears to have been an attempt as late as the 1820s to introduce tenants from the north to the Wicklow estate [5]. Evidence of the policy could be found as late as 1870 [6]. Everywhere vigorous estate management went hand in hand with the maintenance or increase of the Protestant estate population. The increase was for instance dramatic on the Foster estate in co. Louth. It was even more striking on the vast Ballintemple estate in co. Tipperary, a county in which rural Protestant communities were few and small, where there were a mere eight Protestant families in the parish of Ballintemple in 1766. The Hawarden estate was vigorously developed from the 1770s. In 1831 there were 157 Protestants in the parish [7]. The policy was denied of course. Foster denied the charge in co. Louth [8], and the clergyman agent, Horatio Townsend, denied that a preference existed for Protestant tenants in co. Cork [9]. But the preference was in fact widespread and the cumulative consequence of its practice on many although by no means all estates was to call into question in the less paternalistic and increasingly politicised nineteenth century the basic fairness of landlord choice and policy. In a religiously mixed county with a tradition of active as opposed to passive estate management the charge could easily be made, responsibly or irresponsibly, and once made was corrosive of good relations. The Coopers of Sligo were accused of substituting Protestants for Catholics in the early nineteenth century, and the Wynnes were also regarded as sectarian in their choice of tenant [10]. The charge seems justified in the Sligo instance by the evidence of a significant rise in the number of Protestants in the eastern parishes of Sligo between 1749 and 1831. The support of some landlords for the evangelical movement in the 1820s added to the climate in which no good could be expected from a Protestant landlord. A bitter sectarian tension was beginning to divide landlord and tenant long before the so-called land war took place. Some of it was occasioned by national political issues — for example the stand taken by a landlord on emancipation — but it was profoundly reinforced by more mundane issues related to the management of the estate.

A preference for Protestant tenants and the attraction of Protestant outsiders represented one means of defending the Protestant establishment. Another approach was the conversion of Catholics, an aim which was furthered by the draconic property laws and was sometimes strongly espoused by individual Protestants. The conversion of Catholics as measured by the convert rolls, increased sharply in years of putative Jacobite plots or prospective invasion when Protestant fears were heightened and the social and political pressures leading to conformity must have been most acute. Conversions rose to a peak in 1709 and 1710, following the projected invasion of 1708 (itself reflected in the penal law of 1709); they soared again in 1719 when a Jacobite invasion was widely feared [11], and sectarian tension, acute in the late 1720s and early 1730s, was reflected in a significant rise in the number of conversions in 1728, 1731 and 1734. An attempt was made to close Catholic religious houses in 1731, recruiting for foreign service, condoned by the public authorities in the 1720s, was roundly condemned by Protestant public opinion, and the Charter Schools intended to convert Catholics were launched in 1733 against this background [12]. At the same time the Church of Ireland was directed by the House of Lords in 1731 to take a census of population and in the following two years efforts were made on the basis of the hearth money returns to determine the respective numbers of Catholics and Protestants [13]. These, the first census-type operations in the history of the country, were engendered by religious uncertainty. The outbreak of war in 1739 led to a fresh return of Protestant householders made by the hearth money collectors [14]. There was a rise in conversions in 1740 and 1741 and the Jacobite invasion of Britain in 1745-6 was followed by a sharp rise in 1747. No less than twelve Charter Schools were opened in 1748 and 1749, reflecting the tensions and fears unleashed by the '45. Significantly the population of Tipperary was enumerated in 1745 on the order of the county's high sheriff [15], and a census of the population of Elphin distinguishing religions survives for 1749. The outbreak of war in 1756 was followed by a sustained rise in conversions, the highest annual figure so far recorded occurring in 1761, the year following Thurot's landing at Carrickfergus. The high tension triggered off by the landing and fears of plots during the remaining years of war led to pressures reflected in new peaks of conversion in 1766 and 1768. Dean Woodward's Easter sermon to the charter society in Dublin in 1764 leaves no doubt about the depth of fear that a near-invasion had stirred up [16]. Catholic conversions were reported with alacrity in the press on no less than 118 occasions between 1762 and 1769 [17], illustrating the unique pressures evident in this decade. Garrett Nagle, guilty of abducting a Protestant heiress, had subsequently conformed, but had to go through a second ceremony to secure his safety in the frenzied year of 1766 in Munster [18]. Another Nagle, tried and acquitted on a charge of treason, conformed in December 1766. Martin Blake, a propertied Catholic in co. Galway, old and envisaging the successions of his son and grandson to the estate, sought ecclesiastical opinion in Rome as to whether the family should not sell and emigrate, for fear the pressures might not be irresistible for an heir inheriting the estate [19]. Conversions as recorded in the conformity rolls correspond to the actions of propertied or ambitious individuals who had need to certify their conformity: although from the rolls and from other sources the pressures leading to more popular conversions are sometimes hinted at. The recording of the conversions of fifteen couples, mainly farmers and their wives in the parish of Clogheen, co. Tipperary, in 1747 is hardly fortuitous [20], and the twelve conversions recorded in the parish register of Kilmaine, co. Mayo, in Christmas week of 1760 took place against a not dissimilar background [21]. In the critically tense year of 1766 the House of Lords ordered a religious census by parish and diocese for the entire island [22]. The 1760s stand out as an acutely sensitive decade for the rise in conversions and for the widespread belief in a Catholic conspiracy. Charter Schools continued to open, and the number of children accommodated reached a peak at the end of the decade. The 1770s witnessed a dramatic reversal from the fervour of the 1760s. The number of children had already reached its peak, and no less than ten schools were closed during the decade. Even the withdrawal of troops on the outbreak of the American revolution or the war with France in 1778 failed to bring on the frenzy evident in 1744 and 1756. The 1760s were a threshold, marking the last conflagration of anti-Jacobite fears, one which by its Munster excesses alienated moderate Protestant opinion.

The pressures were particularly critical in regions where proprietors of Catholic origin were few. On the other hand, in areas like Galway and Mayo, where many Catholic landowners had maintained their lands intact and later conformed to the established church, landlord hysteria was absent in time of crisis. While there is every reason to believe that, whatever the initial reason for conversion, converts quickly espoused the aspirations and beliefs of their social class, their background gave them immunity from the hysterical fear of Jacobite uprising and acted as a healthy leaven on the Protestant gentry of their counties. The 'converts' stood out in Protestant eyes as a distinct and reassuring category in time of political crisis. [23]. They also dominated political life: Lord Arran remarking in 1768 that 'I shall always bet of the convert side in Galway' [24]. Despite the massive Catholic numerical superiority, only eight Charter Schools out of the total of over fifty were established in the west, two of them, one in Sligo supported by the Wynnes and one in Roscommon town supported by the Sandfords being in regions with some tradition of determined Protestant colonization. Of the remaining five, three, backed by the Cuffes (Ballinrobe), Eyres (Eyrecourt) and the Frenches (Monivea) were founded by families who shared unreservedly the evangelical aim of the Charter School movement. Quite untypically as described by Primate Stone, French of Monivea had also in addition to the settlement of outsiders 'prevailed upon a far greater number of the old inhabitants to conform to the established religion, the consequence of which has been that there is now a face of industry, sobriety and decency in that district unknown to any part of the province at heart . . . ' [25]. Despite their establishment of a school at Loughrea, the Clanrickardes were lacking in evangelical zeal: in 1831 there were few Protestants on their estates. While the Daly family had endowed schools in both Galway town and Mountshannon the school at Mountshannon was closed as early as 1753. Coquebert de Montbret made a point of remarking in 1791 that there was not a single Protestant in the Daly parish of Dunsandle, the Dalys themselves being content with private worship within the great house. In the south-west the situation was entirely different. The local landed establishment lacked the moderating influence from a significant influx of Catholic gentry. The proclaiming of influential Catholics as harbourers of tories in 1691 and the sustained and sometimes coordinated forays by tories and privateers on isolated Protestant communities between 1691 and 1712, remained a painful memory on both sides. Fears of a Jacobite uprising seemed real to Protestants, and for their part the Catholics, who, unlike the Catholic landowners and merchants of Connaught, had not been eager to reach a peace settlement in 1691, smarted under the recollection of their defeat.

The *aisling* — or vision poem — genre of poetry is a poor reflection of Catholic interest in a Jacobite restoration — the most prolific writer, Eoghan Rua O'Súilleabháin, wrote his in the 1770s when poets had in fact abandoned interest in the Jacobite cause [26]. More significantly an influential poet like Seán na Raithíneach O Murchadha whose poetry had little reference to the Jacobite cause wrote a very explicit poem in 1744 welcoming the prospect of a Jacobite return [27]. Protestant landowners and their agents were in no doubt about the feeling, and their alarm must have been heightened by reports of the loose talk in 1744-5 among Jacobite sympathizers abroad and even in London. The earl of Egmont was told in 1744 by one of his agents that the Catholics were greatly elated by the prospect of invasion [28]. In Clare, as early as July 1745, following disturbances one member of the county's gentry lamented 'our poor county . . . (being) left defenceless without even one redcoat in it', and recommended 'strong watches appointed for the night'. By October Ievers, the recipient of this advice, thought that 'after the example of other counties we ought to be as early in our association and rewards to apprehending the disturbers of the peace as possible' [29]. The tensions in 1745 were in fact greater than Lecky implies in his history. The guarded gates of the walled towns, the closing of the chapels at the height of the crisis, illustrate the apprehension not solely of an invasion but of an internal rising.

The deeper tensions of the Jacobite tradition affected the south-west alone: the prospect of Jacobite invasion had links, emotive as well as practical, with a tradition evident in the strong support for the cause of James II in 1689-91. The loyalty of Catholics, even of propertied ones, was suspect. In a tense situation, relations were exacerbated by elections. It was by no means uncommon for non-voters to participate in elections with the purpose of exercising pre-ballot influence on the voters. Elections even without sectarian issues at play caused ill-will well into the nineteenth century, and were on that account never relished by agents. Religious differences could make other differences on occasion unbearable. Sir James Cotter had already distinguished himself in an election disturbance in Dublin in 1713 [30]. Catholic participation can be detected in some of the elections in co. Cork [31], Burke advising his Catholic relatives, the Nagles, in 1768 that they should 'have the good sense to keep themselves from taking any part in struggles in the event of which they have no share and no concern'[32]. The vigorous espousal by Catholics of the cause of Thomas Mathew of Thomastown, co. Tipperary, several of whose forebears had been converts to the established church and who was himself claimed by his opponents to be a Catholic, and the defeat in April 1761 of his strongly Protestant opponent Sir Thomas Maude raised a furore in Tipperary. Mathew was disqualified, but his initial victory and the Jacobite association in his family background — a member of the family had been married to the illfated Sir James Cotter — brought to the surface the hatreds and fears unleased earlier in the Cotter affair. In war time with the traditional fear of invasion more inflamed than ever in the aftermath of Thurot's landing, it was inevitable that the reaction to the events in Tipperary should be a violent one.

Fear on the one side, resentment on the other, produced throughout the century a social tension in Munster unparalleled in the other provinces, reflected in truculent and provocative Catholic attitudes towards Protestants which did not hold elsewhere. Such tensions were not of course wholly absent outside Munster — the killing of the 'papist' Mullenneaux by John Mills in Galway in 1730 and the fear that the Catholics would succeed in packing the jury — is a proof of that [33], but such episodes in the west were quickly forgotten — the Mullenneaux duel lies obscurely in a single letter in estate correspondence for instance whereas the Catholic protagonists of the south-west received popular sympathy at the time, and quickly became heroes in poetry and legend. Sir James Cotter, the reckless Jacobite executed in 1720, had on the evidence of both history and tradition a record of taunting his Hanoverian opponents. He set a pattern of later behaviour on the part of lesser gentlemen with a smaller restraining interest in property and lacking the justification of a close Jacobite tradition for their actions which were not in themselves overtly political. While Cotter had probably ravished the Quakeress Miss Squibb in 1719 or at any rate public opinion believed he had — 'it was a general report that Mr Cotter made a bad husband to me' wrote his wife in July 1720 [34] — what incensed Catholics was the belief that the charge had been siezed on to provide the excuse for a judicial assassination. No less than twenty laments in Gaelic poetry register the profound impact of the event on Gaelic Cork [35]. It was easily the most traumatic political event of the first half of the century in Ireland, having no parallel in the rest of Ireland and providing in recollection on both sides the spark which set alight the sectarian tensions in Munster in the early 1760s.

The unrest in Munster in the early 1760s was the first serious manifestation of widespread agrarian trouble. It set the pattern for the recrudescence of serious revolt broadly in the same region again in the 1770s and in the 1780s. The unrest in the 1760s was associated in Protestant eyes with treason, and a frenzied effort was made to implicate propertied Catholics in its leadership. In the 1770s agrarian unrest was still an ambiguous force difficult to distinguish in the contemporary view from active disloyalty, but in the mid-1780s, when tithes were the main issue, Protestants themselves were guilty of what they had accused Catholics in the 1760s — opportunistic involvement in local discontents. The agrarian unrest in the early 1760s was hallucinatory to contemporaries, because, as the first occurrence of widespread agrarian discontent, the fact that it took place during war could, and did, give it a sinister significance. The fear of combination between local discontent and invasion remained near to the surface: it was behind the gentry-inspired Volunteer bands formed in 1778 on the outbreak of war with France when the country was denuded of troops, and the United Irishmen in the 1790s dreamed of an alliance between plotters and rural groups of Defenders. The unsuccessful French landing at Carrickfergus in 1760 seemed the concrete evidence of the danger, and it was easy to turn the invasion and later signs of unrest into a widespread Jacobite conspiracy. Inflamed Protestant imagination peopled the Munster countryside with French officers and their Irish conspirators. Even before the frenzy had taken full hold, Edmund Burke had written of 'the horrors of a Munster circuit'[36] and in the following years a widespread witch-hunt attempted to implicate well-off Catholics in Tipperary, Waterford and Cork in charges of treason, the culmination being the execution of the parish priest of Clogheen, Nicholas Sheehy, and others in 1766. The witch-hunt was confined to Munster, emphasizing the local and special character of the circumstances. Through the Cotter-Mathew link, it was a peculiar reincarnation of the frenzy of 1720. Coincidentally it came near to having another abduction or ravishing incident near its centre. Garrett Nagle's abduction of a Protestant heiress could have had tragic consequences: the two-fold conformity by Nagle emphasizes how close an escape he had. His cousin, Edmund Burke, had demurred at intervention, though 'expecting no better issue of it', as his word would carry no weight 'against the finding of a jury of the greatest county of the kingdom and that upon the most unpopular point in the world'[37]. The episode illustrates more dramatically than most the pressures leading to conversion. The savagery with which the unrest was put down reflects the depth of the Munster frenzy, and contrasts with the leniency with which purely agrarian offences, no longer a novelty, were punished in later decades. In the 1780s the landed class was widely considered by public opinion to have given very direct countenance to the anti-tithe agitation.

Despite upper-class sympathy for the tithe revolt in the 1780s, a sharp contrast exists between it and earlier unrest which highlights a weakening grip by the upper classes on the rural mind. Jacobite movements, for what they were worth, were gentry-inspired and gentry-led. Even the more specifically agrarian unrest of the 1760s may have had well-off Catholics and priests involved on its fringes. However, continued rural unrest was in the long run to reveal the rifts in the support for rural rebels. As early as the 1770s, they were in conflict with the Catholic clergy and comfortable Catholics of Kilkenny, the Whiteboys in 1775 attacking the Catholic estate village of Ballyragget. Protestant support for the spirited Catholic resistance to the Whiteboys in 1775 was equivocal, Catholic readiness to successfully resist popular onslaught being feared as much as the unrest itself. In giving the anti-tithe movement in the 1780s countenance the gentry were following public opinion and abdicating their traditional role of unqualified support of law and order. The movement had emerged without their patronage, and spread into and survived in the neighbouring Leinster county of Kilkenny despite the opposition of the Catholic clergy and the surviving Catholic gentry of the county. The Whiteboys reflected a widespread ability on the part of country people to vindicate their own stand — subtly implied also in the change of style from Whiteboys to Right Boys in the 1780s and in the constricting impact of emerging popular opinion on the exercise of landlord power in rural society. Significantly too the written word commanded a greater role in the Right Boys, and their system of passing intelligence from parish to parish was commented on at the time.

However powerful landlords were, ultimately there were serious limitations on their powers as a class even before the 1780s. Contrasts in settlement patterns emphasize this. Despite landlord desire to protect the Hanoverian succession against the Pretender, prospering Protestant communities existed only in areas where settlement had been extensive before 1660 when the country was relatively underpopulated. Successful post-1660 settlement in Ulster was itself due more to the opportunities offered to independent Scots by what was still the most backward and underpopulated of the four provinces than to landlord initiative. In other words such settlement had emerged in very different conditions to those of later times. The limitations on landlord power were most evident in the prosperous eastern counties: Louth, Meath, Kildare, Kilkenny, south Wexford, Carlow, and farther afield Tipperary. In Louth, for instance, where a strong pocket of Protestant settlement had been created around Dundalk, the only extensive new colony in the eighteenth century was on upland, still largely unreclaimed at mid-century. In Tipperary despite the presence of many ultra-Protestant gentry, and 'red-hot Protestants'[38], new settlement took place only on the fringes of the Slieve Ardagh and Slieve Felim hills: on the Kilcooly Abbey demesne on the Slieve Ardagh hills; and on the slopes of the Slieve Felim hills to the west at Newport, to the east at Ballintemple. One reason for the absence of change was of course that in these areas some large Catholic landlords preserved their lands. This is true of north Dublin and Meath, of the Kavanagh lands in Carlow or of the Butler lands in Kilkenny and Tipperary, some of the Butler family remaining Catholic, others conforming late and sharing the distaste of converts from the old order for too radical change. There was almost as little change on lands passing into Protestant hands as lands remaining in the hands of old families, the estate villages involving outside settlement were few and Protestant communities around these villages remained small. Even wholesale change of landownership into Protestant hands did not guarantee successful Protestant colonization. The Limerick countryside remained, despite a Protestant landed class, solidly Catholic and Irish-speaking, the Palatines introduced by the Southwells and the Olivers creating a distinctively local internal frontier of cultural conflict.

The contrast between the east Leinster counties and Galway or Mayo was sweeping. The rural Protestant communities were fewer and less populous in the east, even long-established ones like Duleek or Oldcastle. In Connaught in 1831 the population in each of the three largest landlord-sponsored towns was not only larger than that of any rural parish in north Leinster, but was far larger than the Protestant population of any of the Meath towns. In Kilkenny the

Protestant population remained minute in such landlord strongholds as Knocktopher, Inistioge and Gowran. At Piltown, in the Fiddown union, centre of the Ponsonbys, the Protestant community grew from a mere 300 persons in 1731 but it still remained a modest settlement embracing only 483 persons — some 80 families — in 1800 [39]. Even at that figure it was the largest rural settlement in Kilkenny, apart from the untypically large Protestant communties in the parishes of Mothill and Castlecomer on the bleak limestone of the north-east of the county. The reason for the general absence of change was ultimately that landlords, whatever their own cultural outlook, could achieve little change in settlement patterns in already developed and densely populated regions. The presence of a relatively large local population, and of a highly developed rural society revolving around commercial tillage, was too much of a challenge for both settler and would-be sponsor. The prospects of resistance and the capital costs were dauntingly high in return for an uncertain outcome.

Kildare, north Dublin, Meath, Kilkenny and south Wexford were the most advanced agricultural region of Ireland, their farmers already held up at the end of the eighteenth century by agricultural experts for standards of farming and domestic comfort unequalled elsewhere in Ireland. Mixed farming, regular food surpluses which fed the capital, and in the 1760s the first modern flour mills illustrate its technically and commercially advanced state. At the same time, though unevenly distributed in the region, the presence from an early stage of two-storey thatched farm houses bespeaks an indigenous imitation of upper-class life-styles unparalleled elsewhere within Ireland. The greatest continuities in Irish social history are to be found in this region, and beyond it although less impressively in Tipperary or Limerick. By contrast, the midlands, the south and the west, disturbed by thin but extensive immigration, by mobility among the indigenous population who moved with little cost and resistance in a region which remained thinly populated into the late eighteenth century, and profoundly transformed by belated and massive population growth after 1780, have much less continuity in culture. The more settled regions absorbed changes with less profound cultural transformation than less settled areas where indigenous traditions were in fact poorer because their population was small, their life style influenced by immigrants, native and non-native, and their economic resources more meagre. In the more developed regions, archaic features in material as well as oral culture, deeply rooted in a resilient society, often resisted outside influences more successfully than in other regions. A striking instance is the survival of the quern to grind grain in many Kilkenny homes into the nineteenth century. Even the Irish language survived with marked success in Anglo-Norman Limerick and south Kilkenny into the nineteenth century. By contrast in the entire midlands it was little spoken by the end of the eighteenth century.

Landlord ability to bring about change was more limited in the advanced regions than in others. Indeed, the modernizing role of the landlords was to some extent redundant in such regions, because their relatively advanced agricultural state, Anglo-Norman in character, predated eighteenth century landlord reforming initiative. New Protestant settlement was limited, and thinnest in fact in the most advanced districts within these regions: more evident for instance in what were still in 1600 the woodland fastnesses of Wicklow or north Wexford than in the agricultural south of Wexford or the prosperous plains of north Dublin, Meath, north Kildare or the river valleys of Kilkenny. Landlord inability to create new settlements was paralleled in failure to transform existing rural structures as profoundly as elsewhere. In Dublin or Kildare vestiges of the open field system still survived. As late as the time of the ordnance survey in the 1830s, some vestiges of the Norman open fields could be traced in the clusters of farm houses contrasting with the absence of housing within the surrounding fields. In south Kilkenny the presence of landlord demesnes did not lead to the rearrangement of the surrounding farmland that it did elsewhere, clusters of farm houses remaining characteristic, and the small area of re-arranged land around a powerful demesne as at Bessborough stood side by side with farm communities dating from medieval times. At Boolyglass, a farm community had attached to it a square or open space: in its total lack of other features of landlord rearrangement, a unique instance of rural adaptation to market requirements.

A striking indication of the limited landlord impact on agriculture in these regions is the uneven distribution of orchards, often encouraged in seventeenth and eighteenth century leases. The most massive concentrations are to be found in areas experiencing extensive early seventeenth century English immigration: the shores of Lough Erne in Fermanagh, the south-west of Antrim, north Armagh, and north Wexford. On the other hand their presence was very uneven in counties Cork, Limerick, Tipperary and Waterford, although giving rise to strong local traditions of cider making, betokening a very uneven impact of landlord initiative on farmers' lifestyles. Orchards were few in 1840 in Louth, north Dublin, Meath and Kilkenny around the houses of farmers — as opposed to gentry houses — illustrating the unchanged indigenous traditions. In Wexford, there is a sharp contrast in the relative scarcity of orchards in the prosperous south of the county compared to the heavily colonized parishes within the north of the county.

The contrasts between regions which experienced profound changes and those which did not betoken a cultural frontier. Where such a frontier existed, conflict could take place. A cultural frontier does not necessarily have well-defined boundaries — some of the tensions were coterminous with the bounds of the island — but where patterns of immigrant settlement had emerged the frontier was a clear-cut spatial one. External settlement had been almost exclusively seventeenth century, and in a underpopulated island was in the long-run, despite the resentments mirrored in the 1641 rebellion, relatively easily absorbed. By contrast, the potential impact of later immigration even on a limited scale in an already well-settled region is reflected in the tensions caused by the settlement of some one hundred Palatine families (i.e. Protestants from the German Palatinate) in the Rathkeale region in county Limerick. In 1766 some 12 to 16 per cent of the parishes of Rathkeale and Nantinan were Protestant, and almost a third of the neighbouring parish of Killscannell [40]. The initial introduction of Palatines in the Rathkeale region and their subsequent distribution to other locations in the county created a deeply-felt resentment, the Palatines being 'for a long time . . . objects of great hatred to the native peasantry' [41]; significantly the Defenders launched frontal attacks on the Palatine villages of Kilfinnane and Bruff, at the former place being twice repelled by the Palatines under the direction of their landlord Oliver. The introduction of textile workers from the north throughout the south in the eighteenth century was resented, but village-based and frequently short-lived, such settlers did not threaten a local rural community as fundamentally as the replacement of existing tenants by farmers from outside. The most intense exasperation was likely to emerge where a shifting line of settlement existed, and settlement was primarily rural. The two outstanding examples are south Armagh and the south

Wicklow/north Wexford region. Large successful immigrant communities created relatively few tensions: one side or other dominated local society; a stable pattern of townlands dominated by one or other group had emerged at a relatively early date. A more tense situation existed, however, where a stable frontier did not exist, and where the new settlement was either vigorously infiltrating native areas or was vulnerable to counter attack. Stability was lacking, and both sides had much to gain or to lose. The conflict between Palatines and natives in county Limerick represents a localised instance; it was the sole significant rural settlement of outsiders in the eighteenth century in Munster, and the Defender attacks represented an onslaught which had no parallel since the tory forays of the 1690s and of the first decade of the eighteenth century on the isolated Protestant communities in west Cork and Kerry.

Anti-Palatine feeling was evident again in 1821-2 with both successful and abortive efforts to burn churches. But real though the resentment was, the localisation of the Palatines and their conspicuous lack of mobility prevented them from being a fundamental threat to rural Catholics. They lived, in every location in which they were found, close to their sponsors and failed conspicuously to fan out into the surrounding countryside. The real strength of the Protestant community in Limerick lay in the Protestants of English origin supported by the Burys at Pallaskenry, the most outstanding Limerick sponsors, the Quins at Adare (like the Frenches at Monivea in Connaught a rare case of convert zeal) and the Crokers and Lyons at Croom. Away from the lands on both sides of the Maigue, Protestant settlement lacked dynamism despite the patronage of the Southwells at Rathkeale or the Olivers near Kilfinnane; in west and east Limerick it never recovered the ground lost in 1641, and the zealous Protestant landlords of mid-Limerick were counterbalanced in the late eighteenth century by a number of landlords sympathetic to the Catholic cause. More significant examples of conflict because longer drawn out or involving a larger extent of countryside were the frontier conflicts in south Armagh and along the Wicklow/Wexford borders.

The south Armagh region was a centre of tory activity into the eighteenth century, and to the outside visitor it still presented the picture of a remote and primitive region as late as 1760. It was only towards mid-century in fact that this region, close geographically to the advanced regions of North Armagh and Louth, began to experience rapid change. The presence of a few triangular greens in villages in the region suggests some conspicuously unsuccessful pre-1641 attempts at settlement. Only under the celebrated Johnston of the Fews, remembered in hostile legend, in the first quarter of the eighteenth century, was law and order finally established in the region and outside settlers successfully brought in. At the beginning of the eighteenth century an abortive attempt was made to establish a town at Johnston Fews, and a castle was erected for the protection of the settlers. The subsequent establishment of military barracks did however complete the military pacification of the region [42]. The huge parish of Creggan which embraced much of the barony of the Fews was controlled by the landlord-rector Hugh Hill from 1728 to 1773. Hugh Hill's purpose was reflected in his foundation of a Charter School at Creggan in 1737, one of the first seven opened in the entire island. Under his impetus, the pioneer work of Johnston was carried to fruition, leases were set at advantageous rates to outsiders, the success of the policy being reflected retrospectively in substantial communities of members of the Church of Ireland in the parishes of Creggan, Newtownhamilton (carved out of the north part of the parish of Creggan in 1773) and Forkhill. The large rectangular square which dominated the village of Crossmaglen testifies in architectural terms to the most formal attempt at urban creation in south Armagh. The square appears to have been taking shape already at the time of Rocque's map of the county in 1760 [43]. As early as 1760, Baron Willes commented that 'some gentlemen who have land there being determined to improve it, it is much civilized to what it was' [44]. Church of Ireland dominance over Presbyterians in the parishes of Creggan and Forkhill illustrates graphically the comparative success of landlord patronage. The continued colonization of the region is reflected in the creation of the town of Newtownhamilton in 1770 and the creation of the separate parish of the same name three years later. The landlord-sponsored immigration was compounded by spontaneous Presbyterian infiltration into Creggan and more particularly into Newtownhamilton where by 1831 they outnumbered Anglicans by three to one. In contrast to the compact clusters of members of the Church of Ireland, the Presbyterians were widely scattered across the farm land of Newtownhamilton. It was in these two parishes along with Forkhill, centres of long-standing traditions of determined Protestant colonization, rather than in the small parish of Jonesborough with a negligible Protestant community, that the most acute racial and sectarian tensions existed. The eighteenth century Gaelic poetry of the region reveals a much greater consciousness of the spread of English as a vehicle of speech than does the poetry of Connaught and Munster, testimony to the contemporary and abrupt advance of English within the region. By the late 1780s, the tensest situation in colonization seemed to centre on Forkhill, so far the parish least subject to sustained settlement from the outside among the three major parishes. Under the will of a local landowner, Jackson, who died in 1787 provision was made for a school and for the founding of a Protestant colony on wasteland on the Jackson estate. In January 1789 hay, corn and turf at the glebe of the parish of Forkhill, the property of Rev. Edward Hudson who adminstered Jackon's will, was burned, and in July an attempt was made on his life. In 1791 Barkely, the Protestant schoolmaster at Mullaghbawn near Forkhill, and his family were maimed [45].

The tensions were most acute in south Armagh, but the region itself can not be divorced from isolated Church of Ireland colonization elsewhere and widespread Presbyterian infiltration along an extensive frontier between Ulster and Leinster. South Armagh looked to Drogheda as its capital in the earlier eighteenth century, so that tensions and rumours spread effortlessly within the region. But in a less general fashion similar tensions existed along a north/south frontier as far afield as Mayo and Sligo. A large Protestant community existed in the barony of Dundalk and farther afield in the same county, the colony at Collon, founded only in the 1760s, accounted — if we rely on the 1831 returns — for one quarter of the population of the parish. In the 1780s and early 1790s much of the agrarian unrest along this frontier expressed itself in forcible repossession of land. Forcible repossession of land in itself did not prove sectarian tension, as for instance in the Burke/O'Connor episode in co. Mayo, but it illustrates the presence of social tensions which could be particularly explosive in a mixed community. Ardbraccan in co. Meath, even as late as 1831, when its Protestant community had already declined sharply, was the largest rural Protestant community in co. Meath. The sectarian nature of the unrest there is reflected in the murder of the Rev. Butler of Ardbraccan in October 1793 [46]. Farther afield in co. Kildare, as late as 1796, the border counties of Meath and Westmeath were regarded as the region 'from whence most of the Defenders come down to us' [47]. The highhanded behaviour of Joshua Cooper of Markree Castle, co. Sligo, in a region where Presbyterian infiltration was strong in preceding decades, is recorded in Coquebert de Montbret's account of conversation with him in 1791 in which Cooper stated that Colloony 'is nothing but a nest of robbers' and that 'he would dearly like to wipe it out', an aim which according to the traveller 'he has already largely succeeded in doing. Colloony recalls *The Deserted Village*, a poem by Goldsmith' [48]. Cooper's residence at Markree, and Castle Tenison in Roscommon, were both singled out for frontal assault in widespread Defender unrest in north-east Connaught in the spring of 1793. The presence of settlement tensions in this region is strongly implied in comparison of the 1749 and 1831 figures of the population at parish level. Sharp increases in Protestants in the eastern parishes of Sligo correspond to the policies of the Wynne, Cooper and O'Hara estates; there were in addition massive increases in the rural part of Sligo town parish and in Drumcliff, and in Roscommon large increases on the King and Sandford estates [49]. The movement to and fro between Armagh and Mayo was the channel by which sectarian tensions were conveyed from the overcrowded north to the less crowded but growingly restive west.

Many of the landlords of the region through their interest in the linen industry encouraged Protestant settlement. In Sligo, the Wynnes, Coopers, Fitzmaurices and O'Haras were involved from the third quarter of the century, as was a little later the Earl of Arran who seems to have created his settlement at Mullefaragh half-way between Killala and Ballina around 1783 [50]. By 1798 when the village was ransacked no less than three times by the rebels, and the Presbyterian church destroyed, it was a community of 1,000 persons [51]. Strong pockets of Presbyterians were to be found across Mayo, their compact location reflecting their sponsored and industrial origin in contrast to the small but older and more scattered Church of Ireland community in Erris. Significantly, while seats of landlords were singled out for destruction both in 1793 and 1798 in the north of Connaught, the systematic burning of houses as in Wexford/Wicklow was not evident. Though resentment of infiltration was real, the recent, compact and usually industrial character of the settlements meant that hostility was neither as general nor as deep-rooted.

10
The '98 rebellion in Wexford and Wicklow

The character of the '98 rebellion has always presented difficulties. The contrast between the rebellion in Wexford and elsewhere has puzzled historians: the rebellion was most ferocious in a region held even at the time to be relatively quiet and very prosperous. The region was also comparatively free of the primitive, almost medieval non-sectarian disorder which characterised neighbouring co. Kilkenny. Explanations of the ferocity have often taken refuge in agrarian unrest — which is not a convincing explanation in a prosperous region, largely of resident landlords — or in fears among Catholics in Wexford of the atrocities committed by Orangemen elsewhere. The latter explanation poses even greater difficulties, as it raises the question why Catholics in other counties were not equally afraid or why their fears did not lead to a like result. Some explanations stress savage suppression on the eve of rebellion as a provocative factor, but military measures had been even more draconic in many other counties.

Wexford in the 1790s was a more complex county than meets the eye on a superficial examination, and it is in this complexity, and in a chain of interrelated circumstances that lie the explanation of both the origins and the character of the rebellion in the county and on its borders. Above all — a surprisingly neglected factor in the study of the region — Wexford and Wicklow were the most successful Protestant settlements outside Ulster, and shared with Armagh the distinction of being the strongest Anglican rural communities in the entire island. Any major trouble, whatever its cause, was bound to take on a sectarian character, and the Anglicans of the region had followed closely the progress of events in Armagh with its beleagured Anglican population since 1795. Wexford's gentry, moreover, was divided into two warring factions: in itself a significant division, all the more serious because ironically so many of its gentry were resident. The gravity of this division was made all the greater because lesser discontents coalesced around the two factions. Political rivalry added to the social emulation, expenditure and growing indebtedness among the county's upper class[1]. There is little doubt also that in a very prosperous region social mobility was much more marked than elsewhere, and that existing tensions were aggravated by the aspirations and anxieties of families whose standing was ambiguous or required affirmation.

Catholics were numerous among the small gentry and rising middlemen families in the north of the county — much more so than among the tenantry below them: social rivalry was thus further bedevilled by religious distinctions. It was this group in the north of the county, Catholic and Protestant alike, beleaguered by economic pressures and social rivalries, which drove Wexford to rebellion. Many of its members became members of the United Irishmen and Orange Order respectively; they were also responsible for many of the deeds — or misdeeds — which immediately led to the outbreak of rebellion. Moreover, the north Wexford gentry and near-gentry precisely because of their social standing, had connections further afield, and through these links of blood and marriage they embroiled other families in their impending tragedy. They had many links with several prominent families in the south of the county. These families, politically opposed to the county's landed establishment, had quite independently dabbled in the philosophy and activities of the United Irishmen. Thus, kinship and participation in the United Irishmen drew together the destinies of many of the northern families, and of the rich and socially prominent southern families of Colclough, Grogan and Harvey. Among the northern families the Byrnes had collectively a central prominence: rising aspirations whetted by the successful careers of members in Dublin and on the continent, family ties across both counties, and above all close ties with their own immediate kin across the border who were the only Catholics to maintain a social position in co. Wicklow.

The view of the Protestant rebel, Holt, in the aftermath of the rebellion was that the uprising had been provoked by the unbridled behaviour of the Orangemen and extreme Protestants in the region, but that once the rebellion began the Catholics responded with equal savagery [2]. Once the rebellion began, it took on the appearance of a vendetta in which the Orange faction were eager to get rid of the strong Catholic middle class in the region, a fact confirmed too in the more vindictive stance of the Protestant ascendancy in Wexford after the rebellion was crushed than elsewhere. It thus took on the appearance of a witchhunt of the Catholic established families in the region and of their connections. It is significant too that the head of the Kavanagh family at

Borris which had held out against conformity throughout the century despite their landed interest, conformed in this year. The desperation of the comfortable Catholics of the region which impelled them towards measures which by 1797 must have seemed increasingly hazardous for propertied individuals may have been coloured too by their family connections with Kilkenny families. Many of them were long connected by marriage with prominent Waterford and Kilkenny families, all of whom had painful memories of the witch-hunt launched in Munster in the 1760s which affected even families living in Kilkenny. In one sense too some of the protagonists in the growing troubles of the 1790s had some affinities with the turbulent small gentry of Tipperary and Cork of earlier generations which had created many of the disorders of the south-west in the first half of the century. The picture of old Garret Byrne, puffed up with pride in his family, 'esteemed and feared' by those who associated with him [3], able to shoot down a swallow in flight from his front door, and horsewhipping a rival, harks back to the truculence only to be found in such notorious instances as the Cotter case of the 1710s, the O'Sullivan-Puxley enemity of the early 1750s or the O'Leary-Morris rivalry of the early 1770s. Such hostility might not have led to disastrous results in calmer times, as it had certainly failed to do previously in Wexford, but the survival of some of the attitudes associated with past truculence in the growingly charged 1790s could only portend disaster. Another affinity in this situation was the prevalence of younger men, either young men who had just succeeded to estates like Garret Byrne, or the eldest sons of comfortable farmers — men with little of the caution of older and wiser landholders. The south Wexford gentry became embroiled in the United Irishmen or in the rebellion in part through their long-standing identification with opposition to the county's traditional Protestant establishment group. But there were enough personal and family links between them and the Catholic families of the north of the county to suggest that more intimate family links may have reinforced their traditional political opposition in leading them along the road to destruction in the 1790s. Cornelius Grogan and his brother both held land in the north of the county. John Knox Grogan was well thought of by Catholics, and his local connections were close: a cousin was innkeeper at Monaseed, a hotbed of United Irishmen organization. While John Knox Grogan remained faithful to the government and died at the head of his yeomanry before Arklow, the close northern connections of the liberal Grogans may have created the links with sedition that brought about the downfall of John Knox's elder brother, the aged Cornelius, unwilling leader of the insurgents. The Colclough family was linked to the Byrnes, and this link may have been the one that embroiled some of the family in the United Irishmen. Gregory Byrne was married to the sister of Bagenal Harvey of Bargy Castle. The thread of land and marriage linking predominantly northern families with the handful of liberal southern families is a distinct one in the shaping of the tragic destiny of the rich, enlightened and tolerant landed families in the south of the county.

Wicklow had the largest proportion of Protestants of any county outside Ulster, and Wexford's Protestant population, next largest to Wicklow's, was heavily concentrated in the northern areas of the county. The vicinity of Gorey rivalled Carnew in south Wicklow as the most Protestant region in both counties. North of a line from Kilmuckridge through Enniscorthy to Killann, upwards of 15 to 20 per cent of the population of most individual parishes was Protestant. This fact and its importance has generally been overlooked. Pakenham has commented on the absurdity of Catholic fears in a region where Catholics outnumbered Protestants by thirty to one [4]. But in fact, the reality was quite different, and was not quite lost on contemporaries: Arthur Young was surprised in 1776 in Courtown to find a large congregation at service on Sunday: 'this is not often the case in Ireland out of a mass-house' [5]. In fact, the proportion of Protestants was higher if tenants only are taken into account. In the parish of Ardamine in 1831, just south of Courtown, 21 of the 40 tenants of 20 Irish acres and upwards were Protestant, including six of the seven largest [6]. Beyond the borders in Wicklow, the proportion of Protestants generally was even higher, in 1831 amounting to 33 and 40 per cent in the Fitzwilliam parish unions of Carnew and Rathdrum, 40 per cent in the Powerscourt and Delgany parish unions adjoining one another in the north of the county, with almost equally dense settlement along the east of the county from Delgany to the Wexford border. Moreover, in both counties of the Wicklow/north Wexford region, with few towns and little industrial tradition, the rural population, in contrast to the industrial population in some of the main midland concentrations of Protestants, was engaged almost exclusively in farming, and in Wicklow the flannel-makers were farmer-weavers. Along the western slopes of the Wicklow hills, the situation was not dissimilar with strong Protestant settlement in Blessington, Donard, Baltinglass, Hacketstown, Kiltegan and Dunlavin. Tullow parish farther afield was the most Protestant part of the diocese of Kildare, Tullow containing more Protestants than the entire section of the diocese lying within the county of Kildare [7]. The adjoining parishes of Aghold and Barragh and the parish of Clonegal straddling the borders of Carlow, Wicklow and Wexford, constituted a region where Protestants accounted for roughly twenty per cent of the population, the most extensive rural Protestant enclave along the west of the spine of the Wicklow and Blackstairs mountains.

In such communities, sectarian tensions further afield could readily find a response of fear and hatred. Carnew and the neighbouring village of Tinahely were centres of two of the three Orange lodges set up in co. Wicklow [8]. In both areas the yeomen even at their institution in 1796 were predominantly Protestant [9]. Their officious activity in the course of 1797 set a pattern followed in north Wexford in early 1798. The massacre of prisoners by the yeomanry at Carnew on 25th May 1798 was the spark which set off the powder keg in the region. The most serious focal point of unrest was, however, around Gorey. Here there were four compact parishes each with in 1831 not less than a 30 per cent Protestant population. In Liskinfere or Clough parish, the proportion was 45 per cent, in Kilmichaelogue 35 per cent, and in Kiltennell and Kilnahue 30 per cent. The central point of tension between the religious groups was the parish of Kilnahue which consisted of two clear-cut sections, a northern one where Protestants were only 20 per cent of the population, and a southern one where they accounted for 56 per cent. There was a clear physical contrast between the two sections, the southern section covered with small gentry seats and numerous orchards, the northern section relatively barren of such features. Close to this frontier, in the southern section was Mount Nebo, seat of Hunter Gowan who became a yeoman captain and magistrate in 1798, the only Wexford or Wicklow grand master present at the first meeting of the National Grand Orange Lodge in Dublin on 9th April 1798. Two miles away at Monaseed was the residence of Miles Byrne, one of the United Irish leaders in the county. Hunter Gowan's character is best known from Miles Byrne's memoirs, and the judgment is that of an enemy. But the sense of intense social rivalry predating the late 1790s comes across strongly in the memoirs: old Garret Byrne in co. Wicklow had brought up his family 'with high notions of what they owed to their ancestors', Miles Byrne rejoiced in relating how long before the rebellion Garret Byrne had horsewhipped Gowan as an upstart for daring to ride to hounds; and he saw the Catholics replaced in his landlord's yeomanry by 'his poor Protestant tenantry'[10]. Fraser a few years later in an unpolemical context made the observation that from Oulart to Gorey the land was largely in the hands of middlemen [11], in Wexford parlance comfortable farmers of several hundred acres, part worked, part sublet. In Wexford the United Irish leadership came from the Catholic middle class [12]. Who threatened whom economically in this charged atmosphere is not clear. A report from Ardbraccan, co. Meath, in 1814 which suggested that Catholics were more frugal than Protestants and in consequence progressed better materially seems to imply that at least there Protestants were on the defensive economically [13]. But it is not clear for Wexford, although significantly after the rebellion rampant yeomen were responsible for threatening notices proclaiming leases for Protestants only [14].

It is certain, however, that from 1797 Yeoman behaviour was openly provocative, and for their part the United Irish including Miles Byrne were already deliberately fomenting the fear of an Orange pogrom [15]. In a tense and finely balanced community, such fears were credible. Reports of the Carnew atrocity sufficed for the fears spreading in this economically and socially cohesive region to lead to an uprising. It began in fact on 26th May at Boolavogue and Oulart which were in parishes fringing the outlier parish of Kilnemanagh with a 40 per cent Protestant population surrounded by parishes with a much lower proportion of Protestants. Rebellion spread quickly throughout the entire north of the county. It was also characterized throughout its duration in north Wexford and in Wicklow by systematic burning by both sides of the houses and businesses of their religious adversaries. Scarcely a single good house was left standing in west and south Wicklow at the end of the rising[16], and if the damage was less around Rathdrum, it was only because the notorious yeomanry of that district had been on active service from 1797 protecting loyalists in the surrounding countryside from destruction [17]. Given the more extensive urban destruction in the more highly urbanized county of Wexford, losses in Wicklow measured by the claims of 'suffering loyalists' for compensation seem little lower than in Wexford.

The claims in Mayo were not much smaller than in Wicklow, but they afford little evidence of the systematic house burning characteristic of the rebellion in Wicklow and Wexford and the border areas of Carlow and Kildare. Outside the north of the county with its inherited sectarian tensions, most of the damage in Wexford seems to have occurred in the path of the rival armies who carried their sectarian animosities with them and which on the rebel side were manned and led to a disproportionate extent by countrypeople, lesser gentlemen and clergy from the troubled northern parishes of the county where the rebellion had originated. There was no coherent Catholic leadership group from the southern half of the county; the prominent place in the leadership of the rebellion into which the rebels elevated several disaffected Protestant gentlemen, already members of the United Irish movement, reflects this. While no part of the county escaped totally unscathed, the destruction was light beyond the swath cut by the contending armies. Of Tintern, in the south-west of the county, with a small but by the standards of rural south Wexford sizeable Protestant population, Ceasar Colclough's brother, John, after an initial expression of fear for the survival of the tenantry, was able to report a month later that 'I understand Tintern has not suffered much, that very few of the people have been killed, and the rest have all returned to peace and industry'[18]. In Forth and Bargy which, except to the east of the mountain of Forth, had escaped the fury of the rebellion, order was restored quickly by the beginning of the harvest [19]. In Whitechurch parish, south of New Ross, calm was maintained in 1798 [20].

Wexford and Wicklow landlords as a body had not helped the situation. The bitter post-1800 opposition of the landed class of both counties to emancipation seems to reflect an attitude entrenched well before 1800. The Ram family in co. Wexford was the only family, apart from the Southwells in co. Limerick, to settle a significant number of Palatines in the 1710s, both at Gorey and at Old Ross, the latter the largest purely rural Protestant community outside the north of the county; all the Palatine houses at Old Ross and their church were burned down in 1798. A bitter Protestant party existed in Wexford from an early date. In the disputed election of 1754 many freeholders were objected to on grounds of religion [21], evidence of a religious dimension in electoral politics on a scale at that stage uncommon in Irish elections. Lady Louisa Conolly observed in 1798 that 'at Wexford there has, so far back as 36 years to my knowledge, existed a violent Protestant and Catholic party' [22]. Not a single Catholic was said to have been admitted to the Volunteer corps of co. Wexford in 1782 [23]. Even as late as 1870 it was observed that 'Lord Courtown ... adopts means for sympathy in religion between his tenants and himself which a degenerate age will hardly applaud, publicly advertising for "a solvent *Protestant* tenant" ' [24]. In the 1790s successful efforts were made to oust Catholics from the newly formed yeomanry [25]. In the 1797 elections the votes of Catholic freeholders were successfully challenged, both the candidates of the Protestant party, Loftus and Ram, being in consequence returned for the county [26]. The minority who supported the Catholic cause may have done so to an extent simply because of their opposition to the ruling county establishment. As early as 1773 Blacquiere noted that Cornelius Grogan, member for the borough of Enniscorthy, and his patron and brother-in-law Vesey Colclough 'always act in opposition to Loftus as well in this county as in parliament' [27]. Grogan and his cousin John Colclough of Ballyteigue lent countenance to the United Irishmen in the 1790s. The Tintern branch of the Colclough family had in the 1790s given their uncle Grogan the disposal of the Colclough interest, but had a view of Grogan's political abilities as poor as Blacquiere's a quarter of a century earlier. In the aftermath of the collapse of the rebellion, Tottenham, one of the leading members of the Ascendancy party, and others sought to suborn witnesses to swear against John Colclough of Tintern who had not been involved in the misjudgement of his Ballyteigue and Johnstown relatives [28] and Wexford politics became even more bitter. The underlying sectarian streak in Wexford and Wicklow life was reflected in the protracted white terror which succeeded the crushing in July of the rebellion. As late as August 1799 bishop Troy wrote that 'no priest can appear in the northeast parts of that distracted county nor in the neighbourhood of Arklow' [29]. Between August 1798 and October 1800, no less than 27 Catholic chapels were burned in the diocese of Ferns and fifteen in the Wicklow districts of the diocese of Dublin; a mere four chapels, by contrast, were burned in co. Kilkenny, four in Carlow and four in the rest of the island [30].

The contrast between the Wexford/Wicklow region and the rest of the country is striking. While everywhere in Ireland sectarian feelings sharpened very perceptibly in the 1790s, in no place did they lead to the pogroms and house burning characteristic of Wicklow and Wexford. Kilkenny was strikingly free from the troubles evident in neighbouring Wexford and Carlow, and the insurgents when they broke out of Wexford, found recruits only — short-lived ones at that — in Castlecomer, a religiously divided parish, being eyed with suspicion by the country people elsewhere in Kilkenny, Carlow and Queen's [31]. Some counties had a gentry as illiberal as that of Wexford or Wicklow, without this in itself leading to a violent reaction. Even severe disarming in early 1798 is not in itself a material explanation of the uprising. While Queen's had been disarmed firmly but fairly, the bloody disarming of Kildare did not produce a sectarian bloodbath. The reason for the contrast was essentially that the Protestant community was proportionately larger in Wicklow and north Wexford than anywhere outside Ulster, and that communal ability to resist the strains of rising sectarian tension was on both sides proportionately weaker. This is the probable answer to the unanswered question which Charles Dickson, one of the historians of '98 in Wexford, poses as to why atrocities led to rebellion in Wexford but not in Tipperary [32]. Moreover, in many counties as for instance in west Cork which retained its bitter and undying Jacobite memories, the rural Protestant community was almost non-existent: Broderick's proposal in 1694 to plant Protestants in Muskerry was expressly juxtaposed against fears for the safety of Protestants [33]; in 1704 Hedges, an active coloniser in Macroom had noted the absence of 'any Englishman of note in fifty miles of a barbarous country' between Dunmanway and Kanturk [34], and Protestant communities remained few and isolated in subsequent decades. Even in the rest of the county, with town settlement included, the proportion of Protestants was small. Above all, Protestant settlement was not expansive. Paradoxically, eighteenth century religious censuses, for all their evidence of a small proportion of Protestants, had given Protestants a wholly false sense of security; while counts of Protestant householders were accurate enough, Catholic households were underreturned, and a proportion between Catholic and Protestants more reassuring than the reality was produced. While comparison of the 1766 returns with the 1831 and 1834 census-linked returns presents difficulties because it is not in all cases possible to make comparable diocesan groupings for both periods, most sharp increases in the number of Protestants were only apparent because family returns were wanting in 1766 for a significant number of parishes in the dioceses of

Dublin, Limerick, Meath and Ossory. Overall, the figures give an impression of sluggish growth, especially once allowance is made for greater understatement in 1766 than in 1831 and 1834. Indeed by 1831 under the influence of the strong evangelical movement, the number of Protestants may have been inflated at local level. The substantial number of Protestants in some remote parishes of Galway and Mayo may reflect the headway of the evangelical movement even more than the real but belated thrust of colonization in these regions. In the diocese of Kildare, despite the thriving Protestant community of Mountmellick in Queen's county, the number of Protestant families had fallen. In King's county, too, the Protestant community was probably in decline as the combined data for Kildare and Meath dioceses which embrace the county suggest, despite the vigorous late eighteenth century Bury management of Tullamore (Meath diocese) which at that time contained an estimated 1500 Protestants. By contrast, the number of families had almost doubled in the dioceses of Ferns and Leighlin, combined in the summary returns for 1766, an exaggerated rate of growth no doubt but one which reflected the probable growth of a successful and vigorous community. The Wicklow areas of the diocese of Dublin no doubt reflected a corresponding vitality. Thus Wicklow and Wexford were probably unique at the end of the century. First, because the proportion of Protestants was far larger than in any of the rural areas in the south. Second, the community may have continued to grow: some of the registers for Protestant parishes in co. Wicklow for instance show a rise in both the birth rate and the death rate in the decade after 1798. Thirdly, the community was largely a farming one.

The Protestant communities which survived best in the south were the ones with a prosperous farming class which spread out into the countryside widely, and the weakest, depending more directly on a landlord or entrepreneur and consequently concentrated rather than diffused over an area, consisted of artisans, smallholders or industrial workers. Strong farming communities might have owed their origins to a founder or promotor but where a farming community prospered, its economic dependence, perhaps slight to start with, became even slighter. The most striking examples of such communities are the Presbyterian farmers in the north whose spread was to some extent frowned on by landowners in the seventeenth century, and the communities in north Wexford and south Wicklow. Similar communities were established in the midlands, but unlike the Wexford/Wicklow ones they never displayed the same vitality. In some instances as in Geashill, co. Offaly, while dominant among the gentleman farmers and large farmers, Protestants were relatively few among the middle sized and smaller farmers [35]. The community in consequence, while very successful, constituted a relatively small proportion of the total population (13 per cent), and lacked the highly integrated character of the more vital communities. In other parishes, notably in north Tipperary, south Offaly and Queens, the proportion of Protestants was much higher. But though the proportion was in some instances quite high: Modreeny, co. Tipperary (29 per cent), Shinrone, co. Offaly (28 per cent), and Borrisokane, co. Tipperary (23 per cent), a relatively high proportion was economically dependent. In other words, the population consisted less of independent farmers than in co. Wexford or Wicklow, and more of artisans and smallholders, both more directly beholden to the support or patronage of a landed family. Here as in Offaly Protestants frequently predominated among the very large farmers, but were less well represented among the smaller farmers, and there were conspicuous clusters around the villages dependent on landlord seats. This was very evident in the case of the two parishes with the highest proportion of Protestants as opposed simply to the largest absolute number in the midlands: Shinrone which had been the centre of a Charter School, and Cloughjordan (parish of Modreeny), a Dunally village [36]. All these communities were of course successful by any standard, and retain strong Protestant associations to this day. But the point is that they were less successful than the communities of Wicklow and North Wexford where Protestants held a higher proportion of farmland than their proportion of the population suggested, where they were well-represented at all levels of the farming population, and where their distribution across a parish illustrated their independence of landlord patronage. In north Wexford and Wicklow, Catholics predominated among the smallholders and the landless; in the main Protestant parishes of the midlands there is at first sight no evidence that poor Catholics were relatively more numerous than poor Protestants. The vitality of the midland communities may have been affected also by relatively heavy emigration in the eighteenth century from its non-conformist communities. The midlands had been a particularly strong centre of Quaker penetration, and heavy emigration affected many of the less successful settlements especially in less fertile districts.

Mobility itself is of course a complex factor. Some mobility in rural communities was essential if farms were not to become fragmented, and if the inhabitants were to preserve a structure dominated by comfortable, secure holdings. Presbyterian emigration to America both reflected the resilience of the Presbyterian communities as well as contributing to maintain it. Likewise, it seems that there was more mobility from the strong rural areas of North Wexford and Wicklow than from areas where the rural community was less strong. Individuals or families emigrated, moved to the cities or even to neighbouring districts as in for instance the apparent Protestant colonization of Mothill in north Kilkenny in the early nineteenth century. Thus, while in co. Wexford and in co. Wicklow migration helped to maintain the vitality of the community, migrants from the midlands were drawn more from its independent elements than from its smallholders, the movement contributing to weaken the social structure of local Protestantism rather than to strengthen it. The Palatines, brought in from Germany and settled then or later at several locations in Munster were the most arresting illustration of the consequences of the immobility of a dependent group with its consequent absence of movement either internally or towards the outside world. The Palatines failed conspicuously to maintain their economic position. This needs stressing because the fact that they had higher standards of hygiene and cleanliness than the native population has led commentators to exaggerate their economic vitality [37]. In the midlands though Protestants were found in all parishes, concentration was evident in parishes around successful industrial centres such as Mountmellick, Maryboro, Rosenallis, Mountrath or Castlecomer or burgeoning market centres like Ballinasloe, Castlebar or Tullamore. However, even in these industrial or urban centres the Protestant population exceeded twenty per cent in 1831 in the sole instances of Rosenallis and Maryboro. With a smaller proportion of Protestants to Catholics, especially in rural parishes, than in Wicklow or north Wexford, a situation in which an existing numerical ascendancy could be challenged or a new one established did not exist, and competitive social tensions especially in the farming and leaseholding classes were fewer than in the tense north Wexford scene where on all the evidence a state of social disequilibrium existed at the end of the century.

Outside Wicklow/Wexford and the south midlands,

Protestants were not only a small minority apart from a handful of exceptional parishes, but their absolute numbers were often in decline even before 1800. In co. Kilkenny while the Protestant population expanded in a few favoured locations, it fell in most centres [38]. In Rochfort, co. Westmeath, where a landlord-sponsored colony had been established in 1745, a mere ten Protestant families survived at the end of the first decade of the new century [39]; while a Protestant colony and school had been established in Kilrush in 1730, only 3 or 4 families remained in 1808 [40]. Within the short space of 26 years from 1785 to 1811, the number of Protestants was almost halved in the parishes of Slane and Rathkenny [41].

The parishes where Protestant communities thrived were ones where the farming community was widespread across the arable land, where Protestants were to be found at all social levels, and where they were the predominant element among the larger farmers. Such parishes with Catholic and Protestant communities intermingled at all social levels were ultimately more explosive than parishes where Protestants bunched around villages or estates and where they were in consequence predominantly smallholders or artisans. In such regions they were not able to compete for farms: despite official support from landlords, they were poorly represented sometimes even among the larger farmers and generally among the middlesized farmers. The Palatines in Limerick, numerous though they were, were not able to create dynamic communities. Instead of moving to adjacent farms or moving off the land altogether they subdivided land. This is very evident in the tithe applotment books (i.e. books recording the division of tithe) around 1830 [42]: but the pattern already existed twenty years earlier. Wakefield commented on the fact that in Kilcooly the Palatines had been granted 32-acre farms originally; in 1812 there were 6 or 7 families to each farm. Both there and in Adare, according to him, none migrated: in Adare he described them as sunk to the level of the surrounding Catholics [43].

North Wexford and Wicklow stand out as the centres of the most vigorous and successful communities outside Ulster. In 1732 and 1733, one third of the households in Wicklow were returned as Protestant by the hearth tax collectors [44]. In Wexford, the total is misleading because of the concentration of the county's Protestants in the north of the county. But in 1732/33, strong communities were evident in a number of parishes in the northern baronies [45]. The fact that the proportion of Protestants was smaller in many parishes than might be expected in the light of the reliable 1831 returns, especially given the tendency of eighteenth century religious returns to overstate the proportion of Protestants, suggests that the north Wexford community was still growing, destined to consolidate its position over the century. There is a clear contrast, however, between Wicklow where the Protestant ascendancy was entrenched and north Wexford where though the Protestant interest was ascendant, Catholics retained, though unevenly between parishes, a place on the social ladder. The contrast is confirmed by the fact that far fewer Catholics conformed in Wicklow than in Wexford [46] suggesting that Catholics had less substance to protect by conformity. Moreover — a further sign of the strength of north Wexford Catholics and of their wealth in land or advantageous leases — intermarriage between Catholics and Protestants was not uncommon. Some members of prominent Protestant families were Catholic: for instance, the three sisters of the prominent Orange leader Beaumont were Catholic, one of them married to a Talbot of Castle Talbot [47]. In Wicklow, where the substance of Catholics was smaller, there was no comparable pattern of intermarriage. Very few Catholics conformed to the established church of Wicklow: some twenty in all [48]. A number of individuals with Wicklow names conformed in Dublin, but they appear almost all to belong to branches of Wicklow families who had established themselves in the capital or its environs.

The fewness of the conversions is quite striking in the case of the numerous members of the Byrne family who continued to reside in the county. Even including conversions in the dioceses of Ferns and Leighlin, there were a mere four conversions; Catherine Byrne in 1746 at Mayglass in the diocese of Ferns, Marianne Byrne in 1752 at Mochury, co. Wexford, Michael a farmer at Derralossary in 1757, and John at Ballyoren in Wicklow in 1776 [49]. In fact the bulk of the Byrne conversions — 24 in all — took place in Dublin. This reflected not only the relatively modest resources of those Byrnes who remained in Wicklow but the drawing force of Dublin on many of the young or ambitious members of Wicklow families whose rural horizons were proportionately more narrow than those of Catholics in other counties. In all the Byrne conversions there was a single one of an esquire, that of George Byrne of Cornellscourt or Cabinteely. This branch also had come originally from Wicklow: in 1745 George Byrne himself, though resident in

Cabinteely, was still registered as a freeholder at Ballinaclash in south Wicklow [50]. Edward Byrne, the most prominent Dublin merchant in the late eighteenth century, was reputed to be a member of a branch which had migrated from Ballintlea to Dublin: he considered that his origins were gentle, and that he had been deprived of a patrimony by the conversion of a younger brother [51]. The modest social position of the Byrne family is reflected in the fact that a sole member applied to have his genealogy verified by the Ulster herald of arms: significantly a member resident overseas, John Byrne of Bordeaux in 1757, sprung from the Cabinteely branch [52]. None of the other branches, even that of Garret Byrne of Ballymanus who was so conscious of his gentility, seems to have taken this step. The Byrnes were the crucial link in uniting the Catholic gentry and middlemen of Wicklow and Wexford. The Byrnes in both counties were intimately related. Moreover, Miles Byrne's father was married to a Graham from Castlemacadam, and young Miles had spent much of his youth at the home of his mother's people on the banks of the Avoca in Wicklow.

If conversions in Wicklow were few, the contrast in Wexford was striking: some 38 conversions within the county plus another 14 in the diocese of Ferns the bulk of which would have been within the county boundaries of Wexford. Catholics represented a solid group within the gentry of Wexford, both the greater part of their numbers and the richest individuals being concentrated in the north of the county. The two richest families were both in the north, the Talbots at Castle Talbot just east of Enniscorthy and the Mastersons in the very north of the county on estates both at Monaseed and at Castletown. The heads of both families took the oath of loyalty prescribed for Catholics in 1775, both being singled out for comment, Mathew Talbot as having 'considerable land property' and Luke Masterson as having 'considerable land and property' [53]. Both families were intermarried, and they were also married into the two most prominent Catholic families in the south of the county, the Colcloughs and the Suttons. The Colcloughs with branches at several seats in the south were mixed in religion, and the Suttons while they had come originally from Clonard (from which they derived their French title) were widely spread across both Wexford and Wicklow. Eleonora Sutton, wife of William Sutton, gentleman, in the diocese of Ferns, conformed in 1725, and two ladies, Mary and Elizabeth, conformed in the Wicklow parish of Derralossary in 1766.

Along with several Byrnes, three Suttons were the only Catholic names among the freeholders of co. Wicklow in and after 1745 [54]. Even as late as 1832 a member of the family held no less than 632 acres at Kilcommon [55]. In 1742 Thomas Sutton of Clonard married Phyllis Masterson, daughter of John Masterson of Castletown. At least three of their children appear to have been born in Wexford prior to their emigration to France where Thomas Sutton had a dazzling success along with another Wexford family, the Rothes, in the East India Company, and was to emerge as the most venturesome of French financiers in the 1770s. Moreover, the marriages of his children created a powerful interlocking business association which included through the marriage of a daughter to a Bordeaux MacCarthy and of a MacCarthy daughter to Edward Byrne, alliances with a house whose head was consul of the Bordeaux *bourse* in 1768 and with another house destined shortly to be Dublin's largest. Thomas Sutton's younger brother married a daughter of William Talbot of Castle Talbot; his first daughter married in 1768, John Howard Kyan of Mount Howard, co. Wexford and Ballymurtagh, co. Wicklow, whose family was to become embroiled thirty years later in the 1798 rebellion. Talbots, Mastersons, Suttons represented along with the Esmondes and the Hays the north Wexford gentry. Below them there were lesser families, comfortable, aspiring to gentry status or related to gentry, and extensively intermarried: Edward Fitzgerald of New Park in 1798 was the richest of these. The Suttons, who had never failed even in residence abroad to cultivate their Wexford ties, came back to Wexford temporarily during the Revolution: the second comte de Clonard married Anastasia Crosby of Wexford in 1802 and the future third comte, their son, was baptised at Crossabeg in 1807 [56].

There were very intimate links between the powerful Wexford Catholic gentry and the more modest Wicklow families. These links centred principally on the Byrne and Sutton families. One of the youngest daughters of William Talbot (died 1689) married James Byrne of Coolrehorery. Edward, second brother of Luke Masterson of Monaseed married Frances, daughter of John Byrne of Cabinteely. John Byrne's mother was a daughter of Colonel Dudly Colclough of Mochurry, co. Wexford. Marianna Byrne, a spinster who conformed in Mochurry in 1752 and 1753 was probably a daughter of this marriage. The Colclough connection with the Byrnes obviously ran quite deep: one of old Garret Byrne's sons at Ballymanus was named Colclough.

The Byrnes were not only linked indirectly with the Suttons: there was a more direct link. The Mary Byrne who conformed in Wexford in 1778 was described as 'alias Sutton'. The Byrnes held land both on the Wexford borders and in Wicklow. The head of the family within Wicklow in the late eighteenth century was old Garret Byrne of Ballymanus where he held an estate and 'brought up his family with high notions of what they owed to their ancestors'. Further south in Kilnahue Miles Byrne remarked of his own father: 'how often had he shown me the lands that belonged to our ancestors now in the hands of the sanguinary followers of Cromwell, who preserved their plunder and robberies after the restoration of that scoundrel Charles II'[57]. Both Miles' father and old Garret were tenant farmers but their way of life was that of landlords in the sense that they had tenants under them, and in the case of Miles, it is clear from the terms used in his autobiography that he regarded the well-off Catholics living on profit rents as constituting a gentry and even aristocracy. Young Garret Byrne seems to have occupied the demesne and wood at Ballymanus, thus holding what was in effect a seat indistinguishable except from its modest proportions from other gentry seats. In exile in Hamburg after the rebellion of 1798 his concerns were typical landlord ones. He was concerned at depredations in the woods at Ballymanus, and also was seeking to lease the demesne. In the bad year of 1799 after a disastrous harvest rents were slow too, Garret lamenting in April 1800 that 'I believe in my soul that all Edward's tenants and mine would be gratified in hearing of our being starved here, a circumstance they must suppose will be the case if they don't pay us . . .' In typical gentry fashion, Garret and his fellow-exile and brother Edward had their portraits painted in order to be able to send their likenesses home[58].

Strong though the Catholics were in north Wexford and closely knit with the Catholics across the borders in Wicklow, their position was far from secure. In fact the position of Catholics in north Wexford may have been weakening in the 1790s. Some of this was a consequence of the disappearance of the Mastersons as a landed family. Members of the family certainly survived as tenant farmers such as Michael Masterson occupying in 1807, 134 acres at Tominaule as a middleman[59], but the estate at Monaseed and Castletown appears to have passed from the Mastersons into the hands of John Knox Grogan from the south Wexford family of Grogan from Johnstown[60]. As the change was not resented, and Grogan though a Protestant was well-regarded by Catholics in Monaseed, the change must have taken place in consequence of a marriage link. However, the passing of the largest Catholic interest in the north of the county into Protestant hands, even if liberal Protestant hands, could not but weaken the Catholic interest as such. At the same time as this happened, in the very same parish — the huge parish of Kilnahue — the Gowan family, parvenu and strongly Protestant in outlook, were expanding their fortunes. Miles Byrne's memoirs suggest that the Gowans' origins were modest and their success recent. But whatever the justification for this, Hunter Gowan merited the style 'esquire' from contemporaries, and his losses in the rebellion suggest that his possessions ranked second only to those of the greatest landowners and a few business people in the towns. The patronizing tone of Byrne in saying that Hunter Gowan 'called his place Mount Nebo, and planted his land with trees of different kinds'[61] suggests retrospectively resentment at the rising economic and social success of a thrusting rival and its reflection in the outward symbols of gentry status. The tensions revolved around the decisive unbalancing of the religious interests in the parish. Middlemen tenants themselves were vulnerable in a period in which the competition for lease-held land increased: landlords were eager to replace the middleman by letting directly to occupying tenants. The Byrnes at Monaseed failed to get the lease of the townland where Miles had been born — Ballylusk — renewed. Their immediate landlord, a middleman himself, wished to take it into his own hands for a residence. From the retrospective evidence of the 1840 ordnance survey map, Foxcover seemed poorer land than Ballylusk, and had a poorer residence. The change may have been an adverse one from the point of view of the Byrnes. Even Gowan's position may have been vulnerable in the sense that he may have held land on lease as well as in fee. While the 1852 valuation shows that the family held land in fee including the village of Hollyfort, focal point of the parish, it also shows that Mount Nebo itself, seat of the family or of its representatives in 1798 and 1825, was no longer in its possession [62]. It is conceivable therefore that it was held on lease and that it passed out of the occupancy of the family in the interval.

Catholics who had held a relatively strong position despite many obstacles could not but resent deeply the course of change. They were all the more likely to do so because as a body they were linked to very successful co-religionists, both in Dublin, such as Edward Byrne, universally recognised as the richest merchant in the city at this time, and on the continent in the form of members of the families who had pursued successful careers in trade or in army service. These links gave them keen awareness of status and an urge to keep it. The rivalry between Byrne and Gowan which had begun when old Garret Byrne had horsewhipped Gowan after the paths of their packs of hounds had crossed had led to a long-drawn-out legal action which the Byrnes lost [63]. The contrast between the somewhat uncertain fortunes of the Byrnes and the rising star of Gowan's success at Mount Nebo could only serve to deepen the enmity. A deep social competitiveness was thus evident in the 1790s, the more bitter because families like the Byrnes and Gowans alike, had in point of gentry status a somewhat ambiguous standing. Even a generation later the tension is still evident in the attitude betrayed by the compiler of the tithe applotment book of the neighbouring parish of Ardamine. Although the largest tenant in the parish who bore a Catholic name was not listed with the style 'Mr', the next five farmers, in order of size of holding and all bearing Protestant names were so described [64]. The close links of Catholic families with the towns to which many of them had emigrated and where they had succeeded meant that they imbibed from early in the 1790s the radical sentiments which were spreading through the capital. As far as Catholics were concerned, the radical issues revolved around Emancipation. Miles Byrne, for instance, when he was only twelve years old had met at his own home James Devereux of Carrigmanon who was chosen some years later to accompany Edward Byrne and others to present the Catholic petition to George III [65]. Finally, the men who adopted radical opinions were all young. Garret Byrne had just succeeded to his father's estate at Ballymanus, and Miles Byrne had just inherited his father's holdings in 1798, at eighteen years of age. The emphasis in Miles Byrne's memoirs is frequently on the sons of the respectable farmers as leaders rather than on family heads. Such young men were more headstrong than others, and the accident of age in families helped to explain some of the contrasts in the degree of involvement of individual families.

Through intermarriage the south of Wicklow and north Wexford were a single region. Catholic strength was essentially concentrated in three parishes in south Wicklow: Moyne and Kilpipe — which between them included Ballymanus as well as other districts — and Ballintemple [66]. Even 30 years after the rebellion the majority of land holders bore Catholic names, and in parts the preponderance of the Byrnes was striking: it was the Byrne stronghold within Wicklow. In Ballintemple the Grahams were still present, perhaps descendants of the family of Miles Byrne's mother. From Kilpipe the region of Catholic preponderance in land occupancy stretched into the Wexford parish of Kilnahue which though a Protestant parish had Catholic majorities among landholders in the north and west. The parishes were however surrounded by parishes with Protestant majorities among the middle sized and large landholders. To the west were Carnew and Tinahely; to the north the Macreddin district within Ballinacor and farther north Rathdrum; to the east Castlemacadam and Dunganstown. As late as c.1830 Protestant dominance was everywhere evident in Wicklow among occupiers of 50 acres and above: in Rathnew 12 of 16 occupiers, in Glenealy 19 of 31 and no less than 31 of 42 in Carnew. Carnew was the most striking instance of all of Protestant dominance in south Wicklow; there were no less than thirteen small esquires — an exceptional number for an Irish parish — quite apart from the 31 Protestant occupiers of 50 acres and above. The town of Carnew itself was probably the most Protestant small town in all of southern Ireland. From Kilnahue, a belt of six parishes stretched eastwards to the coast: Kilnahue itself, Liskinfere, Kilmichaelogue (Gorey), Ardamine, Ballycanew and Killenagh, in which on the evidence of the tithe applotment books around 1830, Protestants predominated among the middle and large farmers [67]. Moreover, given that these were parishes into which there had been immigration of external families, the variety of surnames is surprisingly small suggesting that immigration consisted of a relatively small number of farming families which spread out across the parish in successive generations in contrast to the larger but much less stable immigration into parishes elsewhere, where immigrants had been sponsored, but failed to dominate local land occupancy.

Complex religious and racial frontiers ran across north Wexford and south Wicklow. Carnew's staunchly Protestant character is comprehensible especially as it bordered parishes where Catholic dominance was equally marked. Straddling the borders of the two counties, and adjoining the sharply divided parish of Kilnahue, it was a key parish in the mental configuration of the two counties. It was no accident that an Orange massacre of prisoners took place in Carnew on 25th

May 1798 as the culmination of lesser atrocities in the preceding days and that it was the spark which set the entire south-east of Leinster alight. Tensions within this region would in turn spread to the parishes immediately to the south of the Protestant belt where the farming class was fairly evenly divided and where growing fears on both sides were potentially explosive. In Clone, seven of 16 farmers of 50 acres and upwards had Irish names, including three of the five occupiers of 100 acres and upwards. In Ferns, 12 of 23 were Catholic including four of the nine with 100 acres or more [68]. It was the tensions in the more northerly parishes which had set the scene, but the actual revolt, triggered off by the Carnew massacre, in fact began to the south of the Protestant belt. It was in the mixed parish of Monamolin that Fr John Murphy raised the standard of revolt on the afternoon of 26th May, as news from Carnew filtered through, and soon the blazing thatch on the roofs of Protestant houses heralded the outbreak of civil war. The strength of the Catholic middle class in north Wexford explains why with the exception of the Byrnes almost all the Catholic leaders were from north Wexford. The sheer dominance of the Protestant community within Wicklow also helps to explain why that county had what was a curiosity of the '98 rebellion in the sectarian south-east, a prominent Protestant rebel, Joseph Holt, who held out in Wicklow till November 1798. Anthony Perry of Inch in Wexford was of course a Protestant, but he had come from the north, and was an outsider to the region [69].

In north Wexford, as already explained, the middlemen farmers were progressive farmers renting roughly 300 Irish acres, working half of it, and subletting the rest. The Byrnes as a family group held far more land though in very fragmented form, than any other Catholic family in the parish of Kilnahue even as late as 1825, a generation after the rebellion, despite the eclipse in 1798 and subsequent exile of the most prominent Byrne in the parish. In the north of the parish they held some 337 acres either singly or jointly with others. The family also held 108½ acres in the intensely Protestant middle and south of the parish. The fact that Miles lived at Monaseed on the frontier between the Catholic north and Protestant south of the parish underlines further how the menacing religious configuration of the county had pressed hard upon the Byrne family.

The middleman system was breaking down by the end of the century with large farms being replaced by direct lettings to the sub-tenants. The remarkably large size of farms in Kilnahue as late as 1825 by comparison with other regions in the south-east of Ireland seems to be a fact which warrants very positive inference that still larger holdings had existed at an earlier date. Former middlemen could hope no doubt to retain in many instances the lands they had farmed directly and on which they resided, but were likely to lose, as leases expired, the lands which they had sublet. This process entailed a loss of income, and also of social status; in effect demotion from quasi-gentry status to that of comfortable working farmer. In the tithe applotment book in 1825, there were only four holdings of an extent of 120 Irish acres and upwards in the parish, i.e. on the scale that would support a gentry-style fashion of life. Yet within the parish, excluding a further house in an enclave of the parish of Carnew, there were, in 1840, no less than nine houses of the type associated with the gentleman farmer: house surrounded by park and woodland, with drive, gates, and in some instances a small cluster of dependents' houses. In other words the physical evidence of the 1840 ordnance survey combined with the details of the 1825 tithe applotment book suggest a process of re-organization on such a scale as would have taken more than a generation to have reached the stage at which it stood in 1825.

Too dogmatic a view should not of course be drawn from the tithe applotment books. As tithes were paid by occupiers, and not all tithe applotment books have sufficient detail to distinguish between occupier and middle interests, the number of acres rented by a middleman from a head landlord may be understated: on the other hand, the fact that Wexford middlemen even originally were relatively small ones and that the process of re-organization was strong, underlines the fact that the contrast between the houses and the smallness of the acres to maintain them is not a purely apparent one. At Monaseed as the evidence of Miles Byrne's memoirs shows, the family had to give up one holding before 1798. If this holding (Ballylusk) was held simultaneously with the other townland of Foxcover, the amount of land rented by the Byrne family could have fallen from a total of not less than 362 Irish acres to 180 acres. The post-1798 structure of the Gowan land seems to suggest that not all of Hunter Gowan's land was in fee and that occupiers like Gowan even if presenting an image of security may have been more vulnerable than appearances might suggest. The fact that in the post-1798 period the coherent holdings of land in the hands of the Byrnes at Kilnahue or Ballymanus and of the Gowans at Mount Nebo had become fragmented illustrates the underlying difficulties which middlemen faced in keeping together the small lease-held estates which were essential to attaining — and preserving — economic and social status.

Holt, the detached Protestant rebel in Wicklow, observed that 'it was private wrongs and individual oppression, quite unconnected with the government, which gave the bloody and inveterate character to the rebellion in the county of Wicklow. The ambition of a few interested individuals to be at the head of affairs first lighted up the flame everywhere' [70]. His account of the indiscriminate attack by a prominent landholder, unidentified in the published manuscript, on the houses of a number of tenants including Holt's, suggests a conflict of social interests whose real dimension can only be guessed at this stage but is not inconsistent with the likelihood that middle interests entertained a dislike of the smaller occupiers who could and were displacing some of them from some of their acres. Fraser, in his account in 1801 of Wicklow referred to a policy of replacing middleman tenants by occupiers on a number of estates [71].

The fact that typically around 1830 in north Wexford parishes several individuals with the same name possessed large holdings suggests that the middlemen were strong enough to ensure that at least immediate relatives remained among the beneficiaries of re-organization, and the number of acres held by members of a family may suggest the approximate size in the immediate past of the family's middleman interest within a parish. These strong forces must have confronted both Catholic and Protestant. They could be explosive in a region where Catholic and Protestant farmer alike were threatened by the impersonal forces of reorganization, which could easily be personalized in the form of resentment, or fear, of Catholic or Protestant neighbour. Miles Byrne and Hunter Gowan, near-neighbours along the Monaseed-Hollyfort frontier between north and south Kilnahue, caught up in the social fears and rivalry of the vulnerable middlemen of the region, were the human expression of the irresistible forces driving north Wexford to inevitable civil war in the emerging sectarian tensions of the late 1790s. Undoubtedly, the situation was made more explosive by the termination of the subsidy on land transport of malt to Dublin in 1796. This was predominantly a tillage region with barley the main crop, not only in the rich lowlands of north Wexford but in the border hill country. Short-term economic fluctuations with their disastrous effect on barley prices must have seemed to threaten still further the very stability of economic life, and to reduce the possible loss faced by comfortable rural farmers in undertaking violent courses that might not be contemplated in more normal times [72]. It was uncommon in the 1790s to find the initiative to establish the Orange Order at the social level of Hunter Gowan; equally it was unusual for rural gentlemen as comfortable and literate as Miles Byrne to risk their substance in movements such as the United Irishmen and in rebellion. These were no ordinary times; and the reactions of individuals and the attitudes they formed were powerfully influenced by social conditions in their own region.

11
Education and cultural change

After the 1798 rebellion, things could never be the same again. The rebellion revived memories of the 1641 massacres, its main location occurring moreover in a region characterised by severe strife in 1641-2, and seemed to justify all that timid Protestants had said in the course of the eighteenth century. But the underlying religious and racial tensions which gave to it its sectarian character outside Ulster were not the sole cause of the rebellion or of the rising social gulf. One factor was the emerging breakdown of social deference. The deepening opposition to tithes, the only universal feature in social unrest, was learned from the upper classes: 'it is common table talk before servants, and even the labourers in the field; can we therefore wonder at the opposition it receives from the lower orders'[1]. The breakdown in deference was first evident among Presbyterians in the north-east in the 1760s and 1770s; whereas Munster violence was vented on isolated tenants or tithe proctors, Presbyterian resistance had a radical and egalitarian underlying philosophy. For the first time, agrarian unrest was characterized by the direct intimidation of the landed classes: the threat to burn their homes. Houses were attacked in pursuit of this threat, and in the ensuing atmosphere of intimidation and fear, 'most gentlemen's houses here are like garrisons', a resident near Portstewart wrote in 1772[2]. Catholic imitation of Presbyterian methods followed in co. Armagh. Indeed, early Defender companies in 1785 seem to have included many Protestants or to have been armed by Protestants opposed to the excesses of the Protestant Peep O'Day Boys[3]. The competitive arming by Catholics and Protestants spread into the neighbouring counties in north Leinster and Connaught. Arms in quantity were to be found only in the houses of the upper classes and with the breakdown in deference raids on houses spread across the northern half of Ireland, being imitated unevenly even farther afield. Raids invited resistance, resistance at times occasioned loss of life on one side or both and the escalating cycle of raid and spreading fear proceeded. The raids were not necessarily sectarian in origin — the search for arms was the motive — but raids in the main by Catholics almost exclusively on Protestant houses necessarily had a sectarian outcome. Sentinels at strategic points, armed guards on houses, had created a novel and terrifying atmosphere in much of the countryside.

For the upper classes, this novel unrest was alarming. In Louth and Meath in 1793, for instance, scores of Defenders were executed or transported, while traditional agrarian offenders in co. Waterford were receiving lenient punishments of three months in jail or a shilling fine. The mounting cycle of fear was also fed artificially by conservatives anxious to discourage countenance for popular agitation. The pamphlet by Bishop Woodward of Cloyne saw anti-tithe unrest as part of a conspiracy against the establishment [4]; so did Fitzgibbon who lashed the upper classes of Munster at the height of the tithe revolt. The idea of maps of old land divisions being carefully preserved by Catholics had long existed among Protestants, and was given a new lease of life by Woodward's defence of what he saw as a threatened establishment and by Fitzgibbon's public reminder to Protestants that the origins of their property lay in confiscation [5]. The circulation of the map of the forfeited estates, of which the lord lieutenant Westmoreland early in 1792 enclosed a copy to London, gave fresh alarm to Protestants [6]. At the end of 1792 a sombre Westmoreland commented (with some exaggeration in fact as not all Protestants shared the fear): 'You cannot have an idea of the alarm in every part of the country. Man, woman and child dream of 1641' [7]. The fear was also influenced by the quixotic events in Ballintubber where Alexander O'Conor, brother of the O'Conor Don, seized the castle and estate in 1786. The fact that this upper class act of forcible repossession involved another old family — the Burkes — was ignored, and opinion dwelt on the trampling of the prescriptive rights of a hundred years' occupation of the property by the Burkes. It was mentioned in parliament 'as the commencement of an insurrection of the natives to regain the former possessions' [8]. The French Revolution with the doubts it threw on the certainties of the social order added to upper-class fears. In the face of the United Irishmen conspiracy and the unsettling raids for arms, the nerve of the upper class broke in some counties in the early months of 1798 and the gentry sought the refuge of the garrison towns.

Education spread rapidly in the closing decades of the century. It was itself a powerful factor in the incipient breakdown of deference and in Presbyterian leadership in changing class relations. In the north-east alone were apprentices sought through the medium of newspaper advertisements, and the demands of co. Down United Irishmen in 1795 included one that the price of newspapers should be reduced, as part of everyman's 'rights for a newspaper' from 2d. to ½d. [9]. But while less dramatic than in the north-east, literacy increased in the country at large in the course of the eighteenth century. The transcription of manuscripts in Ireland actually increased [10], reflecting a growing number of transcribers and a widening circle of readers. The transcribers of manuscripts and poets were originally dependent on patronage, sometimes afforded as by the Brownlows of Lurgan by Anglo-Irish families themselves. Patronage was sometimes repaid by tutoring as well as in manuscripts or in praise poems. As patronage declined, transcribers and poets increasingly became schoolmasters to maintain themselves, and in turn the prospect of an income from schoolmastering made it possible for a growing number to transcribe manuscripts rather than the favoured few who before mid-century could count on patriarchal upper-class patronage. Such teachers were therefore increasingly self-sufficient, and also no longer linked to the upper classes by the umbilical cord of patronage, they were less imbued by the virtually medieval sense of deference of their early eighteenth century predecessors who accepted rewards from and praised Anglo-Irish families as readily as native families where patronage was forthcoming. Schoolmasters both created and served the demand for literacy. With several thousand openings at the end of the century, teaching provided the main outlet for the literate, and a growing demand for literacy in a still only partly tapped market gave it an irresistible appeal for the literate person of no means. There was a growing need in an increasingly commercialized society for literate individuals. At Castlecomer employment as clerks in the mines was readily obtained by pupils [11], and even in remote and poor Leitrim people found occupation as 'smart pedlars, shopkeepers and dealers' [12]. Teaching itself provided the largest single outlet for the literate; the number of teachers, already rising rapidly in the last two decades of the century, exceeded 12,500 by 1825. In the person of the teacher, increasingly a man dependent on his own initiative rather than on patronage, two traditions fused — in radical or republican one unleashed by the revolutionary forces of the 1790s and the older aristocratic one of the seventeenth century contained in many of the compositions which teachers transcribed or imitated.

In the first years of the new century, there was a growing belief that education was in the hands of persons who were morally dissolute and politically subversive. One observer in 1819 commented on the effects of such teaching from 'particularly that pernicious little book "the articles of Limerick" of which several thousand copies are sold every year through every part of the nation which it is impossible for children to read, without instilling a spirit of disloyalty to the government and hatred of the present royal family and English connection' [13]. In the class room historic resentments — aristocratic in their origins but now depending increasingly on the separate racial identity they implied rather than loyalty to the restoration of an aristocratic social order — fused with the heady democratic sentiments of the French Revolution. Thus *Cox's Magazine*, while revolutionary in flavour, gave a considerable amount of attention to historical instances of injustices. Read to crowds of villagers at cross-roads, it reached and influenced a wider audience than merely its subscribers [14]. It is not surprising therefore that teachers identified with the United Irishmen in the 1790s. Obvious in the case of known poet-schoolmasters like Michael O'Longáin in Cork or Riocard Bairéad in Mayo, the phenomenon is more obscure in other instances. But their presence can be detected in Wexford [15], and even in less literate Mayo, in the wake of '98, in the barony of Clanmorris where four years later 'the common schoolmasters are much fewer than before the rebellion'[16].

Literacy — and with it education which was a key to its control even more that to its formation — was vital. It is this which explains the interest in and struggle over education in the first three decades of the nineteenth century. Literacy and schooling had spread solely because of popular demand and the teachers themselves. Neither the state nor the churches had played an effective role in education in the eighteenth century. Landlords were as a rule indifferent or hostile, and where schools were supported by landlords the purpose was to instil order or discipline rather than to provide literacy. Even the Charter Schools, despite their cultural as well as practical vision, were heavily oriented in their curriculum towards practical tasks; only two hours a day were allotted for formal education. At the outset of the nineteenth century with emerging mass instruction in the hands of subversive schoolmasters, schooling could no longer be ignored. It had to be controlled and landlord-sponsored schools provided for that purpose: a pattern of systematic duplication of teaching effort for which there is no parallel in western Europe was abundantly evident in the early decades of the century. The State, too, sought from 1811 to develop and extend control of education. Faced with the prospect of education dominated by Protestant landlords and establishment, the Catholic Church's interest became equally strong for similar though conflicting reasons. Popular education had suddenly acquired its potential for sectarian rivalry, and nationally and locally the issue was to remain a source of ill-will and polarization of other animosities, it was frequently the battlefield on which other tensions were spent.

Changes in literacy were immensely important in nineteenth century social development in Ireland. O'Connell's Catholic Association in the 1820s rested on mass public opinion: such a movement would have been logistically impossible as little as twenty years previously. By 1851 half the population was literate. The Laurence Stone thesis that revolutions took place when half the population was literate has an Irish application. There was no concatenation of circumstances which could bring about a revolution in 1851, but from the middle of the century public opinion hardened and deepened irreversibly in a remarkably homogeneous form of expression, a phenomenon often wrongly attributed to the Famine. The 1861 census commissioners commented on the widespread circulation of journals; the Fenians drew on public opinion and on articulate support from a low social level which had previously lacked a voice, and the importance of journalists and newspaper owners in the popular cause in the emerging land war illustrates the ultimate advance of literacy.

At the same time circumstances were changing irreversibly in various other directions as well. The distribution of rural wealth as between landed classes and tenants shifted significantly from the beginning of the century. There had of course always been relatively well-off regions with a tradition of comfortable farming families in Kilkenny, Wexford, Kildare, Meath, north Dublin, where housing was better, diet more varied, and agriculture had always been characterized — and not only as in poorer areas from the end of the eighteenth century — by a surplus of grain. In such counties, in contrast to the dairying counties of Munster, farmers had almost invariably provided their own dairy herds. The two-storey farm house already existed. Even the slated house had sometimes made its appearance among indigenous farmers, untypically perhaps in the case of the successful dairy farmers like the Aylwards who had expanded the land under dairies in turbulent south Kilkenny and saw the advantage of slate to 'guard against malicious burning or robbers' [17]. But even in Tullaroan on the Kilkenny slopes of the Slieve Ardagh hills, in the long single storey houses, 'the division of rooms, plastered walls, built up fire places and grates' were making their appearance [18]. In the first half of the century widespread improvement in housing took place. Greater privacy, even the conversion — or enlargement — of a single room cabin into a two-room cabin, implied an almost revolutionary change in aspirations. There was a marked increase in privacy in rural housing throughout the nineteenth century. The diversity of housing standards and the real comfort and privacy that indigenous housing offered were often overlooked by high-minded upper-class advocates of reform, for whom as for Townsend, thatch was a 'covering that necessity alone can justify' [19], or Coote whose outburst about the 'unreclaimed barbarity and uncivilization of the peasantry of Ireland' was prompted by housing [20]. By the end of the eighteenth century, some rise in living standards was not only reaching down the social scale but affecting less advanced counties. Significantly, the tenant response in economic crisis of abandoning his farm, had become much less common, suggesting the presence of a much more stable and comfortable peasantry. In eighteenth century Cork, there was a decided progression in the emergence of a cattle-owning farming class in dairy districts [21]. Throughout the eighteenth century the rise in rural migration and in the hiring of living-in servants measured interestingly a more marked differentiation between labour-employing and labour-selling families. As early as 1749 even within a relatively poor region like the diocese of Elphin a contrast can be found within the region between servant-importing and servant-exporting districts. While graziers or dairy farmers often threatened smallholders or labourers, the rise in cattle numbers in such districts implied some benefits farther afield in the form of more ready sale or higher prices for the young stock that smallholders could not carry themselves.

The outstanding economic feature of the early decades of the nineteenth century was the emerging rigidity of rents. While landlords' rents sometimes rose because they appropriated the surplus formerly enjoyed by the middlemen, rents paid by occupying farmers rose little if at all after 1815. Significantly, the land surveyor rule of thumb about the proportion of produce absorbed by rent changed from one third to one quarter. Rigidity of rents reflected both the policy of improvement under which with a prevailing preference for the capable tenant, the tenant enjoyed a greater bargaining power, and the enhanced ability of all tenants, if necessary in combination, to acquire the same terms that the landlord felt obliged to concede to the improving tenant. The failure of occupier rents to rise significantly after 1815 explains the ability of tenants to finance improvements. It had already been preceded by the windfall gains in the 1790s and 1800s of many tenants who on their twenty-one year leases benefited from the subsequent wartime rise in prices, and which had fuelled rising pre-1815 aspirations. Material improvement has always implied independence. Almost two centuries earlier, this was the view taken of tenants and labourers, favoured by the exceptional circumstances of the 1650s [22]. The dramatic prosperity of the early 1750s was thought to have the result that 'many who lately were half starving appear now like gentlemen and cannot be spoken to' [23]. Kilkenny's leadership in the anti-tithe movement from an early stage right down to the resolution of the question in the 1830s reflected the greater prosperity in this solidly Catholic county than in other counties, the opposition being concentrated particularly among the comfortable farmers who 'seem to consider themselves scarce affected by any other grievance' [24].

Education and material improvement with its implied self-sufficiency heralded the imminent collapse of rural paternalism. This was at first sight paradoxical, because landlord involvement in the life of the countryman was never more direct, intimate and sustained than in the first forty years of the nineteenth century. The landlord emphasis on the quality of the tenant was positive; determined efforts were made to prevent subdivision and in backward areas a renewed attack was made on rundale or fragmentation of land; 'moral' regulation of the tenant was making its emergence and the landlord was vigorously engaged in improving houses, sometimes actually erecting them at his expense, and rebuilding villages.

The breakdown was ultimately not so much a consequence of hostility (although that coloured the conflict) as of emerging tenant self-sufficiency. The landlord improvements themselves were frequently unrealistic, the agents, frequently relatives of the landowners — and significantly, if the landlord was absentee, occupying the big house — better equipped to police the estate than to sell improvements to farmers doubtful of the economic benefit and half believing the fulminations of *Cox's Magazine* against the paternalistic farming societies as an extension of Orange influence. Moral regulations met increasing resistance especially from the 1850s as an infringement of personal liberty. In education, landlord involvement followed rather than preceded tenant interest, and on many estates the new landlord interest in education, however well-intentioned, was ultimately damaging to his popularity.

The landlord could still interfere in 1800 with the same confidence as Charles O'Hara in 1762 who in meeting opposition to the abolition of rundale 'told them that they must be modernized' [25]. In 1800, a village of 200 cabins in a bog in co. Monaghan was broken up, because 'so many families in close compact in the late disturbed times occasioned the necessity of dispersing them, and cabins having been rebuilt on their several farms, they were reluctantly obliged to abandon their favourite village' [26]. To build the Colclough mansion in the ruins of Tintern Abbey, the village was cleared, and the tenants rehoused in the new landlord village of Saltmills. Such change, if less necessary because so much of it had already taken place, was becoming harder to achieve. By post-Famine times, the landlord or agent effort to deal with the remnants of rundale in the west could meet with tenant intimidation.

Thus, landlords found themselves engulfed by deep cultural changes around them whose significance both they and later historians have often misunderstood because they related the development exclusively to political and sectarian issues. The weakening of the landlord's rural status was mirrored sensitively in his relative economic wealth. Sharp though the rise in rents was between 1775 and 1815, the increase was slower than in the past, and landlord rentals actually began to level off after 1815. Absolute rent levels after 1815 seem to imply a weakening of the landlord's position, because tenant and townsmen's incomes continued to rise. In relative terms the decline was sharper, and began even earlier. Some rise in tenant living standards, the growth of the towns and the emergence of rural and village entrepreneurs suggest that after 1770 the landlord ceased to have the relative monopoly of wealth he had at an earlier date in the countryside. Significantly, the landlord's role as an industrial entrepreneur was coming to an end, the promotion and financing of industrial ventures in the countryside passing increasingly into the hands of merchants. In 1770 landlords received perhaps 20 per cent of national income; a hundred years later the proportion was probably down to 12½ per cent. Thus, the waning political fortunes of landlords corresponded to a deteriorating relative economic situation. Surrounded by a new merchant class in the towns and countryside, landlords not only retreated from the industries which they had once established and the trades into which they had sent their sons, but despised the social status of trade. By the end of the nineteenth century, while Protestant townsmen did not share the political outlook of nationalists, both shared an intense dislike of the landed class.

At the end of the eighteenth century, in the run up to '98 and in its aftermath, a bitter and lasting sectarianism came to pervade Irish life. In the past, with many families recently converted or still divided in religion, a relatively easy relationship often existed. But after the 1790s the landed classes were increasingly conservative, the pre-1798 division between conservative and more radical families gradually disappearing. Even the surviving Catholic landed families no less than the others moved to the right, a number also conforming such as the Kavanaghs at Borris. At this stage the divide in Irish society became a social one as well as a religious one. A bitter indictment of landlords as a class began to develop from the middle of the century. Sectarian landlords had not necessarily been bad landlords. In fact landlords who actively sought Protestant tenants were often the most improving landlords and for the duration of his lease at least the Catholic tenant benefited as much as the Protestant from landlord benevolence. Wexford landlords as a class were very good. Cloney, one of the '98 leaders, a large tenant farmer, a 'middleman' in Wexford terminology, spoke well in recollection of his landlord, Lord Carew, and the staunchly Protestant Rams were remarkably good. Abel Ram for instance, was praised even by the cynical Blacquiere as 'a good kind of man and an excellent landlord in so much that should a man offer him more for his land than he judged it to be worth he would be offended and only take what he thought reasonable' [27]. As a class, landlords have suffered in modern historiography by the acceptance of the stereotypes created by Barrington's memoirs, and by a misunderstanding of Maria Edgeworth's books which are a parody in which a sense of reality is created by the accuracy of everyday detail and of speech, but where the novelist enjoys a wide freedom of imagination by putting the scene safely, as in *Castle Rackrent*, in an irrevocable past.

As a class the gentry were not as rakish as they have been painted. There were solvent families as well as insolvent families. Insolvency was never an uncommon feature of the landed scene. It could affect any family, and could also be reversed dramatically as in the case of the second earl of Aldborough who paid off the large debts he inherited and despite building his town house, the last of Dublin's great stone houses, could still save some thousands each year. It is pointless to seek a date at which landlord indebtedness worsened, because it was never a fixed condition of landed families. Equally, revisionist interpretation in regarding invigorated estate management as a response to post-1815 rent arrears and insolvent tenants underestimates the numerous precedents in the two preceding decades for more active management, and overlooks the fact that this emerging feature was but the final phase in a well-defined century-long evolution of estate practice. Members of parliament had the same virtues and vices as their class as a whole except more publicly. Blacquiere's notes on the three hundred members of the Commons in 1773 only mark four as either indebted or grossly extravagant, four as drinking to excess, two as maintaining or having maintained harlots, two as notorious gamblers, three as leading unspecified frivolous or dissolute lives, and even one as having begun his career as a smuggler ('pirate'). This can not be regarded as a very complete catalogue of the sins of the prominent gentry, especially as Blacquiere recorded only traits of character which influenced members' political usefulness, but neither does it support a picture of an extravagant and unrestrained life, offset as it is by numerous instances of more socially acceptable conduct or gentle weaknesses such as Lord Lucan's propensity to inflict his enthusiasm for the German flute on his guests. As a class in fact, the landed gentry were more restrained and edifying than the ambitious members of its fringe — the large rural middlemen and cadet branches of old landed houses, sometimes indistinguishable — who followed with some time lag the general refinement in manners.

Several features helped to hold the social classes together well into the nineteenth century despite the forces working in the contrary direction. One was the universal passion for horsemanship. As Dineley's sketches around 1680 show, the stables were more modern than the dwellings; a century later, when the house at Eyrecourt already showed some signs of neglect, the magnificent stables were built, almost uniquely at the very front of the residence. Even the patrician third marquis of Downshire had to share the popular passion for horse racing: 'it is only on publick electioneering grounds that I meddle in it ... '[28]. Talk of horses could upset the visiting townsman like Thackeray who had to endure unceasing conversation on the subject between two young gentlemen on a coach journey in Munster, but in his hunt poems a popular poet like Raftery could forget the tensions of the age and region and impartially describe for his large rural audience the hunting prowess of every landowner in the county. The presence of younger sons, too, many of whom remained in the countryside with the prospect, unlike English sons, of portions, promoted social contact. Younger sons crossed social barriers, and mixed with the people even sexually. In fact, often themselves living on profit rents on low-rented lands that their family connections had secured for them, their incomes and life styles were not greatly different from those of the middlemen, who were the laggards of the rural upper classes in the general reform of morals.

A predatory hunt for the favours of country girls was not uncommon. One of the Sarsfields, a Catholic landed family in reduced circumstances, spoke of a relative: 'as perfect and compleat a libertine both in respect of wine and women . . . not content with what women he cou'd get at his service in Corke but wou'd frequently go to the country congregations for the ruin of country girls . . . '[29]. Only a few years previously in 1715 Aoghagan O Rathaile in Kerry had described a middleman, Murceartach O'Griffin 'as a knave, half-Irish, half-foreign and an oppressor of women'[30]. Many years later in the early 1770s incidents among country women seem to have entered into the turbulent background to the quarrel between Arthur O'Leary and the magistrate Morris[31]. Vague assertions about sexual morals by Wakefield correspond to such behaviour[32]. The existence of such behaviour has frequently been taken to be or has been confused with the *droit de seigneur* (or *ius primae noctis*). Belief in the *droit de seigneur* has sometimes been referred to in writings over the last century, a literary fact which is no novelty in itself since as early as the 1690s the lascivious John Dunton had asserted that it had been provided for in the leases of the earl of Cavan[34]. In traditions, either early ones or more spurious ones of later origin created by sexual fantasy, the belief can be traced in Limerick, Galway and Mayo as in other counties. Significantly, the tradition, even if illfounded, seems to be more common in the more backward regions where wayward behaviour was less restrained by conventional limitations on arbitrary action than in the more settled eastern regions. Both Butt and Sigerson among writers in the second half of the nineteenth century hinted at it [35]. In fact, easy going morals should not in themselves be taken as a proof of the exercise of the *droit de seigneur*. The strong or the rich could always exact sexual advantages where they wished, and the prestige they carried in a primitive society meant that their needs were often satisfied readily. It had always been possible for the predatory male to exploit his economic position for sexual purposes, a fact which is not to be equated solely with the position of the landowner or of his grown sons in rural society: more young servants lost their virtue in the houses of comfortable farmers than ever did under the eaves of the big house to the young sons of a great family or to a lustful lord. One of the knights of Glin, for instance, Richard Fitzgerald who died in 1775, had a kept local woman, and a later knight, John Fraunceis (died 1854), nicknamed *Ridire na mBan* (knight of the women), maintained a succession of local girls in houses on the estate [36]. In the socially archaic Kilkenny parish of Slieverue, no less than five unions involving a 'Mr' or an 'Esq.', to whom successive illegitimate children were born, can be traced [37]. A very famous instance in the west was Christopher French St George who, after he had made over the estate to his son, publicly kept a *chère amie* in Kilcolgan Lodge [38]. Some of the later St Georges married down the social scale. All this does not even remotely establish the exercise of the *droit de seigneur* on the estate although for many the St Georges are an unshakeable proof of its existence. After his death, the third earl of Leitrim, a crusty batchelor, was claimed on no substantive evidence whatever to have exercised it, and his assassination in 1878, motivated by agrarian issues, to have been carried out by the enraged tenant father of a defiled daughter [39]. The unfortunate earl has even been described as the last man to have exercised the right: character assassination followed political assassination.

In fact, what has often been confused with the mythical *droit de seigneur* is the very real practice of abduction in which with the support of his followers a suitor kidnapped a girl, and after a form of marriage ceremony ravished her. Maxwell in his *Wild Sports of the West* noted abduction as a frequent occurence in Mayo, distinguishing between mild instances where the girl was abducted with her consent, thus evading parental opposition to a match, and other cases involving 'girls having property' where 'they were less easily recoverable by their families' [40]. In co. Kilkenny the families of rich farmers were particularly at risk in the class war of the mid-1770s: no less than four girls were carried off in a single fortnight [41]. Many of these abductions were carried out by people of some standing at least at local level, and condoned at such a level the practice inevitably lingered on into the 1850s [42]. In tradition the *droit de seigneur* has been confused with such abductions: this is very evident in the case of the dramatist M.J.Molloy who has written a play on the theme but whose traditions mistakenly confuse the *droit de seigneur* with the instances of the abduction of girls with the help of a private pressgang by persons of local note [43]. Abductions were a form of licence or anarchy, medieval in origin, which was spread widely though unevenly in Irish society in the seventeenth and eighteenth centuries, affecting Anglo-Irish families as well as Irish. Abductors were sometimes people of standing, though more commonly they were comparatively young men of some social position but not enough to make a credible match by more orthodox means. Johnston, the would-be abductor of Miss Newcomen in county Longford in 1772, is a good instance: only 22 years of age, recently or still at college, led on by 'villainy, ambition and bad advice' and the encouragement of his friends [44]. What is most striking is that these abductions were not disavowed even by upper class opinion as strongly as they should have been, and executions were rare. The execution of Sir James Cotter in 1720 for his ravishing of Miss Squibb was exceptional; it was regarded as an instance of judicial assassination in which he was executed for his Jacobite leanings rather than his lechery. Even the tory jury which found him guilty had called for a pardon [45]. The trial after the abduction of the daughter of a tenant on another landlord's estate by a co. Limerick gentleman, Henry Grady, illustrates the lenient attitude of the times. The plea to the Lord Lieutenant the Duke of Bedford for leniency laid emphasis first and foremost on the fact that he, his father and grandfather were Protestant: in other words their respectability was pleaded in his favour: 'there are many extenuating circumstances in the case, and the effect on Miss Groves will be deplorable if the law is allowed to run its course against Grady' [46]. Garret Byrne and James Strange, the two abductors of the Kennedy sisters, were both executed in Kilkenny in 1780, the hostility of popular opinion to the executions however showing that disavowal of abduction was still in its infancy in the regions where it had been commonplace.

But times were changing none the less. Upper-class involvement in abduction waned to leave the practice to more modest practitioners, just as the departure of the minor gentry from the faction fights a generation earlier reduced the latter to purely rural and senseless brawls. In 1801, when two abductors were executed, the respiting of a more highly placed third abductor by the justice, under improper representation from the Castle, drove Lord Clare the chancellor to flights of indignation:

Murphy succeeded in ravishing his lady. Sir Henry Hayes attempted to ravish his but did not succeed, because the cock would not fight, and after standing out all legal process for five years, and bidding defiance to two proclamations offering a reward of £500 for apprehending him, he was at length brought to trial, found guilty, and respited by Mr Day, upon a silly doubt in his mind on a point of law . . . Certainly if ever any crime deserved capital punishment, Mr Murphy's, Sir Henry's and Mr Lupton's, did merit it. But it will be difficult to persuade the lower orders that equal justice has been administered to rich and poor [47].

Hinted at in the last line is the difficulty of getting popular support for stern justice in cases of abduction. But times had changed even for Sir Henry Hayes: he was transported to Australia. Moreover, popular opinion itself was also beginning to change. Both abductions and instances of rural women kept by landowners were declining. The rural classes were becoming more resistant to the demands of the brutal petty tyrants of the countryside and less compliant to the allurements of lascivious members of the rural gentry. Young after his Irish tour had remarked that 'landlords of consequence have assured me that many of their cottiers would think themselves honoured by having their wives and daughters sent for to the bed of their master' [48], a statement which is not the proof of the *droit de seigneur* that it is sometimes taken to be but is testimony to the circumstances in which a complaisant morality could exist. Wayward morals were beginning to decline, a trend reinforced by the active role of the clergy. Early eighteenth century clergy were usually members of the Catholic gentry, and could not distance themselves at least in public condemnation from the accepted practices that sometimes took place among their peers. But in the more mobile society of the early nineteenth century the parish clergy, though still from comfortable backgrounds, were from outside the gentry ranks, and found it easier to attempt public enforcement of new and more exacting standards of moral conduct. John Fraunceis Fitzgerald for instance had a long-standing quarrel with the parish priest of Glin occasioned by his kept parishioners [49]. Vague local traditions of landlord-priest hostility as at Kiltullagh, co. Galway sometimes refer to priestly opposition to a maintained lady. The upper classes themselves were changing too quite independently of their tenantry, especially because the sons were frequently better educated, and spent their lives profitlessly and aimlessly at home or as minor gentlemen tenants less often [50]. Life around the great house or in an independent home on a profit rent, though it created familiarity with a wide range of people, was ultimately demoralising. In the nineteenth century, with large intermediate tenancies declining, younger sons increasingly served in the army, in the colonies or even entered the new careers such as journalism in London. For the individual, the change was immensely fulfilling, but the loss of the younger sons from the countryside and its humdrum temptations and pastimes made the great family increasingly remote to the ordinary people.

The contribution of the gentry to Irish life, minimised on one side, has often been overstated on the other by writers such as W.B.Yeats. Their business ideas were frequently extravagant and impractical in industrial projects in the eighteenth century, even a century later in the grandiose farm buildings they erected during the high-farming vogue. Unlike the Scots, they never had close contact with the universities, and the progression of younger sons into trade had been more evident among the Anglo-Norman gentry in the hinterland of Galway and Waterford than elsewhere. Even the landlord impact on agriculture and the environment, very real though it was, should not be overstressed as the most advanced agricultural areas remained the Anglo-Norman regions of north and south Leinster, already the most advanced to start with. Nevertheless the transitional role of landlords was enormous, especially beyond the Anglo-Norman regions where seventeenth century landowners and the immigrants they brought in profoundly changed the countryside and even its language. Irish had ceased to be spoken in north Wexford and Wicklow long before the end of the eighteenth century; there was less Irish spoken in

King's, Queen's and Westmeath than in Meath, north Dublin, or the Tallaght district of the south of Dublin; Kilkenny and Limerick were Irish-speaking into the nineteenth century. Above all it was a colonial society. Settlers were resented more than landowners, the memories of the 1641 'massacres' were revived in blood in 1798. In turn 1798 itself was celebrated a hundred years later as yet another bloodbath centenary. The first modern historians wrote in a poisoned climate in the 1860s, Ireland's tale starting from the massacres and the conflicting estimates of their extent. The settler had been resented in the seventeenth century; in the complicated political, cultural and social unfolding of the nineteenth century, the landowner was rejected as well in the culmination to a long evolution in which his paternalistic role had ceased to be useful, and the self-sufficient tenant and the unsympathetic town nationalist failed across the growing rancours of an embittered century to comprehend the passing landlord world.

12
The character and identity of modern Ireland

Two events in modern Irish history are exceptional: the Great Famine and the 1798 rebellion, and they mirror much of the character of Ireland and of Irish history. The more unusual of the two is the Great Famine, which coincided with the emergence of the sustained emigration from the 1840s to the 1960s. This outflow was larger than the natural increase in population, and is no less unique than the Great Famine itself. Many countries have had famines in the course of their history, but none in western or northwestern Europe has experienced one in such recent times. Nor has famine in any other country been followed by a sustained fall in population: such did not happen even in the case of Finland which experienced a famine even later than Ireland. The significance of the Great Famine lies not only in the actual crisis but in the underlying vulnerability which explains why a food shortage was not a transient crisis but assumed the proportions of a major and ongoing disaster. Assessment of the vulnerability of the Irish economy is complex, however, because the spectre of famine had receded between 1674 and 1740, and though famine recurred at a later date, even regional famine was not experienced again until 1821. The problem is one of appreciating how circumstances admitted to improvement but did not provide a sufficient base to put Ireland like its western counterparts beyond the threshold of famine. Indeed, it is necessary to appreciate that Ireland gradually drifted towards disaster despite a sustained growth in its foreign trade, and what was tantamount to a revolution in its agriculture. Even in wheat, for which its comparative advantages were relatively slight, it led the revolution in flour milling from the 1760s into the 1830s. The essential factor to appreciate is that Irish living standards were extremely low even at the outset of the seventeenth century, and that dramatic increases in output did not raise per capita living standards much beyond subsistence level. Moreover, given the simultaneous occurrence of sustained growth of trade and population, circumstances admitted at the same time of the emergence of comfortable farmers who benfited from trade, and of immiseration at the base of the social order.

Hence the complexity of dietary change is not a detail in Irish social change, but a central aspect of the entire range of social and cultural changes in Ireland. The underlying depth of Irish poverty serves to remind us that the blight of itself is not the basic factor in the Irish famine of 1845-48. It is not the potato but the inability to replace it in crisis which is the most relevant feature. A reversal from the relatively favourable food circumstances of 1674-1740 is therefore highly relevant in understanding the long drawn out background to the Great Famine. The so-called 'gap in the famines' after 1740 is something of an illusion because it glosses over two contrasting trends within the community. By the 1780s food supply at the base of the rural community was becoming precarious again. Dependence on the potato was more general, and cash incomes, which had helped to sustain the rural community, were harder to come by among marginal families or on marginal lands. The complexity of the evolution of food supply is very significant. If the pattern of meals and the character of hospitality is analysed, it is clear that there was a good deal of conservatism in milieus above the lower classes. In fact, given the new wealth of many, the circumstances of many rural dwellers on balance actually improved. The famine of 1845-48, disastrous though it was, was much less general than previous famines. Farmers were no longer at risk in the way that the entire community was in 1740-1. For them the situation was simply one of economic crisis, often of relatively manageable proportions, not one of survival. It entailed some reduction in cash when the potato failed because they ate some of the grain which they would otherwise have sold and because cottiers were unable to pay them the rents of their potato plots.

Irish history and the Famine itself demonstrate the changes in the social structure which created a solid core in the countryside below the various gentry categories. Irish history also illuminates the religious divide in the countryside around which many of the social tensions of the age coalesced. The 1798 rebellion is significant both because it reflects the forces of religious division in Ireland between Presbyterians and Anglicans as well as Catholics and Anglicans, and because religious conflict drew some of its tensions from the underlying evolution of the social structure of the countryside. The 1798 rebellion was the most ferocious civil war in Ireland, and one of the most bitter in modern European history. It is treated with caution in most modern textbooks as a phenomenon which is difficult to account for or which was unexpected. Most have been eager to underplay its sectarian character in contrast to nineteenth century writers who emphasised it vehemently. If its sectarian character is highlighted, it did not really begin in Leinster or in Antrim, but in County Armagh in 1795, and the whole period 1795-98 represented a single period of inexorable progress. Armagh was the central point of the entire trouble. Armagh did not rise in 1798: the northern rebellion in 1798 was non-sectarian and was largely confined to the radical Presbyterians in Antrim and Down. The sectarian troubles which were more characteristic of 1798 stemmed from Armagh: Catholics fleeing from Armagh brought their tensions to Mayo, centre of the rebellion in the west in that year, and the militant defence of the establishment by the most Anglican region in the north was bound to have a response in the most Anglican region in the south, especially as Anglicans in both regions felt themselves threatened by social forces favouring other groups. The key counties in these troubles were the most prosperous in Ireland: Armagh was at the peak of its linen prosperity, while Wexford and south Wicklow were a highly advanced agricultural region of large farmers and small gentry. However, economic change promoted social change, and its ramifications were particularly complex in districts which were evenly divided in religion. Armagh was in religious terms the most diversified county in Ireland with Presbyterians, Anglicans and Catholics often in close proximity; in north Wexford and south Wicklow, 25 to 50 per cent of the population in many parishes were Protestant. In Armagh weavers were encroaching on the county's farmers, and Catholics among the many smallholders were also increasing their social stake through linen. The rise in their status is reflected in the fact that they often had firearms which had been popularised by the Volunteer movement. Firearms were a symbol of status or emancipation: hence the emphasis by Protestant gangs on raiding Catholic houses for arms from the 1780s. In Wexford, the tensions revolved around the small middlemen gentry farmers. In both counties, they reflected economic problems. In Armagh weavers were bidding farm land out of the reach of farmers; the uprooting of orchards in the Anglican areas of north Armagh in 1790s betokened the pressure on land; and the Presbyterians were much less radical than their brethren in Antrim and Down. In Wexford and south Wicklow, a food exporting region in contrast to Armagh which was a food importing county, the class at risk was one with farms often running into hundreds of acres in place of the tens of acres of Armagh's dwindling farm class. But the situation made Catholic and Protestant alike aggressive. As Catholics were better-represented among the smallholders than among larger farmers, the tendency to let directly to undertenants menaced Protestants more than Catholics. It created a destructive competition among both groups to hold or rent land. In their precarious position they were both combative. Comfortable, educated rural Catholics became United Irishmen, Protestants sought the support of the Orange Order, in whose spread in southern Ireland they took the initiative.

The landlords are not central in Irish history; indeed all these issues can be viewed outside a narrow agrarian context. The foundation and spread of the Orange Order originated in popular initiative, and landlord acquiescence or participation followed: some even opposed it resolutely. The role of the landed class has often been written too large in Irish history because of the political obsession with undoing the land system in the late nineteenth century. Indeed the concept of 'land system' suggests a more coherent organization than it actually possessed. The role of landlords was greatest in backward areas, where they often initiated change. As regions developed, they lost much of their influence: indeed, landlords after 1800 were still initiating social changes in the remote west and north-west in a way which was no longer possible or acceptable in the east. Ultimately, the occupation of land was more important than ownership. The biggest impact on Ireland was made by settlers, many of whom were quite independent of their landlords. Indeed, landlords, ever more fearful of radical ideas, distrusted Presbyterians increasingly in the 1790s: northern landlords saw them as a bigger threat to the constitution than Catholics. It was only the threat to the establishment by foreign invasion and Catholic resurgence that created a union between landlord and Presbyterian tenant. But it was an uneasy union. A divide was always there. It was behind the differences between southern and northern unionists in the early 1920s, and more recently behind the failure of the north's gentry who were still in charge of Ulster government to carry Protestant opinion with them in the early 1970s. The Union itself was a defeat for the Orange gentry of the day, a factor which made it easier, incidentally, for Presbyterians opinion no less than for Catholic to acquiesce in the Union in 1800. In fact, the Catholic relief acts of 1778 and 1793, passed for imperial reasons rather than local ones, had already presaged the change which was later to be reflected in the dismantling of many institutions in Ireland in the hope of keeping the Union intact. Within Ireland, the gentry were increasingly isolated as the nineteenth century went on. English public opinion and English statesmen held them more responsible for Ireland's problems than they actually were. Even Anglican townsmen shared the general Catholic or nationalist antipathy for the landed class.

The relative unimportance of the landed class is reflected in the very course of social change in Ireland. The great underlying changes in social life and organization were under way long before the collapse of Irish landlord society. Increasingly, whether in backing the Orange Order, or in seeking to patronise education, an activity in which they had originally little interest, they found themselves responding to changes rather than leading them. They no longer shaped the world as they once had, and in the second half of the nineteenth century the great number of local memorials to landlords erected by the connivance of landed families reflected an awareness that the loyalty of the tenantry could no longer be taken for granted. In most societies, the landed classes have been a source of stability. Even where they have been undermined by revolution as in France in 1789 or in Russia in 1917, the cultural outlook of those who replaced them was not much different from their own. In France the passing of its Ancien Regime nobility had relatively little effect on the nature of French life and institutions. Even in Russia the Bolsheviks cherished the buildings, art and cultural institutions of the old regime. In Ireland, by contrast, although the passing of the old regime was both unbloody and operated slowly, the disavowal of all that it stood for was more vehement than in Russia or France, and with few exceptions the leaders and public opinion alike in the new state were not prepared to care for the buildings, institutions or cultural aspirations of the old order.

There was in the aspirations of the new order little love for older institutions or traditions. Indeed, this feature was but part of the general poverty of tradition in Ireland, even in intimate areas of life. In diet, for instance, the course of change was so sustained that little was traditional. Hospitality likewise changed in a wholesale fashion, and even whiskey, today regarded as a traditional drink, was as a popular beverage an innovation in the eighteenth century spreading out from the more Scottish parts of the country. Indeed, the country's landed establishment with its English values undermined the prestige of local traditions. By 1800, for instance, the prestige of Anglo-Irish landed position had overborne the readiness or willingness of landed families to have close ties with trade. The Irish view of their country and its ways was uncertain and apologetic. The lively and observant French traveller, De la Latocnaye, observed that 'the general wish is to have everything in the English fashion, and this is not good.'[1] An American who had known the Irish both in Bordeaux and in Dublin, observed that one moment they 'appear to worship their country, and the next utter the severest sarcasms against it'.[2] The contrast between Maria Edgeworth and Scott epitomises the Irish lack of self-confidence. Maria Edgeworth looked at her own country with some condescension, whereas Scott exalted Scottish history, culture and even food, marking the crest of a great wave of Scottish self-confidence.

One of the most arresting illustrations of all of the Irish readiness to abandon traditions is the decline of Irish. Contrary to what is often said, there is little evidence that English had made great inroads before 1800. And what is particularly significant is that it was the educational system in the decades before 1831, largely at that time in the hands of teachers with a foot in the old culture, which rejected the language. Ultimately a crisis of identity arose in Ireland. Catholics had few traditions and were anglicised. Protestants, increasingly disowned in English policy, had to find an identity which might give them a role in Ireland. Hence some Protestant intellectuals were behind the interest in creating a distinctive culture and preserving the Irish language. Nationalists, eager to find symbols for their nationalist aspirations, quickly took the movement over, politicised it, and confined it increasingly to the linguistic element, the narrowest and least congenial feature in it. Given the poverty of cherished traditions, an almost mythical past or golden age had to be invented. The interest in archaeology was largely a contribution of Protestant gentry and clergymen to the general awakening to Irish culture, but a fervent belief by all in a golden age in the Island of Saints and Scholars quickly grew. It had the advantage for nationalists too of ignoring changes since the advent of the Normans. History itself has been deformed by the crisis in identity and by the eagerness to find one in the past. The passing in stony official silence of the eighth centenary of the arrival of the Normans in Ireland, the exaggerated official emphasis on early Christian times in the context of the current exhibition of early Irish treasures, or the Wood Quay debacle, emphasise how Irish attitudes have been conditioned, even warped, by the course of Anglo-Irish relations. But ultimately what is significant is not the political dimension of this phenomenon, but its cultural aspects. Because so much change was belated, the surviving contrasts between the new modes and old often give an impression of greater attachment to tradition than is the case. But in fact the continuity is very weak. And the crisis at the end of the nineteenth century was not merely the recurrent one of Anglo-Irish relations but one of finding a satisfying identity, in circumstances in which the likelihood of Irish self-government was greater and in which the progressive collapse of Anglo-Irish institutions made the need more pressing.

Notes

Abbreviations
BL   British Library
NLI   National Library of Ireland
PRO   Public Record Office, London
PROI   Public Record Office of Ireland, Dublin
PRONI Public Record Office of Northern Ireland, Belfast
TCD   Trinity College, Dublin

1 Introduction

1 *A tour through Ireland* (Dublin, 1746). Also attributed to William Rufus Chetwood (see L.W. Hanson, *Contemporary Printed Sources for British and Irish Economic History, 1701-1750* (Cambridge, 1963), p.650.

2 A Young, *Tour in Ireland* (1780); *Travels in France and Italy in the years 1787, 1788, 1789*

3 L.M. Cullen, 'Merchant communities overseas, the navigation acts and Irish and Scottish responses', in L.M. Cullen and T.C. Smout (eds.), *Comparative aspects of Scottish and Irish economic and social history 1600-1900* (Edinburgh, 1977), p. 173.

4 For a survey of the literature on middlemen, see D. Dickson, 'Middlemen' in T. Bartlett and D.W. Hayton (ed.), *Penal era and golden age* (Belfast, 1979), pp. 162-185.

2 Castle, countryside and social change

1 *Rob Roy* quoted in D. Woodward, 'A comparative study of the Irish and Scottish livestock trades in the seventeenth century', in L.M. Cullen and T.C. Smout, ed. *Comparative aspects of Scottish and Irish economic and social history, 1600-1900* (Edinburgh, 1977), p. 149.

2 *Proceedings of the incorporated society for promoting protestant schools in Ireland from February 1733 to March 25 1760*

3 NLI, 16F2, f. 22.

4 *The autobiography and correspondence of Mary Granville, Mrs Delany* 1 (London, 1861), 351, 354.

5 PRONI, T. 2812/2/6/36. Transcripts of O'Hara papers, Wm. Perceval, Belfield, to O'Hara, 21 November 1717.

6 R. Munter, *The history of the Irish newspaper* (Cambridge, 1967), p. 132.

7 T. De Vere White, *History of the Royal Dublin Society* (Tralee, 1955) p. 19.

8 S. Madden, *Reflections and resolutions proper for the gentlemen of Ireland* (Dublin, 1738), pp. 36-7.

9 Dunton's letters in E. MacLysaght, *Irish Life in the seventeenth century* (2nd ed. Cork, 1950), p. 337.

10 PRONI, Transcript of Willes letters, c. 1760.

11 S. Ní Cinnéide, 'A new view of eighteenth-century Kerry' *Journal of the Kerry archaeological and historical society*, No. 6 (1973), p. 87.

12 L.M. Cullen, 'Merchant communities overseas, the navigation acts and Irish and Scottish responses', in Cullen and Smout, op. cit., pp. 170, 172-3.

13 PROI, Blake papers, M 6936/3/1, Martin Blake, 3 April 1808.

14 Francis Jones to Charles O'Hara, 18 January 1793. NLI, Ainsworth report on O'Hara papers.

15 Manuscripts Room, Library, TCD, Clements Papers, letter of 12 January 1795.

16 L.M. Cullen and T.C.Smout, 'Economic growth in Scotland and Ireland' in Cullen and Smout, ed. *Comparative aspects of Scottish and Irish economic and social history 1600-1900* (Edinburgh, 1977), p. 8.

3 The landlord's world

1 *Faulkner's Dublin Journal*, 10 July 1742.

2 See L.M. Cullen, 'Economic and social history, 1691-1800', forthcoming in *A new history of Ireland*, IV.

3 BL, Egmont papers, Add. MS 47011, p. 129, 30 October 1746.

4 PRONI, Transcripts of Abercorn papers, 23 February 1747/8 (no. 6); 10 April 1752 (no. 114).

5 PRONI, T. 2812/19/1, Transcript of Charles O'Hara's memorandum book, especially under the years 1760 and 1762.

6 R. Thompson, *Statistical survey of the county of Meath* (Dublin, 1802), p. 103.

7 NLI, Ainsworth report on O'Hara MSS. Perceval to Kean O Hara, 3 April, 25 May 1718.

8 M. Craig, *Classic Irish houses of the middle size* (London, 1976), p. 39.

9 Craig, op. cit., pp. 39-40.

10 W.A. Maguire, *The Downshire estates in Ireland 1801-1845* (Oxford, 1972), pp. 29, 32-33.

11 A. Clarke, 'Plantation and the catholic question, 1603-23' in T.W. Moody, F.X. Martin and F.J. Byrne (ed.), *A new history of Ireland*, III, 204.

12 Madden, op. cit., pp. 30-31.

13 D.J. Dickson, 'An economic history of the Cork region in the eighteenth century', unpublished Ph.D. thesis, TCD, 1977, pp. 73-89.

14 See A.P.W. Malcomson, 'Absenteeism in eighteenth-century Ireland', *Irish economic and social history*, 1 (1974).

15 Dickson, op. cit., pp. 64-5.

16 See T. Jones Hughes, 'Society and settlement in nineteenth-century Ireland', *Irish Geography*, V, no. 2 (1965).

17 TCD, Library, Manuscripts Room, MS 883/2, pp. 90, 107.

18 TCD, Library, Manuscripts Room, Hartpole-Lecky papers, No. 354, pp. 56-7, 71, 73, 77-8.

19 R.J. Hoffmann, *Edmund Burke, New York agent* (Philadelphia, 1956), p. 283.

20 W. Tighe *Statistical observations relative to the county of Kilkenny* (Dublin, 1802), p. 261.

21 W.S. Mason, *Statistical account or parochial survey of Ireland* (Dublin, 1814-19), ii, 425; J. M'Parlan, *Statistical survey of the county of Donegal* (Dublin, 1802), p. 57; J. M'Parlan, *Statistical survey of the county of Leitrim* (Dublin, 1802), p. 43; W.G. Wood-Martin *History of Sligo* (Dublin, 1892), iii, 297; R. Fraser, *General view of the agriculture of . . . Wicklow* (Dublin, 1801), pp. 91-2.

22 J. M'Parlan, *Statistical survey of the county of Mayo* (Dublin, 1802), p. 85.

23 Dickson, op. cit., p. 217.

24 R.J. Hoffman, *Edmund Burke, New York agent* (Philadelphia, 1956), pp. 321, 323, 359.

25 Madden, op. cit., p. 220

26 NLI, MS 5102, Journal of Mary Mathew, 17 October 1772. I am indebted to Nuala Cullen for drawing my attention to this source.

27 H. Dutton, *Statistical and agricultural survey of the county of Galway* (Dublin, 1824), pp. 344-5.

28 D.B. Quinn, 'The Munster Plantation: problems and opportunities' *Journal of the Cork archaeological and historical society*, LXXI (1966), 30, 39.

29 M. Perceval-Maxwell, *The Scottish migration to Ulster in the reign of James I* (London 1973), p. 168.

30 Quinn, loc. cit., 39.

31 J. Harrison, *The Scot in Ulster* (Edinburgh and London, 1888), p. 62.

32 The so-called '1641 depositions' in the Manuscripts Room, Library, TCD.

33 1641 depositions, co. Limerick volume, ff. 144, 183 b; King's co. volume, f. 77; Kerry volume, f. 124b.

34 1641 depositions, Roscommon volume, f. 4b.

35 G. Boate, *Ireland's natural history* (London, 1652), pp. 97-8.

36 1641 depositions, Queen's co. volume, f. 156.

37 Boate, op. cit., p. 135.

38 Boate, op. cit., p. 152.

39 See Parliamentary papers, 1835, vol. xxxiii, First report of commissioners of public instruction, Ireland.

40 The 1661 poll-tax ordinance specified taxation of every individual above 15, with inter alia distinction between 'yeoman or chief farmer' and 'husbandman or petty farmer', and equated craftsmen with husbandmen, but the 1660 poll-tax ordinance clearly seems to imply a less than comprehensive imposition, its only distinction below gentle status being that of 'yeoman or farmer'. Living-in servants were taxed.

41 A. Clarke with R.D. Edwards 'Pacification, plantation, and the catholic question, 1603-23', in T.W. Moody, F.X. Martin, F.J. Byrne, ed. *A new history of Ireland*, iii (Oxford, 1976), 221.

42 1641 depositions, first Wexford volume, ff. $9^v - 10^v$.

43 Petty, *Political anatomy of Ireland*, 1672 in C.H. Hull, *Economic writings of Sir William Petty* (Cambridge, 1899), 1, 149.

44 Even more so, if their death rate also was lower than among the Irish.

45 Parliamentary papers, 1835, vol. xxxiii, First report of commissioners of public instruction.

46 On Presbyterian immigration, see L.M. Cullen, 'Population trends in seventeenth-century Ireland', *Economic and social review*, VI, 2 (Jan. 1975); A. Gailey, 'The Scots element in North Irish popular culture', *Ethnologia Europea*, VIII, 1 (1975).

47 J.I.D. Johnston, 'The Clogher Valley as an economic and social region in the eighteenth and nineteenth centuries', unpublished M. Litt. dissertation, TCD, 1974, pp. 149, 162.

48 W. Macafee, 'The colonisation of the Maghera region of South Derry during the seventeenth and eighteenth centuries', *Ulster Folklife*, xxiii (1977)

49 P. Tohall, 'The Diamond fight of 1795 and the resultant expulsions', *Seanchas Ardmhacha*, iii (1958).

50 J. Byrne, *An impartial account of the late disturbances in the county of Armagh*, in W.H. Crawford and B. Trainor, *Aspects of Irish social history 1750-1800* (Belfast, 1969), p.74. I am indebted to my student Mr John Glennon for dwelling on the possible significance of this fleeting reference.

51 PRONI, T. 2855, Willes letter, c. 1760.

52 TCD, Library, Manuscripts Room, MS 883/2, p. 71.

4 Village and countryside: landlord and settler

1 T.C. Smout, 'The landowner and the planned village in Scotland, 1730-1830', in R. Mitchison, ed. *Scotland in the age of improvement* (Edinburgh, 1970).

2 On Irish villages, see L.M. Cullen, *Irish towns and villages* (Dublin, 1979).

3 See Dineley's sketch, reproduced in L.M. Cullen, *Life in Ireland* (London, 1968), p. 62.

4 It disappeared soon afterwards; only some physical vestiges could still be traced on the ground by 1893. See R.T.Mitchell's *Survey of Ireland* quoted in D.L. Savory, 'The Huguenot-

Palatine settlements in the counties of Limerick, Kerry and Tipperary', *Proceedings of the Huguenot society of London*, XVIII (1947), 228.

5 S. Lewis, *Topographical dictionary*, 1837.

6 NLI, 21F138, f. 56.

7 Its landlord character would have been more evident at an earlier date with a market house, since removed, sited centrally in the main street.

8 See for a recent survey, R.J. Hunter, 'Towns in the Ulster plantation', *Studia hibernica*, No. 11 (1971). See also R. Gillespie, *Pictorial maps of the plantations in counties Londonderry and Down drawn by Thomas Raven in the 1620s: a set of 20 slides with notes* (PRONI, n.d.).

9 Precise enumeration is difficult, because a triangular appearance can sometimes be created by the juncture of two roads with the apex being cleared. Several of the identifications may be challenged. On the other hand, many villages have not been included because their triangular pattern seems uncertain: early maps, where they survive, sometimes decisively confirm or negate conclusions drawn from other evidence.

10 C. Coote, *General view of the agriculture and manufactures of the King's county* (Dublin, 1801), p. 138.

11 PRONI, T. 870.

12 The character of Newtownards before the creation of its later grid pattern is clear in PRONI, D. 952.

13 PRONI T. 343, copy made in 1812. As the church depicted on the map was erected at an early date (see *Calendar of state papers, Ireland, 1625-32*, p. 497), it is quite likely that the sketch represents the town at a very early stage of its development.

14 B. Adams, 'The diamonds of Ulster and Pennsylvania', *Ulster Folk and Transport Museum Year Book (1975-6)*, pp. 18-20. I am indebted to Dr Alan Gailey for bringing this paper to my attention.

15 NLI, 16D10.

16 R. Loeber, 'Irish country houses and castles of the late Caroline period'. *Quarterly bulletin of the Irish Georgian society*, XVI, nos. 1 and 2 (Jan-June 1973), 16-18, 20-21.

17 The fact that George Rawdon who, as agent for the Earl of Conway, had created several towns in Antrim and Down including Ballynahinch, co. Down, which on later evidence had a central square, laid out Portarlington is probably only a

coincidence, although an arresting one.

18 The open space was probably a seventeenth-century creation, Sixmilebridge having been an early centre of the iron industry, corresponding to the triangular greens in Tuamgraney and Scariff, but the triangular layout could of course be an accident of the steep fall of the terrain to the river. Pre-1641 settlement there, however, suggests the former.

19 NLI, 21F105.

20 NLI, 16D10.

21 I am indebted to Dr C.J. Woods for the reference from Russell and to Mr W.H. Crawford for evidence of the dating of the second square in Castlewellan (PRONI, T.2209).

22 *Report and charter of the incorporated society* 1735; see also *Faulkners Dublin Journal*, 12 March 1734.

23 Ibid.; see also *Faulkner's Dublin Journal*, 13 December 1737.

24 TCD, Library, Manuscripts Room, Crosbie Papers.

25 *Dublin Gazette*, 18-22 October 1737.

26 Madden, op. cit., p. 43.

27 *Autobiography and correspondence of Mary Granville, Mrs Delany*, 1, 376.

28 Ibid., 1, 385.

29 PRONI, D.401/1.

30 Dickson, op. cit., pp. 580-01.

31 NLI, 16D10, dated 1810.

32 *The journal of the Rev. John Wesley*, ii (Dent, [1906]), 414.

33 Both comments are from one of the Baron Willes' letters, c. 1760. PRONI, microfilm.

34 Dickson, op. cit., p. 576.

35 TCD, Library, Manuscripts Room, Hartpole-Lecky papers. Aldborough to George Hartpole, 25 January 1794.

36 See *Shell guide to Ireland*, under Roundstone.

37 J.G. Alger, 'An Irish absentee and his tenants', *English historical review*, X (October 1895), 667-8.

38 *The autobiography and correspondence of Mary Granville, Mrs Delany*, iii, 156.

39 See Young, op. cit., i, p. 111; PRONI, Roden MIC 147,

vol. 17, p. 54 (1749); PRONI, T. 2862/3/1, 25 Feb. 1764.

40 For the Palatines, see Genealogical Office, Dublin Castle, MS 540.

41 See NLI, MSS 15910, 15912-15916.

42 C. Coote, *General view of the agriculture and manufacture of King's county* (Dublin, 1801), p. 110.

43 G.V. Sampson, *Statistical survey of the county of Londonderry* (Dublin, 1802), pp. 505-6.

44 NLI, 16D10.

45 T.J. Barrington, *Discovering Kerry* (Dublin, 1976), p. 235.

46 I am indebted to my student, Rev. R.B. McCarthy, for this information on Cahirciveen.

47 W.S. Mason, op. cit., ii, 422-5.

48 C. Coote, *Statistical survey of the county of Cavan* (Dublin, 1802), p. 255.

49 Young, op. cit., i, 315.

50 Lewis, *Topographical dictionary*, 1837.

5 Social structure and evolution

1 I am indebted in particular to M. Poussou, University of Bordeaux, in both seminars and lectures at Trinity College for information on this issue.

2 Letter of 10 Nov. 1645 from Dean of Fermo to Rinuccini's brother quoted in *Irish Times*, 29 Aug. 1979; *Advertisements for Ireland*, ed. G. O'Brien (Dublin, 1923), p. 43.

3 A. Young, *Tour in Ireland*, ed. A.W. Hutton, (London, 1892), ii, 120.

4 J. Meyer, *Les Européens et les autres* (Paris, 1975), p. 137.

5 B. O'Cuiv, 'The Irish language in the early modern period' in T.W. Moody, F.X. Martin, F.J. Byrne, ed. *A new history of Ireland*, iii (Oxford, 1976), 535.

6 N. Canny, *The Elizabethan conquest of Ireland* (Hassocks, 1976), pp. 11-13.

7 *Spanish Armada, Illustrated account of the Francisco de Cuellar story* (Sligo school of landscape painting, n.d. (1979)), p. 64.

8 L.M. Cullen, 'Economic trends, 1660-91' in *A new history of Ireland*, ed. T.W. Moody, F.J. Byrne, F.X. Martin, iii

(Oxford, 1976), 402-3, 404, 405-6.

9 L.M. Cullen, 'Economic and social history, 1691-1800' in *A new history of Ireland*, IV, forthcoming.

10 PRO, Customs 1/100, ff. 17, 39;6, 18 Nov. 1767.

11 PRONI, T.2812/19/1, Transcript of O'Hara memorandum book.

12 PROI, M2466.

13 See especially L.M. Cullen, 'Income, foreign trade and economic development: Ireland as a case study', unpublished paper at New Orleans seminar on exports and economic growth, October 1975.

14 L.M. Cullen, *Life in Ireland* (London, 1968), p. 45.

15 op. cit., p. 46

16 *Spanish armada, Illustrated account of the Francisco de Cuellar story* (Sligo School of landscape painting, n.d. (1979)).

17 PRO, Adm. 1/2455. Edward Smith to Admiralty, 12 March 1734.

18 A. Young, *Travels in France and Italy during the years 1787, 1788 and 1789* (London, [1915]), p. 25.

19 *Diary of Humphrey O'Sullivan*, ed. M. McGrath, ii (Dublin, 1936), 21-2.

20 See E.L. Almquist, 'Mayo and beyond: land, domestic industry and rural transformation in the Irish west', *Irish economic and social history*, v (1978).

21 Papers presented to the Franco-Irish conference of Irish and French historians, Trinity College, Dublin, March 1977 (to be published shortly).

22 Cullen, op. cit., pp. 41-2.

23 Andrew Borde, *The boke of the introduction of knowledge* c. 1540, reprinted London, 1814.

24 *Spanish Armada, Illustrated account of the Francisco de Cuellar story* (Sligo School of landscape painting, n.d. (1979)).

25 J.M. Synge, 'The people of the glens' from *The Seanachie*, Spring 1907, in *The Aran Islands and other writings by John M. Synge*, ed. R. Tracy (New York, 1962), p. 186.

26 S Ní Chinnéide, 'An 18th-century French traveller in Kildare', *Journal of the Kildare archaeological society*, XV, no. 4 (1974), 379.

6 Social and cultural frontiers

1 TCD, Library, Manuscripts Room, 1641 depositions, Armagh volume.

2 B. Trainor and W.H. Crawford, ed. *Aspects of Irish Social History 1750-1800* (Belfast, 1969), p. 174.

3 PRONI, T. 3041/1/E53, 18 Aug. 1788

4 K. Danaher, *Ireland's vernacular architecture* (Cork, 1978), p. 10.

5 See W. Nolan, *Fassadinin: land, settlement and society in south-east Ireland 1600-1850* (Dublin, 1979).

6 *Caoineadh Airt Ui Laoghaire* (Dublin, 1963), ed. S. O Tuama. *Memoirs of Miles Byrne*, ed. S. Gwynn (Dublin, 1907).

7 R.R. Madden, *United Irishmen*, 2nd series, i (Dublin, 1843), lx. W.P. Burke in his *History of Clonmel* (Waterford, 1907), p. 368n. does however not accept the relationship.

8 L.M. Cullen, 'Merchant communities overseas, the navigation acts and Irish and Scottish responses', in L.M. Cullen and T.C. Smout, ed. *Comparative aspects of Scottish and Irish economic and social history 1600-1900* (Edinburgh, 1977), pp. 170-71.

9 On the Suttons, see various papers in Archives Nationales, Paris, Minutier Central, notarial *étude* XXVI.

10 On the Fitzgeralds' Wexford links, see Archives Nationales, Paris, Minutier Central, *Étude* XC/367, 8 March 1751.

11 Wakefield, *An account of Ireland, statistical and political* (London, 1812), ii, 745.

12 I am indebted to my student Miss Rosemary Reid for details of catholic conformities in Wexford and Wicklow.

13 D. Dickson, op. cit., pp. 64-6.

14 'Test book, 1775-6' in *59th Report of the deputy keeper of the public records in Ireland*, pp. 50-84.

15 S. Ní Chinnéide, 'A Frenchman's tour of Connacht in 1791', *Journal of the Galway archaeological and historical society*, XXXV (1976), 56.

16 The researches of Professor John Mannion are illuminating on this question.

17 I am indebted to Mr. Eugene McCracken of Savannah for information of this colony.

18 See Barton MSS in National Library, and various acts in

the notarial *étude* Guy in the Archives départementales de la Gironde, Bordeaux.

19 L.M. Cullen, 'Merchant communities overseas, the navigation acts and Irish and Scottish responses,' in L.M. Cullen and T.C. Smout, ed. *Comparative aspects of Scottish and Irish economic and social history 1600-1900* (Edinburgh, 1977), p. 173.

20 F.E. Vokes, 'Theology: past, present, future', *Trinity College Gazette*, XVI, 2(15 Nov. 1979).

21 I am indebted to my student, Rev. R.B. McCarthy, for this information.

22 J.M. Synge, 'The oppression of the hills', *Manchester Guardian* 15 Feb. 1905, reprinted in J.M. Tracy, ed. *The Aran Islands and other writings by John M. Synge* (New York, 1962), pp. 180-81.

23 See Bishop Tenison's visitation book for Ossory, PROI, M2462.

24 Church of Ireland, Wicklow, parish registers.

25 L.M. Cullen, *Life in Ireland* (London, 1968), p. 41.

26 J. Bossy, 'The counter-reformation and the people of Ireland, 1596-1641', *Historical Studies*, VIII (Dublin, 1971), ed. T.D. Williams.

27 PRONI, Willes letters (microfilm).

28 Audrey Powell, 'Thatch over your head', *Observer*, 19 August 1979.

29 A. Crookshank and the Knight of Glin, *The painters of Ireland c. 1660-1920* (London, 1978), p. 32.

30 J.M. Synge, 'From Galway to Gorumna', *Manchester Guardian* 1905, reprinted in J.M. Tracy, ed., op. cit., p. 274.

7 Diet in a changing society

1 A.T. Lucas, 'Irish food before the potato', *Gwerin*, iii, no. 2, 8, 30.

2 E.E. Evans, *Irish heritage* (Dundalk, 1942), pp. 34-5; *Irish Folkways* (London, 1957), pp. 11, 83.

3 T.P. O'Neill, *Life and tradition in rural Ireland* (London, 1977), pp. 56, 62.

4 Lucas, op. cit., 11.

5 W. Ellis, *The country housewife's family companion*,

1750, p. 365, quoted in C.A. Wilson, *Food and drink in Britain* (London, 1973), p. 185.

6 G. O'Brien, ed. *Advertisements for Ireland* (Dublin, 1923), p. 33.

7 J.J. O'Meara, ed. *The topography of Ireland by Geraldus Cambrensis* (Dublin, 1951), pp. 14-15.

8 G. Boate, *Ireland's natural history* (London, 1652), pp. 167-8.

9 J. McEvoy, *Statistical survey of the county of Tyrone* (Dublin, 1802), p. 81.

10 G. Griffin, *The Collegians* (1963 ed., Dublin), p. 290.

11 W. Tighe, op. cit., p. 483. A similar observation from the Dungiven area of Tyrone appears in W.S. Mason, *Statistical account*, i, (Dublin, 1814), 308.

12 E. MacLysaght, *Irish life in the seventeenth century* (Cork, 1950, 2nd ed.), p. 338, quoting Dunton.

13 E. MacLysaght, op. cit., p. 315.

14 TCD, Library, Manuscripts Room, 1641 depositions, co. Carlow volume, f. 133.

15 R.N. Salaman, *The history and social influence of the potato* (Cambridge, 1949).

16 *The Danish forces in Ireland 1690-91*, ed. K. Danaher and J.G. Simms (Irish Manuscripts Commission, Dublin, 1962), p. 15.

17 R. McKay, ed. *An anthology of the potato* (Dublin, 1961), p. 26.

18 My mother's recollection of family tradition in south Wexford.

19 Rolande Bonnain-Moerdijk, 'L'alimentation paysanne en France entre 1850 et 1936', *Etudes rurales*, no. 58 (April-June 1975). I am indebted to Professor Isac Chiva for drawing my attention to this paper.

20 *The diary of Humphrey O'Sullivan*, ed. M. McGrath, ii (Dublin, 1936), 315; L.J. Kettle, ed. *Material for victory: the memoirs of Andrew J. Kettle* (Dublin, 1958), p. 5.

21 *The diary of Humphrey O'Sullivan*, i, 197.

22 I am indebted to Nuala Cullen for this observation.

23 C.A. Wilson, op. cit., p. 155.

24 R. Bonnain-Moerdijk, loc. cit., 43.

25 MacLysaght, op. cit., p. 332.

26 R. Fraser, *Statistical survey of the county of Wexford* (Dublin, 1807), p. 95.

27 C. Coote, *Statistical survey of the county of Cavan* (Dublin, 1802), pp. 94, 240. Farmers were said never to use their own butter in the barony of Farney in county Monaghan, Coote, *Statistical survey of the county of Monaghan* (Dublin, 1801), p. 130.

28 W. Petty, *Treatise of Ireland 1687* in C.H. Hull, *Economic writings of Sir William Petty* (Cambridge, 1899), ii, 594.

29 S. Madden, *Resolutions and reflections proper for the gentlemen of Ireland* (Dublin 1738), p. 52.

30 A. Young, *A tour in Ireland 1776-1779*, ed. A.W. Hutton (London, 1892), i, 340, 341, 369, 456.

31 PRO, M2462, Bishop Tenison's visitation book, p. 59.

32 H. Townsend, *A general and statistical survey of the county of Cork* (Cork, 1815), i, 412.

33 W. Tighe, op. cit., p. 386.

34 W.S. Mason, op. cit., iii, 569, 621.

35 M. Carbery, *The farm by Lough Gur* (London, 1942 ed.), pp. 38-9.

36 *The diary of Humphrey O'Sullivan*, ii, 77.

37 *The diary of Humphrey O'Sullivan*, ii, 359.

38 For a particularly relevant observation, see Young, *Travels in France and Italy during the years 1787, 1788 and 1789* [1915, London], p. 56.

39 J.M. Callwell, *Old Irish life* (Edinburgh, 1912), p. 224.

40 A. Dobbs, *Essay on the trade . . . of Ireland* (1729-31), in *A collection of tracts and treatises illustrative . . . of Ireland* (Dublin, 1861), ii, 349.

41 Lucas, op. cit., 15-16.

42 NLI, MS 392, p. 269.

43 S. Ní Chinnéide, 'A Frenchman's impressions of county Cork in 1790', part ii, *Journal of the Cork historical and archaeological society*, LXXIX (1974), 15.

44 Rothe House, Kilkenny.

45 Young, *A tour in Ireland*, ii, 49.

46 Sir John Carr, *The stranger in Ireland* (London, 1806), p. 156.

47 NLI, Ainsworth report on O'Hara papers. Capt. Wm. O'

Hara to Charles O'Hara, 18 October 1784.

48 PRONI, Willes letters (microfilm).

49 *The diary of Humphrey O'Sullivan*, iii, 35.

50 S. Ní Chinnéide, 'A view of Kilkenny, city and county, in 1790', *Journal of the Royal Society of Antiquaries of Ireland*, CXIV (1974), 33.

51 *The diary of Humphrey O'Sullivan*, ii, 141.

52 S. Ní Chinnéide, 'A Frenchman's tour of Connacht in 1791', *Journal of the Galway archaeological and historical society*, XXXV (1976), 62.

53 W.H. Maxwell, *Wild sports of the west* (London, 1832), i, 113.

54 *Diary of Humphrey O'Sullivan*, ii, 23.

55 M. Carbery, op. cit., pp. 20, 39-40.

56 A. Young, *Travels in France and Italy during the years 1787, 1788 and 1789* (London [1915]), p. 60.

57 Ní Chinnéide, ' A Frenchman's tour of Connacht . . .', op. cit., 53.

58 Ní Chinnéide, 'A Frenchman's impressions of county Cork in 1790', pt. 2, *Journal of the Cork historical and archaeological society*, LXXIX (1974), 123.

59 *The diary of Humphrey O'Sullivan*, iii, 175-6. At 8d. per lb. salmon had been uncommonly dear. A year later as late as October it was only 2d. per lb. (op. cit., iii, 243).

60 *The Journal of the Rev. John Wesley* (1906 ed., London), iv. 42.

61 J.C. Walker, *An historical essay on the dress of the ancient and modern Irish* (Dublin, 1818), pp. 201-2.

62 Maxwell, op. cit., i, 276.

63 S. Ní Chinnéide, 'A Frenchman's tour of Connacht . . . ', op. cit., 58.

64 Maxwell, op. cit., i, 278.

65 Ní Chinnéide, 'A journey from Cork to Limerick . . . ', *North Munster Antiquarian Journal*, xiv (1971), 70.

66 C. Lever, *Charles O'Malley* (1841, 1913 ed. London), i, 245.

67 J. McEvoy, *Statistical Survey of the county of Tyrone* (Dublin, 1802), p. 81.

68 PRONI, T. 1062/30, Nov. 1731.

69 *Diary of Humphrey O'Sullivan*, ii, 125.

70 P.H. Ryland, *History, topography, and antiquities of the county and city of Waterford* (1824), quoted in T. Fitzgibbon *A taste of Ireland* (London, 1968), p. 89.

71 Griffin, op. cit., p. 79.

72 Carbery, op. cit., pp. 44-5.

73 S. O'Ceallaigh, *Filíocht na gCallanán* (Dublin, 1967), p. 38. 'You can be drinking for a spell since corn became dear'. For an interesting comment with the same general import, see *Diary of Humphrey O'Sullivan*, i, 209-10.

74 Royal Irish Academy, O.S., Box 39, co. Londonderry, Dungiven parish, 29 Nov. 1834. I am indebted to Mr W.H. Crawford, Public Record Office of Northern Ireland, for this reference.

75 For a discussion of the controversy, see L.M. Cullen, 'Irish history without the potato', *Past and present*, no. 40 (July, 1968).

76 See O Súilleabháin's *Barantas do Dhomnal Ó Dálaigh* quoted in Cullen, 'The hidden Ireland: reassessment of a concept', *Studia Hibernica*, no. 9 (1969), 44-5.

77 TCD, Library Manuscripts Room, 1641 depositions, Carlow volume, f. 24; Wicklow volume, ff. 63, 82.

78 TCD Library, Manuscripts Room, 1641 depositions, Wicklow volume, ff. 170-1. The conversion is calculated on the basis of Arthur Young's figures for the yield per acre.

79 O. Goodbody, 'Two letters of Benjamin Chandler', *Quaker history*, LXIV, no. 2 (Autumn, 1975), 111.

80 I am indebted to my student, Mr Thomas Truxes, for this information.

81 Hennessy archives, Cognac, John Saule, 7 May 1769.

82 Messrs. Delamain, Jarnac, Delamain letter book, 16 April 1768. I am indebted to M. Alain Braastad, proprietor of the firm, for much information and assistance.

83 ibid., 23 February 1768.

84 Hennessy papers, Cognac. The letter is filed among letters for 1772, but Delamain's regular hand is very hard to allocate to particular periods in his life.

85 ibid., James Delamain to Richard Hennessy, 8 August 1791.

86 R. Fraser, *General view of the agriculture . . . of the county of Wicklow* (Dublin, 1801), p. 56.

87 There are several passing references to maize in O'Sullivan's diaries of which the most important are: i, 51; ii, 181, 285, 315; iv, 41-3.

88 W. Tighe, op. cit., pp. 479-80; *Munster Farmer's Magazine*, vi, May 1819, 114-5, *Diary of Humphrey O'Sullivan*, i, 277. I am indebted to Dr David Dickson for the reference from the *Munster Farmer's Magazine*.

89 W.S. Mason, op. cit., iii, 410; Fraser, *Wexford*, p. 79.

90 Faulkner papers in the possession of Mrs Amy Monahan at Castletown, co. Carlow.

91 Young, *Tour in Ireland*, ii, 151.

92 J. Dubourdieu, *Statistical survey of the county of Down* (Dublin, 1802), p. 146; C. Coote, *Statistical survey of the county of Armagh* (Dublin, 1804), p. 277.

93 *Munster Farmer's Magazine*, vi (1819), 114-16.

94 *Diary of Humphrey O'Sullivan*, ii, 313.

95 H. Dutton, *Statistical survey of the county of Clare* (Dublin, 1808) p. 368.

96 Tighe, op. cit., p. 498.

97 Kettle, op. cit., pp. 5-6.

98 *Malachy Horan remembers*, ed. G.A. Little (1976 ed., Dublin and Cork), p. 18.

99 R. O'Foghludha, *Donnchadh ruadh MacConmara* (Dublin, 1933), p. 22.

100 Young, op. cit., i, 150.

101 W.S. Mason, op. cit., i, 198.

102 *Diary of Humphrey O'Sullivan*, i, 93-5.

103 Young, op. cit., i, 428; C. Coote, *General view of the agriculture . . . of the King's county* (Dublin, 1801), p. 164.

104 C. Coote, *Statistical survey of the county of Armagh* (Dublin, 1804) p. 251.

105 D.H. Akenson and W.H. Crawford, *James Orr, Bard of Ballycarry* (Belfast, 1977), 18, 60.

106 *Diary of Humphrey O'Sullivan*, iii, 19, 137.

107 W.D. O'Connell, *Cork Franciscan records 1764-1831* (Cork, 1942). The calculations are approximate as the records have not been published in full, and the bias in the above calculations is probably towards underestimating rather than exaggerating consumption.

108 S. Ní Cinnéide, 'A Frenchman's tour of Connacht . . .',

op. cit., p. 63.

109 *Diary of Humphrey O'Sullivan*, ii, 141, 263.

110 E. O'Muirgheasa, *Amhráin na Midhe* (Dublin, 1933), pp. 53-4.

111 *Irish commons journals*, iv, app. xciii.

112 Young, op. cit., i, 287-8.

113 Friend's Historical Library, Dublin, Diary of Joshua Wight, 1752-6.

114 Danaher and Simms, op. cit., pp. 107, 129.

115 Coote, *General view of . . . the King's county* (Dublin 1801), p. 88.

116 C. Coote, *Statistical survey of . . . Armagh*, p. 125. The beans were generally 'boiled and mashed with oatmeal, milk, butter and pepper . . . previously called stulk'.

117 According to Carleton, 'sthik is made by bruising a quantity of boiled potatoes and beans together. The potatoes, however, having first been reduced to a pulpy state, the beans are but partially broken. It is then put onto a dish, and a pound of butter or rendered lard thrust into the middle of it'. Carleton, op. cit., p. 140n.

118 Young, op. cit., i, 288.

8 Hospitality and menu

1 W.S. Mason, *Statistical account*, i (Dublin, 1814), 312.

2 J. Dubourdieu, *Statistical account of the county of Down* (Dublin, 1802), p. 215.

3 M. Carbery, *The farm by Lough Gur* (London, 1942), pp. 21-23.

4 W.S. Mason, op. cit., iii (Dublin, 1819), 127.

5 W. Carleton, *The courtship of Phelim O'Toole: six Irish tales* (London, 1962), p. 95.

6 G. Griffin, *The Collegians* (1963 ed. Dublin), p. 18.

7 Carbery, op. cit., pp. 21-23.

8 Griffin, op. cit., p. 18.

9 W. Carleton, *The Squanders of Castle Squander* (London, 1852), i, 277.

10 C. Lever, *Charles O'Malley* (1841, 1913 ed. London), i, 69.

11 E. MacLysaght, *Irish life in the seventeenth century*, 2nd

ed. (Cork, 1950), pp. 335, 338.

12 PRONI, Willes letters (microfilm).

13 J.M. Callwell, *Old Irish life* (London and Edinburgh, 1912), p. 224.

14 A. Borde, *The boke of the introduction of knowledge* (c. 1540, reprinted London, 1814.)

15 J. Derrick, *The image of Ireland*, (London, 1581). The engraving is reproduced in L.M. Cullen, *Life in Ireland* (London, 1968), p. 44.

16 D. Corkery, *The hidden Ireland*, 4th impression (Dublin, 1956), p. 44.

17 E. Dillon, 'The lament for Art O'Leary', *Irish university review*, i (Spring 1971), 207.

18 R. O'Faoghludha, *Amhráin Phiarais Mhic Ghearailt* (Dublin, 1905), p. 59 (Translation by the author).

19 NLI, MS, 711, 25 July 1720.

20 *The autobiography and correspondence of Mary Granville, Mrs. Delany*, i-iii (London, 1861).

21 *The letters of Sir Walter Scott*, ed. H.J.C. Grierson, IX (London, 1935), 195.

22 J. Bush, *Hibernia curiosa* (London, 1769), p. 17.

23 W. Carleton, *The Squanders of Castle Squander* (London, 1852), 1, 64.

24 G. Griffin, *The Collegians* (1963 ed.), p. 80.

25 I am indebted to Nuala Cullen for this observation.

26 Sir John Carr, *The stranger in Ireland* (London, 1806), p. 155.

27 I. Weld, *Statistical survey of the county of Roscommon* (Dublin, 1832), p. 342.

28 *Autobiography and correspondence of Mary Granville, Mrs Delany*, vol. ii (London, 1861), 503.

29 S. Ní Chinnéide, 'An 18th-century traveller in Kildare', *Journal of the Kildare archaeological and historical society*, XV, 4 (1974), 381.

30 S. Ní Chinnéide, 'A journey from Cork to Limerick in December 1790', *North Munster Antiquarian journal*, XIV (1971), 16.

31 *Letters of Sir Walter Scott*, IX, 190.

32 *The diary of Humphrey O'Sullivan*, ed. M. McGrath, i, ii (Dublin, 1936).

33 Carleton, *Courtship* . . . , p. 152.

34 *The diary of Humphrey O'Sullivan*, op. cit., i, 21, 185, 197.

35 For a somewhat similar meal, see Carleton, op. cit., p. 120. In a footnote he qualified this: 'this, about thirty years ago, was usual at wedddings and other feasts, where everything went upon a grand scale'.

36 A. Trollope, *The McDermots of Ballycloran* (1874 ed., London), pp. 204, 207.

37 *The diary of Humphrey O'Sullivan*, op. cit., i, 145.

38 J. Brady, *The big sycamore* (Dublin, 1958), p. 72. Fitzgerald is a pseudonym for Browne throughout the book.

39 Lever, op. cit., i, 246.

40 J.M. Callwell, op. cit., p. 242.

41 A. Trollope, *The Kellys and the O'Kellys* (1848, 1929 ed. London), p. 97.

42 W.H. Maxwell, *Wild sports of the West* (London, 1832), i, 25.

43 Carbery, op. cit., p. 233.

44 P.A. Sheehan, *Glenenaar* (1954, ed., Dublin), p. 89.

45 Carbery, op. cit., p. 44. See also Brady, op. cit., p. 72.

46 *Diary of Humphrey O'Sullivan*, ii, 333.

47 For a description of breadbaking in such ovens, see J.M. Calwell, op. cit., p. 225. For a photograph of one, see K. Danaher, *Ireland's vernacular architecture* (Dublin, 1978, 2nd ed.), p. 46.

48 S.O' Tuama, *Caoineadh Airt Uí Laoghaire* (Dublin 1963), p. 33.

49 S. Ní Chinnéide, 'A Frenchman's tour of Connacht in 1791', *Journal of the Galway archaeological and historical society*, XXXV (1976), 58. De Montbret attributes the absence of such bread simply to a lack of barm.

50 e.g. Ní Chinnéide, 'A Frenchman's impression of County Cork in 1790', pt. 2, *Journal of the Cork historical and archaeological society*, LXXIX (1974), 17.

51 *Diary of Humphrey O'Sullivan*, ii, 361.

52 Ní Chinnéide, 'A Frenchman's impression of county Cork in 1790', pt. 2, op. cit., 16.

53 C. Coote, *Statistical survey of the county of Monaghan* (Dublin 1801), p. 175.

Notes

54 J. Dubourdieu, *Statistical account of the county of Down* (Dublin, 1802), pp. 80, 87-8.

55 Carbery, op. cit., p. 65.

56 I am indebted to Dr. C.J. Woods for this reference.

57 Akenson and Crawford, op. cit., pp. 18, 60.

58 W.S. Mason, op. cit., iii, 244.

59 M. Edgeworth, *Tour in Connemara and the Martins of Ballynahinch*, ed. H.E. Butler (London, 1950), p. 45.

60 Oxford University Press edition, 1929, p.6.

61 M. Dods, *The cook and housewife's manual* (9th ed., Edinburgh, 1849), p. 131.

62 J. Bush, *Hibernia curiosa* (London, 1769), p. 84.

63 H. Dutton, *Statistical survey of the county of Clare* (Dublin, 1808), p. XV.

64 A. Young, *Travels in France and Italy during the years 1787, 1788 and 1789.* (1915, Dent, London), p. 31.

65 Dods, op. cit., pp. 609, 613.

66 Young, op. cit., p. 189.

67 Somerville and Ross, *Experiences of an Irish R.M. (London, 1970, ed.)*, p. 248.

68 Maurice Collis, *Somerville and Ross* (London, 1968) p. 68.

9 Settlers and natives: conflict

1 PRONI, O'Hara transcripts, T.2812/4/68, 3 March 1692/3.

2 On the Foster preference for Protestants, see A.P.W. Malcomson, *John Foster, The politics of the Anglo-Irish ascendancy* (Oxford, 1978), pp. 308-9; on the preference on county Cork estates, Dickson, op. cit., pp. 147-53, 243, 245, 256, 260. For western examples, see P.K. Egan, *The parish of Ballinasloe* (Dublin, 1960), p. 135.

3 W.A. Maguire, *The Downshire estates in Ireland, 1801-1845* (Oxford, 1972), p. 230.

4 Francis Jones to Charles O'Hara, 24 December 1784 in NLI, Ainsworth report on O'Hara papers. See also letter of 24 November 1784.

5 Maguire, op. cit., p. 229.

6 W. O'Connor Morris, *Letters on the land question of Ireland* (London, 1870), pp. 80, 114, 152-3.

7 I am indebted to my former student Miss Simonetta Ryan for her analysis of the Ballintemple estate.

8 A.W. Malcomson, op. cit., pp. 138-9.

9 H. Townsend, *A general and statistical survey of the county of Cork* (Dublin, 1815), ii, 175.

10 T. O'Rorke, *History of the parishes of Ballysodare and Kilvarnet* (Dublin, 1878), p. 165; *History of Sligo: town and county*, i (Dublin, 1889), 452.

11 For the fear of invasion in Cork county where the Cotter incident was about to break, see BL, Egmont papers, Add. MS 46984, pp. 60, 61, 76, 78-9.

12 The most recent account of the Schools is in K. Milne, 'Irish charter schools', *Irish journal of education*, viii, I (1974).

13 *An abstract of the number of protestant and popish families in the years 1732 and 1733* (Dublin, 1736).

14 E. Wakefield, *An account of Ireland, statistical and political* (London, 1812), ii, 586.

15 PRONI, Willes letters, fourth letter (microfilm).

16 *A sermon preached at Christ-Church Dublin on the 13th of May 1764 before the incorporated society for promoting protestant schools in Ireland by Richard Woodward, Dean of Clogher.*

17 I am indebted to my former student Mr. Colm O'Floinn for this information based on J. Brady, 'Catholics and catholicism in the eighteenth century press', *Archivium Hibernicum*, XIV-XVII.

18 *Correspondence of Edmund Burke*, ed. T.W. Copeland, i (Cambridge, 1958), 216n, 276n.

19 PRONI, Blake papers, M6935/73/(5), copy of the case sent to Rome 23 Dec. 1769. For the case of the Wyse will in 1775, see W.P. Burke, *History of Clonmel* (Waterford, 1907), pp. 393-4.

20 PROI, Lodge MSS, Conformity Rolls.

21 Parish register of Kilmaine, 1744-84. I am indebted to my former student, Mrs. Brigid Clesham (née Rooke), for this information.

22 PROI M2478, 3582, 3585, 5036; Wakefield, op. cit., ii, 587.

23 PRONI, T.3228/1/75, Harrowby papers, 24 May 1756.

24 PRONI, T3200/1/1/14, 1-11 July 1768.

25 PRONI, T. 2915/7/1, 1 Jan. 1759.

26 L.M. Cullen, 'The hidden Ireland: reassessment of a concept', *Studia hibernica*, no. 9 (1969), 17.

27 'Ta an bhliadhain seo ag teacht' in Torna, *Seán na Raithíneach* (Dublin, 1954), pp. 255-7.

28 BL, Egmont papers, Add. MS 47009, pp. 37, 43.

29 PROI, M5992, Ievers papers, Robert Hickman, 14 July, 1745; Henry Ievers, 11 Oct. 1745 (copy).

30 NLI, Cotter papers, MS 711, p. 131: J.A. Froude, *The English in Ireland* (London, 1881), i, 393.

31 Dickson, op. cit., p. 63n.

32 *Burke Correspondence*, op. cit., i, 346-7.

33 PRO, Chancery Masters Exhibits, CIIO/46, St. George v. St. George, bundle O, no. 3. Owen Gallagher to St. George, Dublin, 19 February 1729/30.

34 NLI, Cotter MSS, MS 711, p. 157.

35 R.O'Foghludha, *Cois na Cora: Liam Ruadh MacCoitir agus a shaothar fileata* (Dublin, 1937), p. 13.

36 Burke Correspondence, op. cit., i, 147-8.

37 ibid., 215-6.

38 Willes' term in 1760.

39 W.S. Mason, op. cit., i, 365.

40 'Protestant householders in the parishes of Croagh, Nantinan, Rathkeale and Kilscannell, co. Limerick, in 1766', *Irish ancestor*, no. 2(1977).

41 Lewis, *Topographical dictionary*, under co. Limerick.

42 Lewis, *Topographical dictionary*, under Newtownhamilton.

43 NLI, 15B5.

44 Quoted in Crawford and Trainor, op. cit., p. 38.

45 W.E.H. Lecky, *History of Ireland in the eighteenth century* (1916 ed., London), III, 422-5; State Paper Office, Dublin, Rebellion papers, 620/22/58, Memorial by Norman Steel, J.P., to Lord Lieutenant, n.d.

46 *Walker's Hibernian Magazine*, 13 March 1794.

47 State Paper Office, State of the country papers, 1015/5, Fenton Aylmer, 14 Feb. 1796.

48 S. Ní Chinnéide, 'A Frenchman's tour of Connacht in 1791', *Journal of the Galway archaeological and historical*

society, XXXV (1976), 64.

49 The 1749 census returns are for Elphin diocese only: as Colloony, centre of the Cooper estate, was in Achonry diocese, the change around Markree Castle itself can not be measured, but on the evidence of changes in adjoining parishes, it could have been sizeable. 21 per cent of the Cooper parish of Ballysodare was Protestant in 1831, the highest proportion of any rural parish in north Connaught.

50 PRONI, T.3200/2/39, Thomas Jones to Lord Arran, 1783 (?).

51 J. Stock, *A narrative of what passed at Killala in the county of Mayo* (Dublin, 1800), pp. 84-6.

10 The '98 Rebellion in Wexford and Wicklow

1 Edward Hay, *History of the insurrection of the county of Wexford* (Dublin, 1803), pp. 35-7.

2 *Memoirs of Joseph Holt* (London, 1838), i. p.14.

3 Miles Byrne, *Memoirs*, ed. S. Gwynn (Dublin, 1907), i,11.

4 T. Pakenham, *The year of Liberty* (London, 1969), p. 143.

5 Young, op. cit., i, 90.

6 PROI, TAB 31/30.

7 T. Newenham, *A statistical and historical inquiry into the progress and magnitude of the population of Ireland* (London, 1805), pp. 302-3.

8 See A. McClelland, *The formation of the Orange Order*, n.d., p.14; Pakenham, op. cit., p. 379, note 24.

9 Miles Byrne, *Memoirs*, ed. S. Gwynn (Dublin, 1907), i, 18.

10 Byrne, op. cit., i, 10-11, 13.

11 R. Fraser, *Statistical survey of the county of Wexford* (Dublin, 1807), p. 84.

12 Pakenham, op. cit., p. 143.

13 W.S. Mason, *Statistical account*, i (Dublin, 1814), 94.

14 Pakenham, op. cit., p. 349.

15 Byrne, op. cit., i, 8-9: Pakenham, op. cit., pp. 143-4, 147.

16 R. Fraser, *General view of the agriculture ... of the county of Wicklow* (Dublin, 1801), pp. 97, 219.

17 Fraser, op. cit., p. 107

18 PRONI, Transcripts of McPeake papers, John Colclough, Dublin, 22 August 1798.

19 Fraser, *Wexford*, 56n.

20 W.S. Mason, *Statistical account*, ii (Dublin 1816), 544.

21 D. Goodall, 'All the cooking that could be used — a county Wexford election in 1754', *The Past*, no. 12 (1978).

22 PRONI, T.3048/13/27, 18 June 1798.

23 Byrne, *Memoirs*, i, 71.

24 W. O'Connor Morris, *Letters on the land question of Ireland* (London, 1870), pp. 152-3.

25 C. Dickson, *The Wexford rising in 1798* (Tralee, 1956), pp. 11-12.

26 PRONI, Transcripts of the McPeake papers, John Colclough, Tintern, 17 Sept. 1797.

27 M. Bodkin, 'Notes on the Irish parliament in 1773', *Proceedings of the Royal Irish Academy*, section c, XLVIII (1942), 220.

28 PRONI, McPeake papers, John Colclough, 22 August 1798.

29 Pakenham, op. cit., p. 349.

30 *Cox's Irish Magazine*, January 1808, pp. 214-25, 'A list of catholic chapels burned by orangemen and others during the rebellion'; Lecky, op. cit., IV, 472.

31 Pakenham, op. cit., p. 270.

32 Dickson, op. cit., pp. 41-2.

33 PRONI, T.3406/4/1.

34 PROI, M757, Hedges letters, 22 October 1704.

35 PROI, TAB 15/28.

36 PROI, TAB 15/44; TAB 27n/14.

37 Young was not greatly impressed by the Palatines, as his general observations on them suggest. Young, op. cit., ii, 34.

38 Tighe, op. cit., pp. 456-61; W.S. Mason, op. cit., iii, 631; Wakefield, ii, 612.

39 Wakefield, op. cit., ii, 626.

40 Dutton, *Clare*, p. 239.

41 Wakefield, op. cit., ii, 619.

42 PROI, TAB 17/91; TAB 17/21. See also the tithe applotment for Kilcooly, TAB 27S/73.

43 Wakefield, op. cit., i, 267, 277.

44 *An abstract of the number of protestant and popish fam-*

ilies in the years 1732 and 1733 (Dublin, 1736).

45 PRONI, T.808/15058. I am grateful to Dr David Dickson for a copy of this document.

46 I am grateful to my student, Miss Rosemary Reid, for this information.

47 Byrne, op. cit., i, 14, 192.

48 Figures from Miss Reid.

49 PROI, Convert Rolls.

50 PRONI, T. 2659/1, 'A list of the gents and freeholders of the county of Wicklow who did not vote at the late election, and others that now have a right to vote'.

51 Sir J. Gilbert, *History of Dublin* (Dublin, 1854), i, 156-9, 354-5; W.J. Fitzpatrick, *Ireland before the Union* (Dublin, 2nd ed., 1867), p. 200.

52 Genealogical Office, MS 162, f. 128-30.

53 *Fifty-ninth report of the Deputy Keeper of the public records in Ireland*, p. 75.

54 PRONI, T. 2659/1.

55 PROI, TAB 32/31.

56 Genealogical Office, MS 161, p. 59; MS 164, p. 21; MS 168, pp. 344-41; MS 179, p. 389.

57 Byrne, op. cit., i, 3, 11.

58 PROI, M5892 5 (iii), 5 (iv), Garrett Byrne to Frances Byrne, Hamburg, 11 April, 30 May 1800.

59 Genealogical Office, MS 814(2).

60 NLI, 21F104.

61 Byrne, op. cit., i, 10.

62 PROI, TAB 31/18; Printed Griffith valuation for Kilnahue parish, 1852.

63 Byrne, op. cit., i, 10-11.

64 PROI, TAB 32/30.

65 Byrne, op. cit., ii, 219.

66 PRO, TAB 32/36; 32/40; 32/47.

67 This paragraph is based on the tithe applotment books for Wicklow and north Wexford.

68 PRO, TAB 31/7; 31/11.

69 Byrne, op. cit., i, 8.

70 *Memoirs of Joseph Holt* (London, 1838), i, 17.

71 Fraser, *Wicklow*, pp. 213-15.

72 T. Powell, 'An economic factor in the Wexford rebellion of 1798', *Studia hibernica*, no. 16 (1976).

11 Education and cultural change

1 H. Dutton, *Statistical survey of the county of Clare* (Dublin, 1808), p. 189.

2 Letter from Mrs. Eliza O'Neill, 27 March 1772 in Crawford and Trainor, op. cit., p. 44.

3 J. Byrne, *An impartial account of the late disturbances in the county of Armagh*, 1792, in Crawford and Trainor, op. cit., pp. 172-3.

4 *The present state of the church of Ireland* (Dublin, 1787).

5 PRONI, Willes letters (microfilm); Townsend, op. cit., i, 101; Young, op. cit., i, 300; T. Newenham, *A view of the natural, political and commercial circumstances of Ireland* (London, 1809), p. 261.

6 PRONI, T. 3319/12, 18 Feb. 1792.

7 PRONI, T. 3319/16, 3 Nov. 1792.

8 I. Weld, *Statistical survey of . . . Roscommon* (Dublin, 1832), pp. 381-2; *Annual register*, March 1786.

9 Crawford and Trainor, op. cit., p. 181.

10 R.A. Breathnach, 'The end of a tradition: a survey of eighteenth-century literature', *Studia hibernica*, no. 1 (1961).

11 Tighe, op. cit., p. 514.

12 J. M'Parlan, *Statistical survey of the county of Leitrim* (Dublin, 1802), p. 68.

13 W.S. Mason, op. cit., iii, 626.

14 W.S. Mason, op. cit., iii, 639-40.

15 Pakenham, op. cit., p. 151. See also Lecky, op. cit., iii, 458.

16 J. M'Parlan, *Statistical survey of the county of Mayo* (Dublin, 1802), p. 99.

17 Tighe, op. cit., p. 384.

18 W.S. Mason, op. cit., iii, 509.

19 Townsend, op. cit., i, 408.

20 C. Coote, *General view of the agriculture and manufactures of the King's county* (Dublin, 1801), p. 20.

21 Dickson, 'Cork region . . . ', pp. 356-7. 361.

22 L.M. Cullen 'Economic trends, 1660-1691' in *A new history of Ireland*, ed. F.J. Byrne, F.X. Martin and T.W. Moody, iii (Oxford, 1976), 401.

23 PRONI, Transcripts of Abercorn papers, 10 April 1752, Strabane.

24 Tighe, op. cit., p. 599.

25 Hoffmann, op. cit., p. 283.

26 C. Coote, *Statistical survey of the county of Monaghan* (Dublin, 1801), p. 143. This may be the village of Blackstaff whose break-up is referred to by Peter Kavanagh in *Patrick Kavanagh country* (Curragh, 1978), p. 24.

27 M. Bodkin, 'Notes on the Irish parliament in 1773', *Proceedings of the Royal Irish Academy*, Section C, XLVIII (1942), 220.

28 Maguire, op. cit., p. 81.

29 NLI, Sarsfield papers, MS 17891 (6), 1725.

30 W. Nolan, *Sources for local studies* (Dublin, n.d.), p. 39.

31 S. O'Tuama, *Caoineadh Airt Uí Laoghaire* (Dublin, 1963), pp. 14-16.

32 Wakefield, op. cit., ii, 755, 757.

34 Quoted in E. MacLysaght, op. cit., p. 358.

35 See L.M. Cullen, 'Economic and Social history, 1691-1800', forthcoming in *A new history of Ireland*, IV.

36 J.A. Gaughan, *The knights of Glin* (Dublin, 1978), pp. 71, 107-112.

37 S.J. Connolly, 'Illegitimacy and pre-nuptial pregnancy in Ireland before 1864; the evidence of some catholic parish registers', *Irish economic and social history*, VI (1979), 16.

38 Gordon St. George Mark, 'Tyrone House, co. Galway', *Quarterly bulletin of the Irish Georgian society*, XIX, nos. 3 & 4 (1976), 25-27.

39 For a very comprehensive restatement of the traditional view of the earl see Father Francis McHugh, 'Who killed the "bad earl" of Leitrim', *Irish Times*, 27 May 1978. For a more critical approach, however, reference should be made to a series of articles by Seamus Brady in the *Irish Press*, 2-7 October 1967, and to the correspondence in the *Irish Times* to which Father McHugh's article gave rise from F.J. Sullivan, R.B. McCarthy (8 June), and Tom Baron (13 June 1978).

Notes

The *droit de seigneur* theme was also recently given a new lease of life by David Thomson's novel *Woodbrook*, and by the review of it in the *Listener* on 12 Dec. 1974 by Caroline Blackwood, followed by a correspondence in the *Listener*, by Brendan Gill, Caroline Blackwood and L.L. Horne, on 17, 23, 30 Jan. 1975. Caroline Blackwood's review and the correspondence were reprinted in the Irish Georgian Society's *Newsletter*, Summer 1975. On the *droit de seigneur*, see also review by L.M. Cullen of A. Feder and B. Schrank, *Literature and folk culture: Ireland and Newfoundland*, in *Times Literary Supplement*, 18 August, 1978.

40 W.H. Maxwell, *Wild Sports of the West* (London, 1832), ii, 148.

41 Young, *Tour in Ireland*, ed. A.W. Hutton (London, 1892), ii, 154.

42 W.J. Fitzpatrick, *Ireland before the union* (Dublin, 1867, 2nd edition), p. 211.

43 M.J. Molloy, 'The making of folk plays', in A. Feder and B. Schrank, ed. *Literature and folk culture: Ireland and Newfoundland* (St. John's, Newfoundland, 1977); also M.J. Molloy's interview with Mary Leland, *Irish Times*, 12 March 1976.

44 PRONI, D.3196/L/IB/I, 1 October 1773. I am indebted to Dr. Anthony Malcomson for this reference.

45 PRONI, T.3315/1, f. 28. Philip Perceval, 31 March 1720. I am indebted to Dr. Anthony Malcomson for this reference.

46 PRONI, T. 2915/1/40, 22 February 1757.

47 PRONI, T.3329/1/38, 19 Sept. 1801, Clare to Auckland. I am indebted to Dr. Anthony Malcomson for this reference.

48 Young, op. cit., ii, 54.

49 See Gaughan, op. cit., pp. 107-112, 115.

50 cf. Gaughan, op. cit., p. 123, for such conditions in Limerick.

12 The character and identity of modern Ireland

1 *Rambles through Ireland* (Cork, 1798), ii, 241.

2 *Sketches of society in France and Ireland in the years 1805-6-7, by a citizen of the United States* (Dublin, 1811), i, p. 220. I am indebted to Peter Solar for bringing this book to my attention.

Index

Abbeyleix, 80
Abductions, 23, 102, 134, 196, 200, 245-7
Absentees, 30
   rents remitted to, 43, 46
   trends in absenteeism, 45, 46
   effects of, 67
Adare, 78, 81, 115, 125, 206, 222
Adderley, Thomas, 76, 77
Agents, 34, 40, 45, 48, 49, 77
   categories of, 49-50
   'moral', 50-51
   of gentry origin, 130, 241
Aldborough, 2nd Earl of, 72, 76, 77, 78, 243
Altamont, Lord, 126
America, 14, 16, 73, 84, 109, 127, 130, 151, 153, 158, 159, 188, 221, 255
   American revolution, 13, 196
Anglican, 12, 15, 16-17, 20, 110-11, 210, 251, 252, 254; see also Church of Ireland
Antrim, co., 22, 27, 52, 55, 56, 59, 65, 111, 163, 164, 167, 186, 204, 252
Ardamine, 213, 228, 229
Ardara, 80
Ardfert, 59
Argentine, 127
Arklow, 213, 217
Arlington, Earl of, 69
Armagh, co., 20, 22, 55, 56, 57, 58, 69, 89, 92, 98, 109, 110, 121, 123, 157, 161, 163, 164, 168, 186, 204, 205, 206, 207, 208, 209, 234, 252, 253
   city, 110
Arran, Lord, 197, 209
Arthur, 118
Askeaton, 59
Athenry, 27
Athy, 179
Aughrim, co. Wicklow, 73
Australia, 157, 247
Aylward, 239

Bagnelstown, 71, 72, 76
Bairead, Riocard, 237
Balla, 79
Ballickmoyler, 69
Ballina, 209
Ballinakill, 59
Ballinasloe, 75, 77, 191, 197, 221
Ballinrobe, 31, 133, 176
Ballintemple, co. Tipperary, 194, 202
   co. Wicklow, 228, 229
Ballitore, 59
Ballycastle, co. Antrim, 76
   co. Mayo, 103
Ballycanew, 229
Ballymote, 76
Ballynahinch, 187
Ballyragget, 201
Ballyshannon, 62
Baltimore, 59
Baltinglass, 59, 214
Banagher, 59
Banbridge, 76
Bandon, 76
Bandon, -bridge, 53, 54, 59
Bangor, 65
Bantry, 103
Barkely, 208
Barker, 78
Barry, 35, 127
   John, 127
Barton, 127, 128
   William, 127
   Thomas, 127
Beaumont, 223
Belanagare, 62
Bellew, 71
Belmullet, 72, 79
Belvedere, Lady, 81
Berkeley, George, 30, 31
Bessborough, 204
Binghamstown, 79
Birr, 53, 64, 69, 71, 72, 73, 75, 76
Blacker, William, 50
Blacquiere, 217, 242, 243
Blake, 32
   Thomas, 126
   Martin, 196
Blarney, 76, 81
Blennerhassett, 78
Blessington, 59, 214
Blundell, 70
Bolton, Cornelius, 76
Boolyglass, 204
Bordeaux, 116, 126, 127, 128, 224, 225, 255
Borris, 70, 212, 242
Borrisokane, 220
Boyd, 128
Boyd, Hugh, 76
Boyle, co. Roscommon, 53, 70
Boyle, family, 85
   Richard, 52
Bray, 62, 179
Breton language, 89
Brittany, 30, 89, 119, 136, 137
Broderick, 218
Brooke, Henry, 76
Brown, 74, 165
Browne, 72, 98, 126, 182
Brownlow, 98, 236
Bruff, 154, 205
Burke, 208, 235
   Edmund, 48, 115, 200
Burlington, Earl of, 49
Bury, 72, 206, 219
Butler, 21, 122, 123, 124, 125, 126, 202
   Rev. Butler, 208
Butt, 245

285

Index

Butter, 18, 23, 94, 100, 104, 141, 142, 143, 144, 145, 147, 148, 149, 156, 159, 162, 164, 165, 168, 169, 170, 181, 189
Buttevant, 179
Byrne, 115, 120, 121, 211, 223, 225, 230, 231
    Edward, 119, 224, 225, 226, 228
    Garret, 212, 215, 224, 225, 226, 228, 246
    Miles, 214, 215, 224, 226, 227, 228, 229, 231, 232, 233
    For other Byrnes, see 213, 223, 224, 225, 226

Cahir, 122, 123
Cahirciveen, 80
Callaghan; see O'Callaghan
Callan, 126, 147, 151, 160, 161, 163, 164, 165, 179, 182, 184
Cantillon, 118
Cappagh White, 74
Carew, Lord, 242
Carleton, 168, 175, 178, 180
Carlow, co., 37, 52, 53, 54, 60, 61, 65, 71, 78, 112, 121, 144, 161, 202, 214, 216, 217, 218
Carnew, 62, 213, 214, 215, 229, 230, 231
Carolan, 98
Carlingford, 156
Carr, Sir John, 153, 175, 178
Carrick-on-Shannon, 182
Carrickfergus, 13, 195, 200
Carrickmacross, 71
Carrowkeel, 79
Carrowmore, 79
Carysfort, 54, 59, 61, 64, 66, 73; see also Macreddin
Cashel, 122, 123
Castles; see Housing
Castlebar, 221
Castlecomer, 76, 114, 144, 150, 203, 218, 221, 236
Castle Carbury, 27, 28
Castle Island, 78
Castlemacadam, 224, 229
Castlemartyr, 59
Castletown, Queen's co., 69
Castlewellan, 72
Catholic, 14, 17, 20, 21, 22, 34, 56, 58, 94, 99, 101, 110, 111, 114, 115, 116, 117, 120, 121, 124, 127, 128, 132, 137, 179, 193, 194, 195, 196, 197, 198, 199, 200, 201, 202, 206, 210, 211, 212, 213, 215, 216, 217, 218, 220, 222, 223, 224, 225, 226, 227, 228, 229, 230, 232, 234, 235, 240, 242, 244, 247, 251, 252, 253, 254, 255
    Association, 238
    Church, 134-5, 138
Cavan, co., 34, 80, 149
    town, 61
    Earl of, 244
Celbridge, 70
Charlemont, 64
Charleville, 59
Charlestown, 79
Charter Schools, 28, 30, 34, 70, 123, 124, 125, 195, 196, 197, 207, 220, 237
Checkpoint, 76
Chichester, Lord, 85
Church of Ireland (Established Church), 14, 17, 30, 38, 55, 56, 102, 121, 122, 127, 129, 132, 169, 195, 207, 208, 209, 223; see also Anglican
Cider, 19, 85, 161, 167, 172, 187, 205
Clancarty, Lord and Lady, 50
Clane, 79
Clanric(k)arde, 73, 125, 197
    Earl of, 39
    Marquis of, 126
Clare, co., 49, 64, 72, 94, 118, 156, 162, 164, 167, 171, 188, 198
    Lord, 115, 247
Clements, 34
    Nathaniel, 27
Clibborn, 59
Clifden, 80
Cloghan, 66
Clogheen, 70, 122, 124, 196, 200
Clonakilty, 59
Clones, 56
Cloney, 242
Cloneygowan, 67
Clonmel, 81, 123
Cloonacool, co. Sligo, 66
Cloughjordan, 220
Colclough, 211, 213, 217, 224, 241
    Dudley, 225
    John, 217
    Vesey, 217
Coleraine, 65, 68, 155
Colley, 27, 28
    Mary, 27
Collon, 76, 78, 208
Colloony, 209
Comber, 65
Ní Chonaill, Eibhlín, Dubh, 177, 184
Conformity, Catholic, to Established Church, 121, 122, 124, 195, 196, 197, 202, 212, 223, 224, 242
Cong, 154
Conyngham, 80, 153
    Lord, 77
Connor, John, 127
Conolly, 43
    Lady Louisa, 216
Cooke, Walsingham, 54
Cookstown, 71, 72, 75, 76
Coolgreaney, 64
Cooper, 194
    Joshua, 208, 209
Coote, 65, 84, 164, 239
    Charles, 53, 168
Cootehill, 75, 80
Coppinger, 120
Cork, 16, 107, 120, 145, 164, 224
    co., 28, 29, 33, 40, 46, 47, 51, 53, 54, 76, 80, 104, 113, 119, 121, 123, 124, 149, 150, 153, 167, 179, 198, 199, 200, 205, 206, 212, 218, 239
    Earl of, 45, 53
Corry, Isaac, 28
Cotter, Sir James, 33, 126, 177, 198, 199, 200, 212
Court Matrix, 61, 78
Courtenay, 28, 45, 67, 113
    George, 45, 53
Courtown, 213

286

Index

Lord, 217
Cox, Sir Richard, 72, 74, 76
Croker, 206
Crookhaven, 103
Croom, 206
Crosbie, 74
Crosby, Anastasia, 225
Crossmaglen, 207
de Cuellar, 90, 92, 107
Cuffe, 31, 133, 176, 191, 197

Dairying, 25, 93, 94, 100, 102, 104, 120, 142, 143, 148, 149, 165, 169-70, 171, 238-9
Daly, 17, 125, 126, 175, 197
    John, 74
Darcy, 62, 80
Day, 247
Defenders, 56, 200, 205, 206, 209, 234, 235
Delamain, James, 159, 160
Delany, Mrs, 28, 31, 75, 178, 179
Denmark, 157, 168
    Danish soldiers, 145, 168
Derry, 12, 55, 65, 68, 110
    co., 22, 65, 81
Devereux, James, 228
Diet, 16, 23, 40, 94, 96, 97, 107, 136, 254
    changes in, 15, 18-19, 95, 140-8, 160, 169
    regional characteristics in, 150, 164-8
    and population growth, 93
    potato in, 140, 141, 144-6, 151, 158-9, 162, 164, 170-1
    farmers', 147, 162-3, 179
    and famine, 168-71
    meat in, 147-8, 149, 151-3, 162-4, 177, 182-3, 186, 187-8
    cheese in, 156-7, 189
    fish, fowl, eggs in, 153-6, 164, 175, 189
    bread in, 175, 183-7
    commercialisation of, 149-59, 161-2, 166, 172-3, 190-1
Digby, 45, 67
Dinely, 27, 152, 243
Dobbs, A., 30, 91, 152
Domestic industry, see Textiles
Donard, 214
Donegal, co., 49, 56, 77, 153
Doneraile, 59, 70
Down, co., 22, 52, 55, 59, 65, 68, 69, 72, 103, 111, 161, 167, 174, 185, 236, 252
Downshire, 44, 70, 193, 194
    Lord, 81
    Marquis of, 244
Drogheda, 26, 29, 208
Dromana, 69, 76, 77
Drumersnave, 76
Dublin, 13, 17, 20, 21, 25, 26, 29, 31, 46, 47, 119, 127, 133, 144, 156, 198, 211, 223, 224, 232, 255
    co., 65, 89, 92, 100, 108. 145, 147, 153, 155, 163, 166, 202, 203, 204, 205, 238, 249
    society, 30, 75
Duleek, 202
Dumfries, 87
Dunally, Lord, 220

Dundalk, 36, 78, 202, 208
Dundrum, 81, 122
Dungannon, 56
    School, 51
Dungarvan, 154, 159
Dungiven, 158, 173
Dunlavin, 63, 214
Dunmanway, 72, 74, 76, 218
Dunmore East, 81
Dunmore, co. Galway, 187
Dunton, John, 31, 148, 176, 244
Dutton, 162, 188
Durrow, 64, 69, 75

Emigration, 109, 126-7, 130, 151, 159, 221, 250
Edenderry, 67, 70
Edgeworth, Maria, 187, 242, 255
Edinburgh, 13
Education, 131, 235, 237. 238. 240, 254, 255
Egmont, Earl of, 198
England, 19, 43, 83, 84, 93, 99, 128, 142, 145, 147, 148, 151, 154, 167, 172, 177, 178, 179, 182, 185, 187, 188, 189, 190, 191, 254, 255
    relations with Ireland, 11
    settlers from, 12, 16, 32, 37, 51, 52, 53, 54, 55, 56, 58, 78, 85, 87, 88, 109, 110, 112, 125, 142, 144, 150, 159, 167, 168, 204
    English character of villages, 65
    English language, 89, 107, 108, 114, 131-2, 208, 255
Enclosure, 26, 29, 36, 47, 48
Ennis, 162
Enniscorthy, 213, 217, 224
Enniskerry, 73, 81
Enniskrone, 154
Enniskillen, 74
Esmonde, 225
Eyre, 75, 197
Eyrecourt, 72, 75, 155, 197, 244

Faction fights, 23, 134, 247
Famine, 30, 40, 91, 96, 168-9, 170-1, 251
    Great, 95, 140, 146, 160, 162, 168, 191, 238, 250
Farmers, 38, 48, 50, 51, 85, 87, 92, 94, 100, 102, 103, 104, 105, 106, 212, 213-4, 219, 220, 221, 222, 238-9, 245, 252-3
    rise of, 17-18, 22, 23, 250, 251
    landlord policy towards, 40-1
    housing of, 29
    income of, 42, 240
    diet of, 147-8, 150, 184, 151, 157, 158-9, 162-4
Faulkner, Samuel, 160
Fermanagh, co., 56, 66, 74, 167, 204
Fethard, 60
Fiddown, 203
Finland, 88, 169, 250
Fish
    in diet, 19, 153-6, 164, 178, 181, 187, 190
    exports, 25, 53
    fishing, 77
Fitzgerald, 35, 118, 119
    Edward, 225
    John Fraunceis, 245, 248

Index

Richard, 245
Fitzgibbon, 115, 125, 235
Fitzmaurice, 209
Fitzwilliam, 45, 65, 213
Flower, 75
Forkhill, 207, 208
Foster, 76, 78, 194
    Baron Anthony, 36
France, 16, 25, 30, 33, 35, 93, 107, 116, 118, 135, 141, 146, 147, 148, 154, 155, 159, 160, 163, 168, 169, 170, 172, 174, 179, 182, 188, 189, 190, 191, 200, 224, 225, 254, 255
    Protestants from, 78
    Revolution, French, 14, 23, 124, 235, 237
Frankford, 66, 74
Fraser, 215
French, 124, 197, 206
    Andrew, 119
    Robert, 27, 76
Frenchpark, 70

Galway, 16, 26, 52, 116, 117, 118, 119, 154, 155, 184, 187, 196, 197, 199, 202, 245, 248
    co., 32, 47, 57, 71, 72, 77, 80, 94, 124, 158, 219
Galwey, 120
Geashill, 45, 65, 67, 220
Germany, 88, 221
    Palatinate, 205
Gentry, 30, 86, 99, 101, 114, 168, 201, 218, 243-4, 248, 253, 254
    gentry sons, 17, 85, 98, 106, 115, 116, 120, 126-7, 129, 212, 244
    housing, 27, 44, 136
    cultural outlook of, 31-2
    old, as middlemen, 33
    role of, 35-6
    regional groupings, 117-9, 120-2
    co. Cork and Galway, 47, 121, 196-7
    Wexford and Wicklow, 121-2, 224-6
    Tipperary, 122-3
    conflict within, 210-13
    life style, 124
    rising families, 125
    and banking, 128
    rentals, 128-9
    estate management, 130-1
    diet, 151, 156, 162, 181-2, 184, 188, 189
    hospitality, 173
    Scottish, 189
    morals, 244-8
Glasse, Hannah, 188
Glenties, 80
Glin, 249
    Knight of, 245
Glover, Mrs, 28
Goldsmith, 35, 209
Gorey, 54, 59, 71, 72, 76, 78, 213, 214, 215, 216, 229
Gormanston, 70
Gowan, Hunter, 115, 214-5, 227, 228, 231, 232
Gowran, 203
Gracehill, 186
Grady, Henry, 246
Graham, 224, 229

Granard, 59, 76
Grandison, Lord, 76, 77
Griffin, Gerald, 143, 175, 178
Grogan, 211, 213
    Cornelius, 212, 217
    John Knox, 212, 226
Groves, Miss, 246

Hacketstown, 68, 214
Hamilton, 52, 65
Harristown, 54
Hartpole, 47, 77
    Robert, 42
Harvey, 211
    Bagenal, 213
    Francis, 149
Hay, 225
Hayes, Sir Henry, 247
Hedges, 218
Hennebry, Fr, 179, 181
Hennessy, 159, 160
Hickey, Michael, 181
Hill, 110
    Hugh, 207
Hillsborough, 76
    Lord, 76
Hodnett, John, 103
Hollow Sword Blade Co., 37, 46
Hollyfort, 227, 232
Holt, Joseph, 211, 230, 232
Holywood, 65
Housing, 29, 31, 47, 48, 50, 99, 100, 107, 113, 238
    tower houses, 26-7, 28, 45, 112, 118, 136, 137
    thatched, 26, 28, 136, 203, 239
    house-building, 43, 44
    housing standards, 239
    Gothic, 44-5
Hudson, Rev. Edward, 208
Huguenots, 16, 78, 159
Hunt, 76
Hunting, 47, 99, 129, 244
Hutchins, 103

Ievers, 71, 72, 74, 198
Immigration, 12, 17, 22, 31, 35, 36, 53, 56, 58, 64, 68, 69, 78, 88, 89, 124, 127, 142, 203
    scale of, 15, 51-2, 54, 55, 84, 87
    changes in, 37, 57
    from England, 84-6, 87, 144, 167, 168, 204
    from Scotland, 87
Income, 137, 189, 251
    national, 41, 242
    per capita in Ireland and England, 92
    of landowners, 44-5, 128-9
    of farmers, 42
Inistioge, 203
Innishannon, 76, 77, 78
Iron mining and working, 42, 53, 59, 64, 85, 87, 88, 112, 114, 124
Irish language, 89, 107, 114, 131, 132, 135-6, 138-9, 204, 248-9, 255
Italy, 135, 155

Jackson, 208
Jamestown, 76
Jefferys, 76, 81
Johnston, 128, 246

Index

Francis, 44
of the Fews, 207
Johnstown, 71, 217, 226
Jonesborough, 207

Kanturk, 73, 218
Kavanagh, 202, 211, 242
Kearney, 120
Kelly, 187
Kenagh, 64
Kenmare, 98
Lord, 76
Kennedy, 246
Kerry, co., 24, 28, 33, 51, 53, 59, 80, 90, 91, 104, 118, 121, 149, 206, 244
Earl of, 77
Kettle, 147
Kilbeggan, 59
Kilcooly, 78, 202, 222
Kilcormac, 66
Kildare, co., 52, 59, 60, 65, 92, 100, 108, 144, 145, 159, 166, 202, 203, 204, 208, 216, 218, 238
diocese, 214, 219
Kilfinnane, 78, 205, 206
Kilkenny, 26, 29, 47, 132, 155, 247
co., 17, 21, 36, 49, 62, 92, 94, 100, 104, 105, 114, 118, 121, 122, 123, 137, 143, 150, 152, 154, 157, 160, 166, 168, 184, 185, 186, 201, 202, 203, 204, 205, 210, 212, 217, 218, 222, 238, 239, 240, 245, 246, 249
Killala, 28, 154, 209
Killann, 213
Killarney, 76, 77
Killashee, 64
Killeleagh, 65
Killenagh, 54, 229
Killough, 69
Kilmichaelogue, 214, 229
Kilmore, 127
Kilnahue, 214, 226, 227, 229, 230, 232
Kilrea, 65, 68
Kilrush, 49, 80, 222
Kiltullagh, 62, 248
King, 70, 72
William, 12, 110
King William's Town, 80
King's co. (Offaly), 45, 52, 53, 54, 64, 65, 66, 67, 69, 74, 79, 163, 220, 249
Kinnegad, 29
Kinsale, 155
Knocktopter, 203
Kyan, John Howard, 225

La Tocnaye, de, 255
La Touche, 125
Lanesboro, 59, 64
Laurencetown, 63, 66, 72
Le Nain, 93
Lecky, 198
Labourers, 91-2, 94, 98, 103, 104, 105, 106, 152, 158, 162, 184, 234, 239, 240
Landlord, landed classes, 14, 16, 17, 23, 32, 60, 98, 99, 106, 204, 219, 253
investment, industry, 40, 42, 74-5, 76-7
landlord villages, 15, 21, 38, 46, 62, 67, 68, 79, 80-1

boroughs, 59
outlook of, 34-5
and tenants, 33, 49-51, 90, 131, 240
leases and leasing policy, 29, 40-1, 42-3, 47, 49-51
income and wealth of, 39, 41, 42-3, 46, 75-6, 238, 240, 241-2
housebuilding by, 43-5
and middlemen, 48, 101-2
estate management, 48-9, 102-3, 243
and education, 237-8
Leinster, Duke of, 80
Leitrim, 49, 52, 53, 59, 236
Earl of, 245
Leix, co.., see Queen's Co.
Limerick, 66, 117, 237
co., 28, 45, 51, 59, 64, 68, 94, 103, 112, 113, 118, 119, 120, 121, 123, 125, 143, 157, 168, 183, 186, 202, 203, 204, 205, 206, 216, 219, 222, 245, 246, 249
Linen, 30, 56, 57, 74, 76, 94, 95, 97, 186, 209, 252
Lisburn, 65, 78
Lismore, 59
Lisnarrick, 66
Listowel, 77
Literacy, 23, 131-2, 189, 236-8
Loftus, 217
Adam, 53
London, 13, 16, 33, 35, 119, 198, 235, 248
Companies, 46, 81
Londonderry; see Derry
Longford, 59, 64
co., 52, 57, 59, 86, 246
Loughrea, 57, 73, 197
Louisburgh, 79
Louth, co., 56, 65, 100, 194, 202, 205, 206, 235
Lucan, Lord, 243
Lupton, 247
Lurgan, 75, 98, 236
Lyons, 206

MacCarthy, 119, 120, 225
MacConmara, Donnachadh Rua, 163
McCormack, 182
MacGearailt, Piaras, 177
Macnamara, 118, 193
Macreddin, 229; see Carysfort
Macroom, 29, 218
Madden, Samuel, 30, 31, 46, 49, 75, 149
Mahon, 81
Malahide, 81
Mallow, 59, 124
Malone, Clements & Gore, 128
Mandeville, 122
Manulla, 74
Marlfield, 81
Martin, 151, 176, 182
Richard, 187
Violet, 190
Maryboro, 69, 221
Mason, W. Shaw, 150
Massacres (1641), 20, 37, 52, 53, 234, 235, 249
Masterson, 224, 226

289

Index

Luke, 224, 225
Phyllis, 119, 225
Edward, 225
Michael, 226
Mathew, 44, 122, 200
George, 43
Mary, 49
Thomas, 199
Maude, 122
Sir Thomas, 199
Maxwell, 155, 183, 245
Maynooth, 80
Mayo, co., 49, 52, 57, 64, 72, 74, 79, 94, 103, 117, 154, 155, 193, 196, 202, 208, 209, 216, 219, 237, 245, 246, 252
Meade, 120
Meth, co., 21, 36, 42, 65, 70, 89, 100, 166, 184, 202, 203, 204, 205, 208, 219, 235, 238, 249
Earl of, 62
Menlough, 126
Middlemen, 21, 23, 42, 98, 114, 175, 243
emergence of, 17, 33
role of, 99-100, 102-3
Wicklow, Wexford, 18, 22, 106, 224, 226, 227, 230, 242, 252
Waterford, Cork, Kerry, 33, 104, 120
housing, 28, 48
Trinity College estates, 47, 99, 102
decline of, 101-2, 103-4, 105-6, 129, 140, 240, 248
morals of, 244
Midleton, 59
Mills, John, 199
Mitchelstown, 45, 69, 72
Moate, 58
Molloy, M.J., 246
Molyneux, 47
Monaghan, 72, 75
co., 56, 91, 92, 149, 166, 184, 241
Monaseed, 212, 214, 224, 225, 226, 227, 230, 231, 232
Monivea, 21, 70, 75, 76, 77, 124, 125, 197, 206
Montbret, de, Coquebert, 32, 108, 126, 152, 154, 155, 165, 179, 184, 197, 209
Montgomery, 52, 65
Mountbellewbridge, 71
Mountmellick, 53, 219, 221
Mountrath, 53, 69, 112, 221
Mountshannon, 74, 125, 197
Moravian, 78, 186
Morris, 115, 212, 244
Morrison, 44
Mothill, 114, 203, 221
Mulleferagh, 209
Mullenneaux, 199
Mullock, Thomas, 79
Murphy, 247
Fr John, 230

Nagle, 198
Garrett, 196, 200
Nesbitt, 35
New Birmingham, 76
New Geneva, 79
New Ross, 126, 216
New Zealand, 157

Newberry Hall, 27
Newburgh, Colonel, 31
Newcastle West, co. Limerick, 45, 53, 67, 68, 113
Newcastle, co. Down, 103
Newcomen, 246
Newfoundland, 126, 163
Newmarket-on-Fergus, 62, 70, 162
Newport, 123, 202
Newrath Bridge, 178, 179
Newtown, 76
Newtown Bellew, 71
Newtownards, 65
Newtownbarry, 71, 76
Newtownforbes, 64
Newtownhamilton, 207
Newtownmountkennedy, 62
Newtownpratt, 74
Nimmo, 77, 80
Norway, 138
Nugent, 126

O'Brien, 71, 124, 154, 175, 183, 186
O'Callaghan, 122, 124
O'Connell, 28, 34
O'Connor, 62, 208
O'Conor, Don, 235
Alexander, 235
Offaly; see King's co.
O'Flaghartie, O'Flaherty, 31, 176
O'Griffin, Murceartach, 244
O'Hara, 124, 154, 209
Charles, 40, 48, 49, 92, 241
Kean, 43, 193
Old Ross, 78, 216
Oldcastle, 65, 202
O'Leary, Arthur, 28, 34, 115, 212, 244
Oliver, 78, 202, 205, 206
O'Longáin, Micheál, 237
O'Maoil Chiárain, Uilliam, 166
O'Murchadha, Seán na Raithineach, 198
O'Neachtain, Seán, 145, 166
O'Neill, 11
O'Rathaile, Aodhgán, 98, 244
O'Rahilly, Egan, 177
Orange, Orange Order, 14, 20, 38, 111, 210, 211, 215, 233, 241, 253, 254
National Grand Orange Lodge, 214
Orchards, 29, 85, 161, 163, 167-8, 204-5, 214, 252
Ormsby, Duke, 103
Orr, James, 164, 186
Orrery, 45
O'Súilleabháin, Eoghan Rua, 29, 158, 198
O'Sullivan, 32
Humphrey, 95, 147, 151, 154, 155, 157, 161, 162, 163, 164, 165, 179, 180, 181, 182
Morty Oge, 32, 33

Palatine, 61, 78, 79, 125, 194, 202, 205, 206, 216, 221, 222
Palatinetown, 78
Palatine Street, 78
Pallas, 64
Pallaskenry, 206
Palmerston, Lord, 49
Pendarves, Mrs; see Mrs Delany
Perry, Anthony, 230
Perssse, 27

Index

Petty, 26
   Sir William, 45, 149
Petty-Fitzmaurice, 45
Philipstown, 157
Piltown, 36, 62, 203
Plantation, 11, 12, 36, 37, 45, 46, 51, 52, 59, 65, 68
Plunket, Sir Horace, 130
Pobal O'Keefe, 80
Poets, poetry, 23, 32-3, 131, 198, 199. 208, 236
Pomeroy, Mrs, 28
Ponsonby, 36, 203
Population, 25, 112
   growth, 15, 18, 25, 55, 83, 89, 97, 143, 193. 203
   growth and diet, 93, 95
   and textiles, 97
   birth rate, 83, 95, 96, 129
   death rate, 83, 96, 97
   marriage ages, 83, 84, 140
   parish registers, 132, 133
   plague and epidemics, 83, 84
Portaferry, 72
Portarlington, 59, 69, 78
Portstewart, 234
Portumna, 39
Potato, 19, 23, 49, 93, 95, 140-1, 150, 164, 170, 175, 181, 188, 251
   evolution of, 144-6, 158-9, 170-1
   growth of, by early English settlers, 159
   and Irish abroad, 159-60
   and crop rotations, 157
   in dairying regions, 165-6
   in diet, 162
   tithe on, 166
   and pork, 151-2
Power, 163
Pratt, 74, 80
Prosperous, 76
Presbyterian, 12, 13, 14, 20, 22, 38, 39, 55-6, 57, 74, 110, 111, 126, 131, 193, 207, 209, 219, 221, 234, 236, 251, 252
Prior, Thomas, 30, 43
Protestant, 18, 21, 28, 32, 34, 36, 37, 54, 78, 106, 107, 113, 114, 115, 121, 122, 123, 124, 137, 138, 194, 195, 196, 197, 198, 199, 200, 201, 202, 203, 205, 206, 208, 211, 212, 213, 214, 215, 216, 217, 218, 219, 220, 221, 222, 225, 227, 228, 229, 230, 232, 235, 238, 242, 246, 255; see Anglican, Church of Ireland, Presbyterian
Puxley, 32, 212

Quakers, 58, 59, 74, 127, 128, 159, 220
Queen's co. (Leix), 42, 47, 52, 53, 54, 64, 65, 69, 76, 81, 87, 89, 112, 218, 220, 249
Quin, 81, 115, 124, 125, 201
   Sir Richard, 78

Raftery, 244
Ram, 54, 71, 216, 217
   Abel, 78, 242
Rathcormack, 59
Rathdowney, 30
Rathdrum, 73, 213, 215, 229

Rathkeale, 61, 78, 169, 205, 206
Rathnew, 229
Rathvilly, 68
Rebellion (1641), 37, 38, 53, 110, 112
   (1798), 14, 20, 21, 37, 38, 210, 226, 234, 250, 251
Rent, 18, 33, 39, 40, 41, 42-3, 44, 45-6, 50, 53, 90, 101-2, 103, 105, 128-9, 193, 239-40, 241
Rice, 126
Ridge, John, 53
Roche, 120
Rochfort, 222
Roscommon, 197
   co., 47, 52, 53, 59, 81, 209
Rosenallis, 113, 221
Ross, co. Galway, 151, 176, 182
Rosses, 95, 155
Rothe, 119. 225
Roundstone, 77, 80
Roundwood, co. Wicklow, 64
Rundale, 48, 79, 80, 204, 240, 241
Rush, 127
Russell, T., 72
Russia, 254
Rutland, 77
   Duke of, 154

St. George, Christopher French, 245
Saltmills, 241
Sandford, 197, 209
Sarsfield, 120, 244
Saule, 160
   John, 159
Scariff, 64
Schools, 23, 54, 62, 236, 238; see Charter Schools, Education
Scotland, 12, 16, 25, 26, 36, 89, 97, 107, 125, 137, 174, 190, 248, 254, 255
   settlers from, in Ireland, 52, 55, 56, 57, 58, 65, 84, 85, 87, 110, 127, 144, 202
   villages in Scotland, 61, 77
   mobility of Scots, 109
   careers of sons in Scotland, 117, 126
   tobacco trade in Scottish ports, 119
   land agents in Scotland, 129
   Scottish diet, 142, 145, 179, 185, 188-90, 191
   famine in Scotland, 168, 170, 191
   Scots Gaelic, 89, 136
Scott, Sir Walter, 178, 179, 188, 255
Servants, 91, 92, 95, 99, 187, 234, 239, 245
Sheehan, canon, 183
Sheehy, Fr Nicholas, 115, 123, 200
   Edmond, 115
Shelbourne, 76
Sheridan, 35
Shinrone, 220
Shirley, 71
Shrule, Queen's co., 47
   co. Mayo, 64
Sixmilebridge, 71, 72, 74
Skerries, 155
Slane, 45, 71, 222
Slieverue, 245
Sligo, 197
   co., 40, 43, 49, 52, 57, 66, 91, 92, 124, 154, 193, 194, 208, 209

291

Index

Smith, 28
Southwell, 113, 202, 206, 216
  Sir Thomas, 78
Spain, 16, 33
Squibb, 199, 246
Staplestown, 61
Stapleton, 118, 126
Stewart, 71
Strafford, Earl of, 45
Strange, James, 246
Stratford-on-Slaney, 72, 76, 77, 78
Strokestown, 81
Summerhill, 70
Sutton, 120, 224, 225, 226
  Eleonora, William, Mary, and Elizabeth, 224
  Thomas, 119, 225
Synge, J.M., 107, 131, 137
Sweden, 84, 88
Swift, Jonathan, 30, 43

Taghmon, 60
Talbot, 81, 223, 224
  Mathew, 224
  William, 225
Tallaght, 145, 166, 249
Tallow, 59
Tea, 28, 149, 150, 164, 175, 176, 186, 187
Templestown, 64
Tenison, 150
Textiles, 38, 41, 42, 53, 93, 94, 95, 97, 111, 172, 205; see Linen, Villages
Thackeray, 244
Thomastown, co. Tipperary, 43, 44
  co. Kilkenny, 155, 199
Tighe, 150, 162
  Mary, 152
  William, 143
Tinahely, 45, 214, 229
Tipperary, co., 35, 43, 70, 76, 87, 94, 112, 118, 119, 120, 121, 122-3, 124, 194, 195, 196, 199, 200, 202, 203, 205, 212, 218, 220
Tithes, 34, 142, 166, 234, 235, 240
  applotment books, 57, 222, 229, 231
Tobin, 119
Toomyvarra, 66, 73
Tottenham, 217
Townsend, H., 150, 194, 239
Tralee, 53, 59, 78
Trant, 118, 126
Trench, 50, 77
  Steuart, 51, 67
Trinity College, 46, 47, 80, 99, 102, 129, 130
Troy, 217
Tuam, 27, 183
Tuamgraney, 64
Tullamore, 72, 219, 221
Tullaroan, 150, 239
Tullow, 169, 214
Tulsk, 59
Tyrone, co., 56, 143, 157, 158, 168, 173, 180
Tyrrellspass, 81

United Irishmen, 20, 38, 111, 200, 211, 212, 213, 215, 216, 217, 233, 235, 236, 237
Unrest, agrarian, 18, 38, 103, 105, 110, 200, 201, 208, 209, 210, 234

Vandeleur, 49, 80
Ventry, 80
Vesci de, 80
Villages, 15, 17, 18, 20, 28, 36, 46, 48, 49, 50, 53, 54, chapter 4, 136, 138, 202, 205, 207, 222
  textile, 38, 51, 74, 76, 77, 78, 79
  establishment of, 58
  slow-down in, after 1640, 86, 112-13
  number established, 61
  few villages founded by Scots, 58, 87

Weld, 178
Wesley, 76, 81
Wexford, co., 18, 20, 21, 22, 36, 37, 52, 53, 54, 60, 64, 65, 71, 78, 86, 87, 100, 101, 106, 108, 112, 114, 115, 119, 121, 123, 127, 149, 165, 168, 175, 185, 202, 203, 204, 205, 206, 209, chapter 10, 237, 238, 248, 252
Westmeath, co., 52, 89, 208, 222, 249
Whiskey, 19, 149, 161, 163, 172, 179-80, 181, 182, 187, 191, 254
Wight, 167
Willes, 154, 176, 207
Wicklow, co., 18, 20, 21, 22, 37, 45, 49, 52, 53, 54, 59, 60, 64, 65, 69, 87, 89, 94, 106, 107, 108, 112, 114, 115, 119, 121, 123, 124, 131, 145, 159, 160, 166, 184, 185, 193, 194, 204, 206, chapter 10, 248, 252
Wingfield, 52, 54
Woodward, dean and bishop, 196, 235
Wynne, 194, 197, 209
Wages, 18, 42, 91, 94
Wakefield, 121
Wales, 89, 136
  Welsh language, 89
Walmsley, James, 103
Walsh, 118
  Antoine-Vincent, 118
  Mary, 180
  Simon, Fr, 180, 181
Wandesforde, 53, 76, 114
Waringstown, 70
Warner, 177
Waterford, 16, 26, 107, 120, 123, 133, 157, 180, 248
  co., 28, 32, 33, 35, 53, 87, 94, 113, 117, 118, 119, 149, 152, 168, 200, 205, 212, 235
  Marquis of, 81
Wentworth, 45, 52, 53, 54, 65
West Indies, 16, 35, 119, 125, 126
Westport, 43, 69, 71, 72, 155, 184
Westmoreland, 235

Yeats, W.B., 248
Youghal, 54
Young, Arthur, 16, 44, 48, 81, 83, 93, 99, 100, 145, 148, 153, 154, 161, 163, 167, 171, 174, 179, 182, 213

/941.5C967E>C1/